KU-263-857

Embodying Health Identities

ACC. No: 02731354

Also by the authors:

Growing Up and Growing Old: Ageing and Dependency in the Life Course
(*co-authored by Jenny Hockey and Allison James*)

Beyond the Body: Death and Social Identity
(*co-authored by Elizabeth Hallam, Jenny Hockey and Glenys Howarth*)

Social Identities across the Life Course
(*co-authored by Jenny Hockey and Allison James*)

Constructing Childhood: Theory, Policy and Social Practice
(*co-authored by Adrian James and Allison James*)

Embodying Health Identities

Allison James
Jenny Hockey

306.461
JAM

© Allison James and Jenny Hockey 2007

All rights reserved. No reproduction, copy or transmission of this publication may be made without written permission.

No paragraph of this publication may be reproduced, copied or transmitted save with written permission or in accordance with the provisions of the Copyright, Designs and Patents Act 1988, or under the terms of any licence permitting limited copying issued by the Copyright Licensing Agency, 90 Tottenham Court Road, London W1T 4LP.

Any person who does any unauthorized act in relation to this publication may be liable to criminal prosecution and civil claims for damages.

The authors have asserted their rights to be identified as the authors of this work in accordance with the Copyright, Designs and Patents Act 1988.

First published 2007 by
PALGRAVE MACMILLAN
Houndmills, Basingstoke, Hampshire RG21 6XS and
175 Fifth Avenue, New York, N. Y. 10010
Companies and representatives throughout the world

PALGRAVE MACMILLAN is the global academic imprint of the Palgrave Macmillan division of St. Martin's Press, LLC and of Palgrave Macmillan Ltd. Macmillan® is a registered trademark in the United States, United Kingdom and other countries. Palgrave is a registered trademark in the European Union and other countries.

ISBN-13: 978–1–4039–1472–9 hardback
ISBN-10: 1–4039–1472–9   hardback
ISBN-13: 978–1–4039–1473–6 paperback
ISBN-10: 1–4039–1473–7   paperback

This book is printed on paper suitable for recycling and made from fully managed and sustained forest sources.

A catalogue record for this book is available from the British Library.

A catalogue record for this book is available from the Library of Congress.

10 9 8 7 6 5 4 3 2 1
16 15 14 13 12 11 10 09 08 07

Printed in China

When we had finished

let me just say
that it's the difference
between jumping up and down on the spot
and trampolining,
between cranking the handle heavily round
and free wheeling,
between pasting a floral paper right up the staircase
and scattering in a scant score of crocus bulbs,
between muttering under the quilt
and singing softly across the canyon.

JH

Contents

1
Problematising Health, Illness and Identity

In Sickness and in Health

One of the vows traditionally taken by the bride and groom in a Christian marriage service, the promise to remain true to one another 'in sickness and in health', locates us already at the heart of some of the theoretical and conceptual issues with which this book is concerned. It points, for example, to the changing social values attached to the physical body over the life course – young now perhaps, but time, we know, will eventually take its toll on the body. Thus it is to their future old age and potential physical and mental infirmities that a young couple are advised to look. Alternatively, our young lovers are being asked to consider the ways in which an unforeseen accident or the sudden onset of disease might, irrevocably, change the direction of their future plans – though fit now, will they feel able to love and care for a sick partner, to look after someone, this seems to suggest, who may no longer be the same 'person' they married?

The challenges to the 'self' and 'other' that illness can bring, implied by the injunctions of the marriage vow, therefore raise a range of interesting questions about the relationship between the body, health and identity and it is this which we seek to explore through the course of this book. What is it about illness that seems to challenge our identity and can lead not only to an altered sense of self, but also to changes in the ways that others see us? What exactly is the relationship between our organic, material bodies and the persons we think we are, and in what ways might the body and its changes in health status mediate our understanding of ourselves and of other people? Through what kinds of social relationships and everyday social interactions do individuals come to understand or make sense of changing physical sensations?

1

How are particular cultural categories of 'sickness' and 'well-being' used by people to make sense of the body's changing state? And, are these bodily or somatic experiences and cognitive processes of sense-making universal and invariant; or do different social and cultural environments provide us with different ways of thinking about – and perhaps even experiencing – body-based sensations, leading to rather different identity outcomes in terms of being 'healthy' or 'ill'? Finally, to what extent are we able to exert some kind of agency in relation to our management or negotiation of health and illness through different kinds of social relationships in our everyday lives; or is it the case that we are not only at the mercy of the 'natural' progression of disease, but also of the doctors and other healers, who diagnose our ills, the technologies which they employ and the medical, economic and political systems within which we live and work? And, if we can have a degree of control over the ways in which 'illness' is experienced and identifies us, how does this occur?

Such are the concerns of our book. However, before we can begin to answer these questions we must set out the parameters within which they are located and, in this first chapter, we introduce some of the key concepts and theoretical tools which we will be using. However, before doing so, we must note at the outset that despite this book's explicit focus on variability, as readers will discover, much of it is written in the first person plural – 'we'. The use of this term is not accidental. Instead, it reflects our concern to develop theoretical insights which are generalisable across social, historical and geographical time and space. That is to say, our use of 'we' signals an inclusive theoretical perspective that can address issues of diversity.

In addition, however, it also demonstrates our awareness of the power and pervasiveness of western medical models, not only within the authors' UK homeland, but also worldwide. Increasingly, bio-medicine *is* a shared experience of healing, albeit one that wields different kinds of authority in different contexts, as we shall go on to demonstrate. So, while the comparative method will be sustained throughout the book, particularly in relation to cross-cultural variation and the different insights into health and identity that this brings, it remains important to recognise the pervasiveness of western medical models and the availability of bio-medical remedies in many parts of the world now. Writing of its impact in Africa, Doyal (1979), for example, argues that western imperialism exposed both commercial colonisers and the indigenous workforce to health risks of all kinds. The introduction of western medicine to the African and Asian sub-continents therefore reflects not only economic interests but also the desire to colonise ideologically via Christianity, a project that was enabled by what Doyal terms the 'kindly influence of medical work' (1979:250). It is therefore in recognition of the importance of these globalisation processes of all kinds within healthcare – whether in relation to the movement of individuals, ideas or technologies – that this volume draws on the work of both medical sociologists and anthropologists to begin to understand how it is that we know we are ill.

We turn first, then, to a consideration of a core sociological problem that is central to our interests in the body, health and identity: the relationship between the 'individual' and 'society'.

Who Says I am Ill? Illness as a Social Construction

It may seem nonsensical to suggest, as we will come to do many times in this book, that 'health' and 'illness' are, in large part, socially constructed, context- specific categories through which we interpret our bodily experiences and then make judgements about the state and status of our bodies. Within western societies at least, the hegemony of a bio-medical model means that objective scientific accounts of health, illness and body-based disease are fundamental to the ways in which healthcare is delivered and, for the most part, to the way we, as patients, understand it. Moreover, on a personal and experiential note, when we say that we feel 'ill' what we are attempting to deal with are physical or emotional sensations or experiences which, however much we might want to wish them away, intrude upon our sense of well-being and incapacitate us in very material ways. To suggest therefore that 'health' and 'illness', rather than being objective somatic states, are instead socially constructed through social practices of different kinds would seem to lack any common sense grounding. And yet, it is relatively easy to reveal the slippery character of these concepts of health and illness and, thereby, to indicate their social embeddedness.

A first point to note, for instance, is the importance of the historical and cultural context to both our understanding and experience of disease. Writing in 1978 Susan Sontag argued that the threat of cancer lies as much in people's perceptions and fears of the disease, as in the disease itself. Worse still, she noted, cancer's ability to stigmatise individual identities, to mark sufferers out as deserving of both curse and punishment, may prevent people from seeking diagnosis at an early stage and inhibit their questioning about the effectiveness of their treatment. In the 1970s, cancer seemed a sure and certain death sentence. However, a decade later, Sontag remarked a new candour emerging in people's relationship to cancer. By the 1980s, she argued, cancer was more openly discussed. Indeed, it had become almost obligatory to show 'diagrams of the rectal-colon or genito-urinary tract ailments of our national leaders on television and on the front page of newspapers' (1988:15). Getting cancer was no longer an individual's greatest fear, voicing its name was no longer a great taboo.

The reasons Sontag cites for this shift in focus and ways of thinking about cancer lay not only in the advances made by medical science, which meant that more people survived cancer more often. She also relates it to the 'emergence of a disease whose charge of stigmatization, whose capacity to create spoiled identity [was] far greater' (1988:16). In 1988 AIDS (acquired immune deficiency syndrome) had taken over as the 'viral enemy' within and had become the new terrifying disease (1988:20). Twenty years later, with the help of new drug therapies, HIV positive people in Western societies are often able to live long lives, making the death sentence of AIDS less imminent. It remains to be seen, therefore, whether current concerns about growing levels of obesity, and the diseases such as diabetes and heart disease that are associated with it, might take over AIDS' stigmatising role in disaster discourses. As Sontag catalogues, from leprosy, TB and cancer through to AIDS 'societies need to have one illness which becomes identified with evil, and attaches blame to its victims' (1988:16).

However, it is not simply history and scientific advancements which mediate our health relationships and our illness experiences through identifying new diseases, offering the possibility of better outcomes for old ones or developing more effective treatment regimes. More fundamentally, as this volume explores, the very ways in which we think about and experience 'health' and 'illness' depend upon a range of other social, political and economic conditions and considerations. What it is to be well or ill is, in a very real sense, context specific. It is in this sense, therefore, that we argue that, *in part*, our bodily experiences of illness have to be seen as socially constructed. They are 'created' through our everyday social interactions and through processes of interpretation that are historically and culturally located.

In approaching the study of health and illness in this way, we must therefore, distinguish carefully between the concepts we use. Here, following Lupton (2004) we define 'illness' as 'the social lived experience of symptoms' and use 'disease', by contrast, as the term to describe 'a technical malfunction or deviation from the biological norm' (Lupton 2004:93–4). Such distinctions are important for, staying with the example of AIDS, it is quite clear that the extent of and manner in which the disease is both acknowledged and experienced as an *illness* depends, very much, on the wider social context. In India, Africa and other developing countries, for example, the AIDS epidemic continues to spread rapidly, the result of the complex interplay between widespread poverty, different cultural practices around sex and gender and, often, political disinterest cloaked with denial. Sub-Saharan Africa, for example, contains 64% of the world's population of AIDS-infected people, even though it contains only 10% of the global population (Copson 2005). In Africa, where drugs are not only expensive but also not readily available, AIDS remains life-threatening and is feared, as much for the social stigma that accompanies it as for its debilitating physical manifestations. By contrast, in western contexts, despite the fact that new cases are continuing to appear, the fear and stigma which surrounded AIDS in the 1980s has now diminished. This is evidenced by a new generation's seeming indifference to the adoption of safe sex practices in a context where successful drug treatment can be easily accessed and there is increased life expectancy for sufferers.

The ways in which AIDS is experienced and understood as an illness, rather than a disease, thus turns out to be neither straightforward nor objective. Instead it is symptomatic of the complex set of social, political and economic relationships that embed the individual within his/her own society. This occurs in any number of different ways, often with radically different consequences. It is in this sense, therefore, that AIDS (along with other illnesses) can be said to be, in part, socially constructed. And, indeed, it is precisely the recognition of the significance of this mix – the cultural variability of the concepts of 'health' and 'illness' and social factors, such as poverty or access to healthcare – which has been – and remains – core to the work of medical anthropology and sociology.

Strictly speaking, however, AIDS is not a single disease. Rather, its presence is signalled through the symptomatic appearance of a range of other bodily conditions, making AIDS itself, as Sontag argues, a 'clinical construction, an inference' (Sontag 1988:21). This means that not everyone who exhibits symptoms of the conditions associated with being an AIDS patient will be HIV positive – and not all those identified as HIV positive will necessarily experience the complete range of symptoms associated with AIDS. The body itself, then, also seems to have an active part to play in the ways in which 'illness' shapes identity. It may be, for example, the voluntary act of seeking out an AIDS test that first indicates a change in an individual's health status and consequent social identity, rather than the onset of specific somatic indicators. And, finally, as we write, in late 2005, a new AIDS conundrum has arisen: a man, identified in 2002 as being HIV positive, appeared by 2003 to have cured himself and no longer has the disease. This bodily change that is currently baffling the scientists, since it defies current medical thinking about the etiology and progress of this condition (*The Independent* 14th November 2005), points to the body's own role in the experience of illness and disease, as we shall go on to explore in some detail.

Questions about the relationship between the body, individuals' agency and the social, economic and political structures and social relationships that help shape health identities are thus core to this volume as we explore the extent to which any individual is free to act in regard to the health and well-being of their body. Individuals who are sick may, for example, feel themselves constrained to act in particular ways – by the medical and scientific 'knowledge' that labels their disease; by the demands made by specific health policies and government

agendas that individuals should change their lifestyles; by the economic strin-
gencies of people's own lives or of the societies in which they live; by their lack
of access to alternative kinds of medical knowledge and treatment regimes; or
by the powerful and compelling tug of cultural beliefs and everyday social practices. In sum, the specificity of the social and cultural contexts within which
disease occurs, and the social relationships that take place within them, are part
and parcel of the ways in which we, as individuals, experience illness and the
changes to health status that this can bring.

Thus one important aspect of the social constructionist perspective that
we are exploring in this volume is the variation in experiences of 'health'
and 'illness' across different societies and historical eras, despite human
beings' common heritage of a body. And we are keen to explore this diversity not only with respect to conceptualisations of 'health' and 'illness' and
their treatment but also, importantly, in terms of those health variations
and structural inequalities, that flag issues of power, rather than simply
those of difference. Thus, although any discussion of bio-medicine requires, as noted earlier, that we adopt a global perspective, health *variations*, or inequalities can also be explored within societies, both in the
western and the developing world.

Marmot (2001) notes, for example, that any complex social system, wher-
ever it is found, will encompass differences within mortality and morbidity
(illness) rates and the steepness of the gradient which divides the sick from
the well can vary profoundly. In addition, while poverty is often seen as a
key source of health inequalities, as Marmot's (1984, cited in Marmot
2001:55) study of UK civil servants demonstrates, it cannot always explain
why some people are more vulnerable to illness and early mortality than
are others. While in the study sample no high-grade civil servant met economic criteria which could be used to define them as 'poor', differences
in health status between civil servants were nonetheless evident and,
significantly, mapped the patterning of civil service hierarchies with aston-
ishing precision. This suggests that the psychosocial implications of *relative*
poverty might be playing a part here for, as Williams (2003) highlights,
stress-related illnesses, indicated by insulin level and weakened immune
systems, may be the outcome of a relative failure to succeed economically
and socially. Poverty therefore emerges as an aspect of individuals' lives
with no straightforwardly causal effect upon their health; rather, it is
the risks evidenced by studies such as Marmot's (2001) which draw
our attention to the implications of an unequal distribution of material
wealth, the relative poverty of people living at close quarters to one
another.

In addition to such examples of health variations in relation to class, as
reflected in economic inequalities, medical sociology and anthropology

have also examined the vulnerabilities associated with gender and ethnic differences, showing how people's differential access to both economic and cultural resources are revealed in health inequalities (Williams 2003). Doyal, for example, points out that gender inequalities continue to impact upon women's health differentially: 'though they have a longer average life expectancy than men, they do not necessarily lead healthier lives' (2002:188). Similarly, as Marmot shows, ethnicity and poverty combine to produce deleterious health effects among ethnic minority groups: poor young black men in Harlem, New York City, 'have six times the average US mortality', an incidence which can be attributed not only to violent death, but also to their greater vulnerability to cardiovascular disease (Marmot 2001:56).

Health Identities and Illness Experiences

In that we are flagging the importance of individuals' different health and illness experiences, within an increasingly global bio-medical context, the question of identity, and the theoretical work associated with it, need also to be considered. A further aim of this volume therefore, and already apparent in our discussion of Sontag's work on AIDS, is to examine the broader discursive links between concepts of health and illness and questions of social identity. That is to say, when thinking about who is ill and who is well, we have, for example, to ask about the ways in which such classifications are made, the kinds of ideas they incorporate and the meanings they embrace and, therefore, the implications these social classifications have, once made, for the individual themselves.

Notable here, for example, is the athletic prowess of the 40-year-old-female-mother-radiographer-marathon runner-long-distance cyclist-cancer sufferer-fundraiser, interviewed in the British press (*The Guardian* May 16th 2004). Is Jane Thomlinson's great sporting achievement – among other things running three London marathons and cycling across Europe – to be acclaimed in spite of, because of, or irrespective of her other identity as someone with life-limiting bone cancer? Is her identity as a cancer patient made more (or less?) meaningful because she is also seen as a fundraiser, an athlete and a mother of three children? And with which of these multiple identities, conferred on her by other people, might she most identify herself – or, might that depend on the immediacy of the social context within which she finds herself and with whom, and when and where she is talking? In her desire to keep on going, and to raise money through accomplishing great feats of physical endurance, does she see herself, for example, as a cancer *survivor*, despite her knowledge that her illness is life-limiting?

Such are the implications for identity raised by individuals' encounters with the ideas about health and illness that abound in society, all of them building further complexities into our subject. So, if as noted earlier, health and illness are to be understood partly within a social constructionist framework of cultural relativity, and as *contextualised*, rather than determined, by bodily experiences, then, necessarily, the process of identification has also be understood as one which is shaped by a similar set of contingencies.

Jenkins, for example, argues that identity is both individual and collective, a process that is the 'practical accomplishment' of the 'dialectical interplay of processes of internal and external definition' (1996:25). As he sees it, a key element in this process is the social recognition of both similarity and difference, both with regard to oneself and to others:

> In identifying myself within any minimally shared cultural setting I render the behaviour of others easier to predict (or imagine). I can imagine their position or orientation vis-à-vis myself. In presenting myself, I may make an active contribution to their behaviour towards me. Similarly, identifying others in particular ways permits me to imagine that I know what to expect of them. I will, more often than not, orient my behaviour towards them in terms of their presentations of identity (Jenkins 1996:124).

Core to this process of identification, therefore, are the everyday social interactions that take place between people as first explored by Mead (1934) through his concept of the generalised other and by Cooley (1964) in the notion of the looking-glass self. For both theorists, how we know who we are and how our notions of 'self-identity' arise, constitute the central puzzle that needs explaining. Mead's answer is to consider why we make the distinctions between 'I' and 'me' and what the effect of doing so is. According to Mead, these distinctions demonstrate that social interactions with other people are core to our self-identity: the 'me' dimension of who 'I' am is constituted, in my mind, through the interactions I have with other people. These social interactions provide, according to Cooley, a kind of looking-glass for my sense of self, something that takes place as an ongoing, internalised and reflexive process of encountering. Most importantly, these mirrors for the self, belonging to what Mead calls the realm of the 'generalised other', derive from the social world. In this sense, they are collective versions of the 'me' perceived by others, reflecting the different social groups to which we belong and from which we learn to see ourselves as others see us. Thus, to return to our example, Jane Thomlinson *is*, at one and the same time, fundraiser, wife and mother, marathon runner and cancer patient.

Remarkably, however, for most of us, these different dimensions of the self are integrated into some kind of coherence within any individual – as the 'I' or sense of self that we have. And yet, as Craib (1998) observes, how that process of identification takes place remains, within sociological theorising, somewhat mysterious. In his view, sociology has yet to fully grasp what exactly is going on *inside* individuals, and simply 'deals with the body from the outside' (1998:10). He urges social scientists, therefore, to engage more with people's subjective experiences in order to make sense of how it is that they come to know who they are.

This underscores, therefore, the importance of agency in processes of identification and, perhaps more importantly the fact of embodiment, for our understanding of the ways in which self-identity develops through the social identities that we take on. Thus, as we shall go on to argue in the next section and throughout this volume, that we both *are* and *have* bodies provides the essential grounding for the ways in which social identities come to make sense for the self. It is our subjective *experiences*, rather than just our understanding, of the ways in which our bodies change – whether through illness or simply ageing – that play a pivotal role in our changing sense of self and identity.

Thus, it could be argued that Jane Thomlinson's greatest achievement is the thorough disruption of commonly held representations of the identity of 'cancer sufferer'. In actively embodying a range of very different identities, she challenges the onlooker, and arguably also herself, to circumscribe her identity through her illness. She 'chooses', instead, to present to the world a very different identity, one in which life-threatening illness is distanced as an identifier for the self. As Jenkins observes, 'who' we think ourselves to be – our sense of personal identity, our individuality and our distinctiveness – may potentially be in conflict with the collective social or nominal identities (Jenkins 1996, 2004) through which others might choose to view us.

Not only does this example represent a challenge to the saliency of 'disease' as the most important identifier or label for the self, but it is also the case that the different, embodied identities that Jane Thomlinson has – as mother, as patient, as wife, as sister – ebb and flow across time, providing different referents for the self in her everyday life through her different experiences of embodiment at different points in her life course. Thus, as we have noted elsewhere, categorical identities 'do not have "life" outside of the person…[and] only become meaningful in terms of the individual's response to them' (Hockey and James 2004:201). The process of *self* identification involves, therefore, a constant tacking back and forth between different aspects of one's *social* identities, a process that takes place within embodied individuals.

As we shall explore through the course of this volume, in relation to matters of illness, individuals can therefore, to some degree, resist or negotiate the health identities that are thrust upon them. Importantly, however, this resistance is not just dependent on the kinds of medicalised discourses through which illnesses are represented; nor is it simply a function of social interactions of different kinds – be they with doctors, neighbours or family members. Our 'health identity' is also dependent upon our actions, as embodied individuals, and the resources that we muster in response to these different identifications of who we are.

The perspective that we adopt in this volume is, therefore, that health identities are not fixed and are certainly never completed or finished. As one feature of social identity they are 'aspects of the ongoing organisation of interaction and everyday life ' (Jenkins 1996:102).

The fundamental importance of this more processual approach to understanding identity has its roots in Goffman's (1968) early book, *Stigma*. Subtitled, 'the management of a spoiled identity', it revealed how bodily disabilities have to be 'managed' by people, lest they discredit their identity and Goffman indicated the variety of ways in which people with disabilities control the kinds of information others have about their condition. Building on these insights, Scambler's (1989) research on individuals with epilepsy revealed, for example, that people diagnosed with this condition feared a change to their identity; they worried that they would be stigmatised and would be seen as unacceptable or inferior by others. They therefore worked hard to draw other people's attention away from their condition, even though ironically, as it turned out, people with epilepsy suffered their greatest difficulties from the 'fear' rather than the 'fact' of being stigmatised. What is missing from such accounts, however, is the teasing out of the practical accomplishment of the relationship between the body, health and identity for the individual – and for this we need to focus more closely on the changing nature of embodiment itself.

What we exemplify throughout this volume, therefore, is the processual nature of identification. Even after death identities can change. For example, the leakage of previously hidden information that someone died of HIV/AIDS, rather than a less stigmatising condition, can radically alter the social identity which persists after their death. Similarly, the recognition that an older woman who died some years ago of a sudden heart attack was a patient of Harold Shipman, the English GP jailed for life in 2003 for murdering 15 patients and under suspicion of killing up to 250 (*Guardian Unlimited* 2005), transforms what might have been seen as a timely and perhaps 'easy' death into the untimely murder of a vulnerable person. In both cases, therefore, the social relationships and interactions that coalesce around these 'health' matters shape the deceased's identity and embodied memory quite profoundly.

Being and Bodies

Despite our overarching concern with the social context of illness experiences and the ways in which health identities arise and are taken on through social interactions of different kinds, a central theme that also recurs in this volume is, as noted above, the implications of the body for identity. What we acknowledge, repeatedly, is that our bodies *do* change, that they *do* get sick, that they *do* or *do not* recover after illness and, therefore, we have also to understand the significance of the body's materiality for health identities.

A final theme in this book is, then, a recognition of the role of the physical body itself as a source of our awareness of whether we are ill or well. All too often within contemporary sociological theorising about health, the brute material facts of sickness, disability and disease, and the physical changes that occur in the body, become bracketed off. They are made somehow incidental to accounts of the social import which these bodily processes have for the individual, or for society more generally (for a critique of feminist work in this mould, see Shilling 2005:3).

And, with respect to mental illness, a similar process can take place. When we make reference to the body-based nature of health and illness in this volume, therefore, we are not referring simply to arthritis and chicken pox, but also to the siting of mental health problems within the body. This is not to say that we posit brain malfunction as the sole *cause* of mental illness; it is simply that, without a body, the individual can experience neither mental health nor illness. And, as we go on to elaborate, it is in seeking to incorporate the body 'in sickness and in health', that we are led to adopt a phenomenological position which, in itself, subverts the Cartesian mind/body dualism, so familiar to us in western societies, which gives the mind, as it were, the upper hand! I think therefore I am; the mind, rather than then body is the source of who we are. By challenging this dualist perspective, however, we can see that 'the body is not simply constrained by or invested with social relations, but also actually forms a basis for and contributes towards these relations' (Shilling 1993:13). Thus, in Leder's words, '[i]f the body as lived structure is a locus of experience, then one need not ascribe this capacity to a de-corporealised mind' (1990:5).

Flagging the corporealised or body-based nature of mind is perhaps a rather provocative step for, as Shilling (1993) notes, not only has the body been an 'absent presence' within mainstream sociology as the taken-for-granted basis of human action, but even within medical sociology and anthropology, where one might expect the body to feature prominently, it has received relatively little attention as a biological entity. Nonetheless, as an entity, in and of itself, the body plays a key part in matters of health and illness. As we discuss in greater detail in Chapter 3, whether naturalistic/foundational or discursive/ constructivist sociological approaches to understanding health and illness are adopted, all too often these theoretical approaches locate themselves outside or apart from the body itself. That is to say, they either take the body's illness as an unproblematic, 'natural' starting point which can then be separated off from the social significance this has for the individual; or, alternatively, they examine the variety of ways in which illnesses are differently constructed and thought about and the impact which social systems have upon the body. In both cases the body is a given. Conceived as a stable entity, it is something that occurs 'naturally' and which society fashions, or something that is produced through social practices of different kinds.

Reasons for this omission, or absence, have been provided from within the sociology of the body. Leder (1990), for example, suggests that our body's capacity to *perceive* what surrounds it becomes possible only because the physical body itself takes a back seat. It effaces itself. Through doing this we have a clearer focus on what we are attempting to perceive. Thus, for example, when we stretch out to stroke a cat, we concentrate on the *feel* of the silkiness of its fur when we stroke it, rather than on the act of touching in and of itself. Without this capacity to sideline the body in this way, Leder (1990) suggests, our western belief in a mind/body split, which seems so 'natural' to us, would in fact be rather difficult to foster.

However, the persuasiveness of sociological accounts that downplay the role of the body can also be seen as a response to extreme forms of biological reductionism and to the powerful dominance of medicalised accounts of the body and its ills (Shilling 1993:68). Arguably, however, not to acknowledge the body at all risks throwing the baby out with the bath water! Whatever our *cognitive* account of sickness and disease in different social and cultural settings, illness *does* have a biological and material basis in the body: 'illness' represents an altered state of physical/mental being that only gains its meaning through contrast with our *experience* of a different condition, the somatic state called 'health'. Whether or not such changes are perceptible at the time of their initial occurrence, our bodies/minds can, nonetheless, recall the difference between the two. Indeed, the 'sick' or 'cured' individual is precisely someone who is able to make such implicitly comparative statements as: my stomach hurts; my head aches; my finger bleeds; my broken arm is mended; my indigestion has gone. And that, as listeners, we can empathise with such statements, from our *own* experience, is also something that has to be explained, sociologically. In our view, therefore, sociological explanations of health and illness must make some attempt to account for the physical body alongside the social one. At present, however, they do so in only a rather limited fashion.

Following Turner (1992) therefore, we argue in this volume that a foundationalist view of the body does have an important role to play within medical sociology and anthropology, since this does begin from a view of the body as 'a material, physical and biological phenomenon which is irreducible to immediate social processes or classifications' (Shilling 1993:10). The challenge we take up in the volume, then, is one of incorporating some recognition of the *physiological* processes that the body undergoes into the *sociological* account of health and illness. However, this needs to be achieved without reducing the complexity of their relationship to a simple 'add-society-and-stir' approach; nor should it underestimate the great significance that culture and the social context have for different health practices and experiences as we have already indicated.

This is indeed a daunting task! However, it is one that finds a solution, as we shall go on to show, through our core focus on embodiment. Adopting this perspective allows us to view the body as not only the site where 'illness' and 'health' are located, but also as the comparative experiential context through which we gain primary knowledge of these states and the health identities that follow: today I feel well, yesterday I felt ill, tomorrow I might feel better. As Craib argues:

> the pulsating organs which I inhabit are a constant part of my feeling and think-ing; I have various physical needs which change throughout my life as my body changes. And the real scandal of being embodied, one which arguably is a governing feature of all our lives, is that our embodiment comes to an end. We die (1998:10).

It is, therefore, the very fact of our embodiment – whether sickly or not – which allows us to explore the 'affects and effects that a body learns' over time – including what it means to be ill or well – and to situate this dynamic process of being and understanding within the complexities of our every-day lives (Latour 2004:227). This approach neither privileges the flesh, nor processes of cognition, but engages with the experience of both and, in Chapter 3, we set out in some detail the way in which this idea can be developed.

The Negotiated and Embodied Body

The approach to understanding health and illness which we adopt in this volume thus begins from a view of the body as not simply an object with some kind of 'bit' part to play within the scheme of things. Rather, we engage with the body as the location at which human 'being' is situated. Without our bodies we do not exist and it is, therefore, from the site of our own embodied being that we come to know 'the body' and its ills in all of the ways which this book will outline. As Leder puts it, when describing how the body appears within the per-ceptual world of embodied human beings:

> The body can itself appear as but another object to be perceived and scientifically described. However, this never exhausts its meaning. The very possibility of objects as we know them, of science, of world, refers us back to that body on the other side of things, the body-as-experiencer (1990:5).

However, linked with the book's commitment to exploring how embodied human beings have generated models of 'the body' in relation to health and illness identities, is another significant concern: the relationship between this process of identification and the bio-medical models of health and illness which posit the healthy body and its functioning as both stable and predictable. As Leder argues, for example:

> Since the seventeenth century the body has been primarily identified with its scientific description, i.e., regarded as a material object whose anatomical and functional properties can be characterized according to general scientific law (1990:5).

Yet as human beings we do not experience the world in this way. Instead, our embodied experience is one of continual change. Thus, for example, we might recall an illness episode – say of influenza – as follows: I woke up with a headache one day that got worse by the evening. I had pains in my limbs the next day and a high temperature which, by the weekend, had intensified. Taking painkillers dulled the ache and reduced the fever. A few days later the pain and fever disappeared. Today, I am now no longer thinking about what is 'wrong' with me; my body has returned to its 'normal' state.

Against these ordinary, everyday experiences of the bodily changes that illness brings can be set others, however, of which we may be less aware on a daily basis. For Allison, it is with a sudden recognition that she looks at her grown up son and realises that his body is now the body of a man, and correspondingly, that her own body has also changed – the skin is less taut, fine lines surround her eyes, her hair has gone grey. She had not noticed these changes happening, but clearly they have taken place; photographs recall the different bodies she and her son once had. For Jenny, the birth of a grandchild acts as a reminder that the body's capacity to reproduce itself transcends the time-limits of its own fertility, as biologically linked reproductive processes extend indefinitely across new generations of the family. Thus, across the life course the body also changes and, as we shall see (Chapter 5), health and illness can acquire different meanings and have different implications for identity depending upon an individual's life course stage.

The approach which this volume develops, therefore, is one which attempts not only to overcome the mind-body distinction that has so plagued recent theorising around the body by reconciling 'the physiological and the phenomenological bodies in a single whole', but one which also gets to grips with a more dynamic view of the body (Latour 2004:208). In our view, the body is not simply the passive site where 'illness' and 'health' are located. Instead it is the fleshy medium through which health and illness are experienced by individuals and therefore has an important role to play in the ways in which somatic states gain social meaning. It is a body that is in constant flux, changing imperceptibly over time as it ages, or more dramatically through accident or the onset of and recovery from illness. Indeed, as Shilling (1993) argues, the human body lacks the kind of fixed properties which typify those of animals who are programmed to survive in quite particular environments. Consequently, for human beings 'the world ... is a relatively open world, a world whose content and meaning must be fashioned from human action' (Shilling 1993:101).

Furthermore, as Freund and McGuire (1991) point out, not only are human beings highly dependent at birth but remain so for far longer than most animals, a period of dependency which results in physiological changes stimulated by the child's social environment. Gerhardt (2004) develops this point with respect to brain functioning and development in babies, arguing that biochemical systems which are integral to life-long emotionality are influenced in particular ways as a result of the child's early social environment. New work such as this points towards the interplay of the social and the biological aspects of human life. However, what Freund and McGuire (1991) also remind us is that, unlike animals, human beings use symbols which allow them to retain and reflect on what has happened in the past – and indeed to give symbolic form to that which may occur in the future. All this, then, has implications for levels of bodily and emotional stress at times of illness. Threats to the human body are not dealt with simply and immediately by 'fight or flight'. Instead, our human capacity for reflection means that, by comparison with animals, we have far more control over our bodies such that, as Freund and McGuire point out, 'while one can *condition* an animal to lower its blood pressure, humans can *place themselves* into states of mind that will alter their blood pressure' (1991:79).

Thus, despite bio-medicine's concern with the stability and predictability of the body and its functioning, as we argue throughout this volume, it is precisely the labile, constantly changing process of human embodiment that makes health and illness such potent markers of identity. In that the 'organic self which traverses the life course... is...in a state of endlessly becoming rather than being' (Hockey and James 2003:136), as reflective social actors, interacting with others, we are confronted constantly by the changes that take place within the biological make-up of our bodies and those of others. A cut finger, a bout of flu or a stomach ache are changes which often lie beyond our conscious control as rational social agents. And, whether we view these as potential disruptions or welcome interventions – the announcement of a new pregnancy, for example, has the potential to do both – negotiating the changes which the body undergoes, whether our own or someone else's, is an integral part of our experience of embodiment. And, through our interactions with

others, importantly, it is also essential to processes of social identification. As
Jenkins notes:

> embodiment is not optional: just as all individual identities are social, so all
> social identities attach to individuals. But while some identities position indi-
> viduals alongside other similarly identified individuals within collectivities,
> others primarily differentiate individuals, as individuals, from each other
> (1996:52).

It is in this sense that the body has to be credited with making its own contribution to social relations, as the site of our lived and ongoing embodiment and
the medium of and for our social interactions (Williams and Bendelow 1998).
However, in order to understand the role of the body in health and illness, we
need to unpick 'the precise ways in which our bodies are made to operate as
both an ongoing location of who we *are* as well as an "object" which we *have*
and need to attend to' (Hockey and James 2003:20). Indeed, as this volume
explores, it is precisely the lived nature of the body which make the biological
changes associated with health or illness so instructive for an understanding
of the classification processes involved in the conferring, accepting and reject-
ing of different kinds of health identities in everyday social interactions. Thus,
it is through negotiating our way through different somatic states of being that
we come to know what it is to be well or ill and also to recognise the ways in
which the changing health status of our bodies contributes to the form and
pattern of our social relations.

For example, the onset of a chronic and debilitating illness may force all
sorts of change in aspects of our lives, which stretch far beyond the confines of
the body itself. In industrial societies patterns of employment may change –
for example, a shift from full-time to part-time work, a change in the kind of
employment, taking early retirement or ceasing work on the grounds of
ill-health. Patterns of leisure may similarly have to alter, with house-bound
activities taking precedence over more communal events. In agricultural, subsistence communities, on the other hand, these options may not be available or
feasible. Here, the body's increasing disabilities may have to be accommodated in other ways such as, for example, relying on the work effort of other
family members, including children (see Christensen *et al*, 1999).

However, aside from these differences in terms of the changed social contexts of people's everyday lives, when the body is threatened by disease, we
also have to note differences in terms of the embodied experiences of individuals. Thus, for example, while for some a diagnosis of heart disease may spur
them to take up regular exercise or prompt greater attention to dietary habits,
other people may choose to ignore this bodily change and alter the everyday
pattern of their lives but little.

And herein lies the importance of our focus on embodiment for, while biological changes in the body *do* occur, the ways in which these changes are incorporated, ignored, championed, dismissed, embraced, or rejected by any individual are not necessarily predetermined – either by the biological processes which have taken place or by the social context within which the individual, embodied self is positioned. Nonetheless, the body does and will change in ways which somehow have to be negotiated. As Hacking (1999) has shrewdly observed, not everything is socially constructed. Some things *are* inevitable. Bodily change and bodily decay are, we suggest, of this order. But how we respond to them is not.

Thus, as 'simultaneously a material object or possession and the site of human experience' (Hockey and James 2003:141), what we describe here as 'the negotiated body' is central to our understanding of the ways in which health and illness are encountered and understood by individuals in society. In that the changing materiality of our bodies is the very site of our embodiment, we must engage in all manner of negotiations to learn to manage our bodies in culturally-appropriate ways. From blowing our noses when we have a cold, coping with the breathlessness of asthma or taking pills to assuage a migraine, all such negotiations are both multifaceted and open-ended. Whether they result from the professional advice given to us by doctors or other healers, from lay understandings of illness gleaned from the Internet and the advice pages of women's magazines, or from casual conversations with a friend, they can profoundly influence our relationship to the organic materiality that is the body. And as we learn to negotiate our bodies and their environments through adopting new body techniques (Mauss [1934] 1973), so any changes in the organic body may not only profoundly alter our sense of who we are but also reshape the way others see us.

Towards Embodiment: The Body, Health and Identity

We begin our journey towards understanding the role of the negotiated body in forging the relationship between health and identity in Chapters 2 and 3. Here we review the ways in which health and illness have been theorised within sociology and anthropology for it is on these disciplinary bases that our approach builds. Chapter 2 examines a range of structural approaches that explore the social factors which impact on individuals' health experiences – for example the links that exist between poverty, social class and poor health. Arguing that these do not provide a sufficient account of the ways in which individuals experience health and illness, we then move on to explore more discursive perspectives. These approaches which examine the influence of particular sets of ideas about health and illness enable us to examine the micro-politics of power that inform the medical encounter. However, in Chapter 2, we also examine agency-based accounts of health and illness and, through this, provide a critique of social constructionist perspectives, while nonetheless arguing for their pertinence, in some important respects, for the concerns of this volume. Here we suggest that what is needed is an approach that explores the interconnections between structural and institutional processes and individual agency in the social construction of health identities. Such an approach that enables us to explore the gamut of everyday interactions that people have – be these with institutions, medical professionals, pharmaceuticals, Internet sites, family members and friends – allows us to begin to formulate an answer to the question: how do we know that we are ill?

However, in Chapter 3 we take this forward in a rather particular way by bringing the body itself into the discussion. Exploring first some of the reasons why medical anthropology and sociology have been drawn towards social interactionist and constructivist approaches, we then set these against the insights to be gleaned from a more phenomenological perspective which is grounded in human embodiment. Locating our exploration at the site of the embodied self, we take on the challenge of finding out how conceptions of the body inform human beings' engagement with not only their bodies but also their wider cultural, social, economic – and importantly health – environments. As Meador (1995) argues, for example, if the hegemony of western medical models draws ever more aspects of human experience within its remit, being 'well', in the sense of lacking any diagnosable pathologies, is likely to become a thing of the past. Within bio-medicine's epistemological framework, well-ness itself is elusive, a condition which is resistant to measurement. Humorously, therefore, Meador describes the seven hours and 13 minutes per day that he estimates would be required to respond to the entire gamut of risk-assessing, health promoting practices now available in western societies – from the Minnesota Multiphase Personality Inventory, through to reverse-osmosis water-filtering systems and the ingesting of 'concoctions of dried seaweed mixed with desalinated sea water, along with a baby aspirin' (1995:425). As Chapter 3 argues, how 'health' and 'illness' are brought into being is therefore a question which needs to be located at the site of the body in the full diversity of its social and historical contexts.

Having set out the theoretical perspectives which frame our thinking, in Chapter 4 we use these to begin to address, empirically, the fundamental question: how do we know we are ill? Here, examining a range of cross-cultural material, we consider the different ways in which concepts of 'health' and 'illness' gain meaning for individuals through their everyday interactions and social relationships. Whether this is through the doctor-patient encounter or through engaging with the lay perspectives that are locally available to them through conversations with friends or family, embodied individuals use these different arenas to begin to make sense of the somatic experiences they have. Chapter 4 explores, therefore, how different theories about the causation of disease, for example, enable individuals to answer the question – why me – in the face of onset of illness, while also acknowledging that, within western societies, health promotion strategies are increasingly laying the blame for illness upon the individual. And, as this process of individual blame begins to expand its remit to include 'good (healthy)' and 'bad (unhealthy)' lifestyles, especially in western societies, so it becomes more difficult to draw a definitive line between health and illness. Given the stigmatising potential of illness, this has, therefore, quite profound implications for identity and, indeed, for our very experiences of embodiment.

Chapter 5 develops these themes by considering in more detail the different representational forms through which individuals gain knowledge about health and illness, knowledge which they may use to interpret, comprehend or reconcile the bodily changes they are experiencing – or which they observe in other people. Whether these representations take the form of lay narratives, Internet sites, advice pages in magazines, TV documentaries and dramas, advertisements or factual reports, each has a kind of 'authority' which individuals must interrogate. Constituting different discourses about health and identity, as the chapter explores, individuals may learn to negotiate a way through them, an experience which increasingly invites challenges to be made to the hegemonic authority of bio-medicine. For some this may mean that the medical model no longer continues to offer a satisfactory account of the experiences of illness and therefore it is to other kinds of representations that people turn.

In Chapter 6, therefore, we go on to ask how representations of health and illness are animated in encounters between individuals and the healthcare system, whether in face-to-face interaction or exposure to health-related materials and media. To this end, we focus on the ritual drama of illness to engage specifically with the embodied experience of sickness. Here, the agency that individuals have with respect to negotiating illness is explored in depth as we trace out the path from health to illness and through to recovery. We ask about the ways in which different structures facilitate or impede individuals making this journey and the strategies through which they, as individuals, manage the experience of getting sick. As a drama which unfolds in an individual's life, sickness is, at one and the same time, a common and shared social experience, but one which is also highly personal in that it has, potentially, profound implications for a changed identity. Chronic illness and disability provide key foci here.

Understanding processes of bodily, and associated social change, is the core subject of Chapter 7 as we explore health and illness across the life course.

Here we witness the power of bio-medicine to define a descent into illness as a 'natural' aspect of the ageing process in western societies such that to be ill is to be old. However, we also explore the ways in which such forms of identification are resisted and challenged – to be sick as a child, for example, is to confound this 'natural order of things'. Cross-cultural material also poses a challenge to such a medicalised life course in that, in many parts of the world, infant mortality is the norm, rather than an unusual event and the diseases of old age are often absent in populations where life expectancy is short. Once more we see, then, in our quest to understand the experience of embodiment in relation to health and illness, the ways in which structure and agency perspectives can both be brought to bear and show that it is the embodied individual whose experiences constitute the site for their interplay.

Chapter 8 explores the impact of medical technologies of different kinds upon health experiences and identities, and pursues this idea further. In that the rapid advances made in medical technology appear to offer ways in which the limitations of the body can be negotiated, if not transcended. Chapter 8 directly confronts the interactions between economic, political and cultural systems that, for the embodied individual, come to constitute the arenas through which health and illness are not only experienced and made sense of but through which identities are shaped. The chapter suggests that through techniques such as IVF and transplant surgery the body is repositioned in many different ways. Not only can it become a commodity to be bought and sold but medical technologies can also intervene to confuse the very boundaries which for westerners divide one body from another. As machines become integral parts of the embodied self or connect individuals to one another, both locally and globally, so these new forms of embodiment have consequences for the health identities that individuals take on and the kinds of personhood they can embrace.

The book concludes with Chapter 9's account of its contribution to medical sociology and anthropology's critical position within contemporary healthcare debates. This reiterates the importance of problematising western conceptions of the 'the body', arguing that a phenomenological approach to questions of health, illness and identity is not only potentially fruitful, but also one which must take account of the cultural and historical specificity of contemporary western embodiment. Health identities therefore emerge as embodied processes which unfold within particular social, institutional, technical and economic environments. Moreover, in that the book highlights the socially constructed nature of the body's 'stability', identification, we argue, involves an ongoing and inevitably incomplete negotiation of changes within our bodies and brains – and therefore within our social identities more broadly. Central to the book's project is therefore an exploration of how identification takes place, how health status meshes with other aspects of social identity, how age in particular relates to health, and what representational and technological processes might be germane to this process – within both contemporary western society and a global future.

2

Theorising Health and Illness

The relationship between the biological changes that take place in our bodies, our somatic experience of these changes and the socially constructed categories which enable us to interpret them is, as noted in Chapter 1, core to this volume's exploration of the relationship between the body, health and identity. If, for example, we decide that the dull ache in our knees is an indication of the 'natural' process of ageing (see Chapter 7), a sign that the passage of time has taken its toll upon our joints, this may have rather different consequences for us than if we decide, instead, that it constitutes a 'symptom' of disease. The first may lead us to take very little action other than seeking reassurance from our friends and family; the second, by contrast, might set in train a whole series of consultations with members of the medical profession. And, which option we choose will also have different outcomes for our sense of self and identity. It may lead to the simple recognition that we are getting that much older; that the game of squash we played the night before was, in retrospect, not a good idea; or by contrast that the arthritis which 'runs in the family' is perhaps about to claim its next victim.

It is therefore through such socially located processes of self-monitoring and reflexivity, processes seen by Giddens (1991) as central to issues of self-identity, that we are led to construct a view of ourselves and of our status as well or ill or, indeed, as just not quite 'right'. Thus, from a social constructionist perspective, it is essentially the translation of somatic experiences into explanatory categories which is seen as fundamental to the generation of ideas of health and illness and to the identities they embrace. And, whether bio-medical constructs or other explanations which cite the spirit world as the 'cause' of somatic distress are used, the different kinds of social relationships and interactional processes that are involved are comparable. Indeed this is what enables the claim that ideas of health and illness are socially and culturally constructed.

However, although this theoretical perspective is a dominant one within sociology and anthropology, and indeed finds a central place in this volume, it needs to be approached with care. First, because this is not the only theoretical resource that has been used by social scientists in their quest to understand and explain patterns and experiences of illness. And second, because it is not, in our view, a sufficient account. If we are to understand how it is that we know we are ill and the ways in which health and illness identities are ascribed to us in the course of our life, then, as noted in Chapter 1, we must see the dialectical process of identification, by which we get to know how others see us, as an embodied process of social interaction. This means, therefore, that we have to explore the nature of the social interactions that take place between ourselves and other individuals, both face-to-face and through our membership of many different kinds of social institutions. Indeed, it is through unpicking the fine details of all these different kinds of relationships, and through seeing them as ongoing and embodied interactions, that we will be able to understand the experiential relationship that exists between the body, health and identity. Only by doing this can we discover the ways in which the process of 'social construction' of ourselves as ill or well actually takes place.

Such complex tasks lie, however, in the chapters to follow. Here we begin by examining some of the ways in which social scientists have traditionally given account of the role of social structure in shaping individuals' health and illness experiences. This will provide us with some initial insights into the relationship between the body, health and identity.

The Individual *and* Society

We start by examining those sociological perspectives which reflect a Durkheimian view of society as being more than simply the sum of its members. In other words, these are perspectives which understand 'society' as a set of overarching structures which, among other things, divide and organise society's members and their everyday lives: for example divisions of class, gender and age. As a top-down or macro-level view, this is a position which makes an abstract model of society its starting point, one which necessarily therefore aggregates the variety of individual experiences into some sort of common structure and sets of collectivities. So in considering health matters, an approach such as this allows us to discover, for example, that people who share a particular social class background (an identity defined by their occupation, income, or post code) are likely to die at a similar age when compared with those of a different class background. Townsend and Davidson's (1982) classic study of geographical variation in mortality rates in England revealed precisely this. Alternatively, in the context of both non-western and western societies, medical anthropologists have explored the ways in which ethnicity works as an aspect of identification and social differentiation in health and illness experiences and in a population's susceptibility to disease (Trostle and Summerfield 1996).

Such structural approaches are epidemiological in nature with a focus on identifying the ways in which social factors such as social class, type of housing, employment status, ethnic background and gender pattern our health status. Referred to as sociology *in* medicine rather than sociology *of* medicine, their job is to call attention to the ways in which social factors impact upon organic processes. They remind us, therefore, that it is 'in the translation of social categories into meaningful reference groups' that social structure is pertinent to questions of social identity (Jenkins 2004:89) for the strength of these perspectives lies in the critique they offer of the more individualistic way in which medical practices, certainly within western societies, commonly frame our everyday experiences of health and illness. As patients we take a set of symptoms to a health practitioner and leave with a disease diagnosed. In adult life, this is an interaction which often, though not exclusively, takes place at a one-to-one level and is a consultation that is focused on the condition of the individual body. Arguably, therefore, this obscures awareness of the influence that broader social factors, such as class differences or ethnicity, may have upon our 'illness' or, indeed, on the ways in which they shape forms and types of diagnosis.

Although our interactions with family members might elicit a somewhat less individualised view – for example, an understanding that our mothers and grandmothers also suffered with a similar condition – and parallel conversations with friends, neighbours and colleagues might suggest that our condition is one which is 'going round' and that there is 'a lot of it about', these remain essentially individualised or localised accounts. And even in societies where the 'cause' or locus of an illness is explained through reference to a wider community of suffering, rather than being individualised within the body (see Chapter 4), the very immediacy of our somatic experience of illness can deflect attention from the larger-scale patterning of disease. Seeing the 'bigger picture', in the manner afforded by structural approaches, allows us, therefore, to move beyond taken-for-granted biological explanations of illness and to give weight to the importance of social factors to our health and well-being.

However, useful though this is, structural approaches cannot necessarily explain the precise *ways* in which these social factors come to play a part in our everyday experiences of health and illness. Thus, although traditional structural perspectives can identify for us the importance of variables such as class or ethnicity, they may be unable to demonstrate precisely how these variables take effect or, indeed, how they interact with one another.

Faced with the quite evident relationship between social class differences and early mortality, identified by their large-scale survey, Townsend *et al* (1988), for example, still did not know what exactly it was about social class which linked it with an earlier death. To address this question they therefore took a more 'local' view and compared two working class towns where levels of poverty and unemployment were very similar yet their mortality rates were different. This was an attempt to fine tune the top-down picture and to give more precise insight into how social class and early mortality might be linked. In this case it allowed these authors to pinpoint a more specific factor – the presence of air-borne pollution in one town but not the other. Janes and Chuluundori (2004), similarly, sought to explain the emergence of stark health inequalities amongst women in post-socialist Mongolia. They argued that the reasons why rates of maternal mortality have recently peaked, rather than declined, can be explained by the unequal access to the 'free market', within which healthcare now operates in that society. Rather than the state providing healthcare to all, the new market system means that rural women, who are poorly educated and as a consequence increasingly impoverished, are less likely to access maternal health-care services.

'Top-down', structural perspectives therefore make an important contribution to our understanding of the relationship between health and identity, by showing up inequalities in health and drawing attention to the fact that illness is not simply a matter of bodily weaknesses or the result of accidents suffered by the individual. Instead, low-income, poor housing, domestic violence, difficult or dangerous work conditions, poor diet, vulnerability to crime, lack of education are social factors which can all undermine health. And, in a more global context, anthropological research focused on the epidemiology of disease within particular social and ecological settings allows us to document the huge variations in life expectancy between members of different societies. Thus we discover that childhood diseases such as measles and whooping cough are major killers of children in societies where their malnourishment is commonplace and vaccination programmes are patchy (Price 1994). Similarly, such approaches show that in subsistence and developing economies, poverty remains as a constant threat to the well-being and subsequent health identities of the majority of the population, in both the short and longer term (Phillips and Verhasselt 1994).

The Individual *in* Society

However, useful as these approaches are, in our quest to explore the relationship between health status and identity and to find out more about the processes whereby we come to take on, or are ascribed the status of 'sick', we need to draw on additional theoretical resources since, as noted in Chapter 1, questions of identity require us to ask about the *process* of becoming ill. We need to know, for example, what counts as an illness and whether the classification of somatic experiences varies between groups, in and between different societies. We also need to understand the social and cultural processes involved in 'getting better', and the kinds of social interactions that are engendered when living with a chronic illness or disability and the ways in which these might shape identity. Such questions cannot readily be answered by structural perspectives which, in capturing the larger scale patterning of experience, tend to freeze the moment, rather than attend to process and change. And they certainly cannot address the embodied nature of that experience. Indeed, individual experience is aggregated within a common picture. Finally, although structural accounts draw attention to social inequalities and highlight the inadequacies of the environments within which people of a particular social class or ethnic background encounter illness, that these individuals might nonetheless have some degree of agency and choice about how they live their lives is less often acknowledged.

One reason for this is that the aim of much research conducted from this perspective is to shape public health policy at a national or international level and so improve the conditions of life for more vulnerable social categories. Yet it is clear that not all individuals belonging to a particular social category will, necessarily, take on a similar health status (for a discussion of variations within the category 'elderly', for example, see Chapters 4 and 7). Thus, without an account of agency, we cannot begin to understand why this might be. Nor can we explain how individuals themselves understand issues of health and illness and what strategies they may devise in their everyday lives for managing them. If our definition of identity is grounded in a notion of process and founded on the dialectic between the external attribution of identity and the individual's internal response, resistance and/or renegotiation (see Chapter 1), then it is clear that we need to find out more about what the individual is up to. We need to draw on more agency-centred perspectives, derived from the work of theorists such as Goffman (1969), that are concerned with the processes of meaning-making in everyday life and which take place in and through social interactions of all kinds. As Jenkins notes, 'individual identification emerges within the ongoing relationship between self image and public image' (2004:71).

Thus, Chapman (2003) for example, seeks to understand why many poor Mozambican women delay seeking prenatal clinic consultations even though these are available and argues that, somewhat ironically, this can be understood as the women's attempts to protect their unborn children. Living in conditions of severe economic hardship, where competition for resources is high, women have to compete with one another for male support and income. Pregnant women, who will require additional resources, are therefore vulnerable to jealousy from others. This is believed to be made manifest in harmful witchcraft and sorcery being practised on their unborn children. Understandably, therefore, the women endeavour to conceal their identities as pregnant women from public knowledge for as long as possible. As Chapman concludes:

> ironically, delaying care in the maternity clinic until late in pregnancy can be interpreted as a preventive and protective health activity within the context of women's conceptions of their own reproductive vulnerability (2003:370).

Comparably, Graham (1987) can explain that in the UK many poor women may choose to smoke, despite potential damage to their physical health and additional drains being made on their already low income. For these women, smoking is a way of relieving the emotional and psychological stress of childcare in difficult circumstances:

> Smoking acts as both a luxury and a necessity when material and human resources are stretched … In a lifestyle stripped of new clothes, make-up, hairdressing, travel by bus and evenings out, smoking can become an important symbol of one's participation in an adult consumer culture (Graham 1987:55).

And, in the African context, where HIV/AIDS continues to threaten poor women's lives at an increasing rate, another, yet comparable, kind of 'choice' is often made: women risk having unprotected sex with their husbands, despite their knowledge of potential infection, in order to conform with traditional cultural constructions of gender identity and concepts of personhood (Grundfest Schoepf 1998).

Additional theoretical resources which will allow us to engage with process, experience and agency therefore seem to be essential if we are to make sense of the ongoing relationship between the body, health and identity. But should we then set structural approaches aside if this is our aim? No – for to do so would be to privilege agency and choice and to fracture the *social* nature of everyday life to the extent that only a loose assemblage of bounded individuals remains. This would be to ignore one important half of the dialectic process called 'identification' which takes place in and through our everyday encounters with other people as well as with institutions. As Jenkins argues, both structure and agency are integral to understanding social identity, this being 'one of the rare concepts that make as much sense individually as collectively' (2004:24).

Thus, for example, although we may choose to resist the 'collective' identities imposed on us via medical practitioners and healers, by our family, friends and, by the representations of self reflected back to us via the media or through broader policy agendas and health initiatives (see Chapters 4 and 5), we cannot adequately account for the experience of health and illness without also acknowledging their impact. Nor must we underestimate the power that such discourses and structures may have in providing mirrors for the self (see Chapter 1). Thus, as Grundfest Schoepf (1998) has argued, for example, one of the reasons why HIV/AIDS has gathered such momentum in Africa, despite the intensive intervention of health workers, is because the efforts of professionals are framed by the concepts and discourses of western bio-medicine. These have failed to counter – or indeed engage with – the more powerful local discourses about gender relations and sexual behaviour that discourage individual condom use. Any account of people's health and illness behaviours therefore needs to acknowledge the structures – be they social, economic, political or ideological – which provide the wider context within which illness is experienced and through which health identities are taken on, negotiated or rejected.

In line with this view, some recent work points to new ways of bringing epidemiological approaches to bear more precisely on the intricacies of the relationship between health, illness and social identity and questions of agency. So, for example, Higgs and Scambler (1998) revisit the relationship between class and health status, arguing that class-based inequalities can still shed light on the quality of individuals' everyday life.

First, they argue that in the past class has been used indiscriminately, as an umbrella term which unhelpfully subsumes a whole range of material factors which can threaten health – from poverty and poor housing to domestic violence and unemployment. As noted in relation to The Black Report (see Townsend and Davidson 1982), this approach can reveal health inequalities in a very powerful way. What it cannot do, however, is identify precisely the mechanisms through which such inequalities are produced. It is too all-encompassing a concept to get at the precise ways in which particular social and material conditions undermine health.

In addition, Higgs and Scambler argue that medical sociologists have not confronted the question of *how* to assign class membership and have neglected 'the political nature of class [in] the debate about inequalities' (1998:83). They have simply used the registrar general's typology of occupational status as a way of pigeon-holing individuals. Such a typology, like many others, makes the intermediate classes its focus, while neglecting not only the power elite who are likely to influence health policy and resourcing at a macro-level, but also the underclass who fall outside any schema based on occupation, yet whose health needs are likely to be the most pressing. But, more importantly, for our purposes here, given the persistence of class-based patterns of inequality which were evident immediately after the Second World War, in Higgs and Scambler's (1998) view, class differences remain an objective condition of identity. Thus, although individuals may no longer be able to claim a class membership, based on relations of production, as Higgs and Scambler contend, this does not mean that class relations are no longer an objective reality. They argue for 'the salience of "rulers" for the differential health of the "ruled"' (1998:97). Although it is through our patterns of consumption, rather than production, that our class-based locations are ascribed, what we wear and eat, the media we consume, are nonetheless important attributes and characteristics through which others 'identify' us, and through which we negotiate who we think we are (see Bourdieu 1984; see also Archer and Francis (2006) for a discussion of the racialised context of class). Thus, even if class no longer contributes to our subjective sense of self-identity, it still shapes the conditions within which we operate. For example, dangers at work can be overlooked as part of a working-class macho culture of risk or over-looked out of feelings of helplessness when risk seems all pervading. What does heavy nicotine addiction matter to people resigned to exposure to dangerous chemicals and with no choice but to live in conditions of air pollution?

For those medical sociologists and anthropologists involved in health research in the context of the developing world, a combination of both structure and agency perspectives is proving to be critical for in many regions patterns of morbidity are changing differentially within *single* populations. 'Modern' health disease profiles, such as diabetes and heart disease, are now being seen alongside the more traditional ones associated with poverty and are thus being seen as distributed along class lines (Phillips and Verhasselt 1994). Additionally, as Lambert (1998) has argued, in relation to understanding the pattern of sexually transmitted disease (STD) in India, epidemiologically focused research and health interventions benefit enormously from the insights derived from more locally based, subjective understandings of health and gender. In the Indian context, she argues, STD symptom reporting need not necessarily indicate the presence of disease for 'in indigenous conceptions, women as well as men have semen and the association of semen with general health and strength can lead to concerns about the loss of this vital fluid' among women (Lambert 1998:1008).

As the above discussion demonstrates, epidemiological and structural approaches, by themselves, offer important but partial explanation of the nature of the relationship between the body's health and social identity. To fully comprehend the processes whereby health identities are taken on we need also to take account of people's understandings and experiences of health and illness. In short, we need to see how illness is made sense of in specific localities and one way to do this is to focus in on the medical encounter. Traditionally, within medical sociology and anthropology, it is the interactions that take place between medical practitioners and other healers, and their patients that have been regarded as one of the most important contexts within which 'health identities' are forged so it is here that we look first.

In this next section we consider what different theoretical perspectives have so far allowed us to understand about the processes involved in the medical consultation.

Theorising the Medical Encounter

We begin with the classic account offered by Talcott Parsons (1951). A functionalist sociologist, Parsons saw doctors as an example of western society's experts, members of a group who had a key role to play in ensuring its smooth running. In Parsons' model illness represents a form of social deviance because illness disrupts individuals' lives and so makes them unable to fulfil their normal social roles. It is therefore the role of doctors, appropriately empowered by the structures of their professions, to treat the patient and to legitimise their withdrawal from society as sick, by conferring on them the sick role. By virtue of their medical training and professional status, Parsons reasoned, doctors are obliged to treat the patient by using expert knowledge, to be altruistic rather than self interested, and to be emotionally detached and to follow professional ethics. These obligations come hand in hand with the right to examine the patient, both physically and emotionally; to act autonomously as a practitioner; and to occupy a position of authority *vis-à-vis* the patient. The patient, for their part, when feeling ill, is obliged to consult a doctor to claim the identity of 'sick'; but, having done so, they can only withdraw from carrying out their normal social roles, as long as they follow the doctor's treatment regime and return to normal functioning as soon as possible.

Writing prior to the development of the more critical stance of the social sciences towards medicine and medical knowledge (see below), Parsons characterised the doctor/patient relationship as appropriately unequal. If the doctor had power, status and prestige, then this was a resource that benefited not only the patient but also society more generally. For Parsons, these asymmetrical relationships between doctor and patient were positive. They ensured that society functions smoothly by having experts in place to deal with society's members when they cannot participate appropriately, and when they need, for example, absences from work to be professionally authorised.

Marxist perspectives on the structure of the medical encounters (see Navarro 1976; Doyal 1979; Waitzkin 1989, 1991) begin from a similar starting point: an assumption that doctor/patient relationships are unequal, that the doctor is the expert and that the patient is dependent on that expertise. However, rather than this being seen as a mechanism for ensuring the smooth running of society, within a Marxist framework, this relationship is viewed negatively, as the shoring up of a particular power structure. The doctor is part of an elite middle class and medicine provides the legitimation for them to reproduce the dominant class ideology. From a Marxist perspective, doctors are therefore seen as agents of social control through, for example, defining health functionally, as the ability to work. In addition, through the consultation process doctors provide a medical framing of what are often social problems thereby deflecting patients' awareness from any social inequalities which may be disadvantaging them (Waitzkin 2000). And, finally, as the benevolent face of capitalism, doctors help mask its more punitive, coercive or exploitative facets through seeming to have the well-being of the population at heart.

Interestingly, though, despite Talcott Parsons having a consensual model of society and Marxist models being inherently conflictual, both are concerned with the structural issues that shape the context of health and illness. Thus, although ostensibly exploring the experience of the consultation process at a micro-level, they tell us little about the particular dynamic that connects doctors with their patients and through which health identities – those of being and becoming sick – are constructed through that interaction. Instead, for Parsons the medical and the sick roles simply represent forms of power which the doctor and the patient have no choice over. His model assumes that the system works in the interests of both parties equally, serving the ends of society by providing a mechanism for dealing with a breakdown of the system. Equally, a Marxist approach often also has little to say about how the individual doctor or patient might negotiate their role or indeed subvert it. Instead it focuses on the structural effects of class differences as they make themselves felt within the social context of the medical encounter. This gives them a relatively deterministic character and assumes that the asymmetrical relations of power embedded in that encounter are always to the benefit of the doctor and not to that of the patient, albeit that for some, Waitzkin (1989) for example, this element of control is an unintentional aspect of the medical encounter.

In addition to not allowing us to see how individuals experience the medical encounter, these top-down theoretical approaches also do not enable us to make sufficient sense of the ways in which medicine and the whole sphere of health and illness have changed across time. For example, the growing proportion of patients with chronic rather than acute illness (Nettleton 1995), means that the Parsonian version of the sick role has lost salience. Chronically sick people cannot simply swallow their medicine, recover from their disease and return to 'normal' function. And, likewise, their doctor cannot fulfil an obligation to treat the patient in the sense of returning 'normal' function since there is no 'cure' for many chronic conditions. There are only ways of alleviating symptoms and preventing associated health problems. More than this, today the patient is likely to be an expert, as well as the doctor (see Chapter 5). With resources such as the Internet and self-help groups available to them, as well as the everyday experience of managing their condition, people with chronic illnesses are no longer solely dependent upon their doctor for help. What this suggests is that, as the understandings and practices around health and illness have shifted, traditional theorising of the structural issues involved in the medical encounter have become inadequate for the task of understanding how it is that people get to know that they are ill. More penetrating questions therefore need to be asked about the processes involved, about the ways in which health identities are actively *produced* or socially constructed in the medical encounter, rather than simply the ways in which it frames identities. For example, Davis (1991) shows that female patients may challenge the socially-legitimated authority of male doctors:

> It was abundantly clear, that just as male doctors could be nice and friendly while exercising control, patients were often surprisingly recalcitrant and rebellious. In fact, the patients routinely exercised power in all sorts of subtle, sneaky and even somewhat unorthodox ways (1991:76).

The Social Construction of Health and Illness

Dominant within contemporary medical sociology and anthropology – and indeed, as noted earlier, core to the concerns of this volume – social constructionism's key theoretical contribution has been its questioning of the western medical model of health and illness. Work in non-western settings which reveals the diversity of health and illness categories has been used to make strange and therefore problematise the taken for granted objectivity of the ways in which westerners 'know' their bodies. Central to this critique is the questioning of the objective and neutral status of medical knowledge through the suggestion that 'medical knowledge' can be regarded as fluid, subjective and context specific. This perspective takes both strong and weak forms. The hardline poststructuralist account views the body, health and illness as little more than the products of particular sets of ideas, relationships and practices. According to this view there is no objective, neutral scientific knowledge about health; all knowledge, including our knowledge of the body and its illnesses, arises in and out of social relations of different kinds. By contrast, the latter, weaker version takes the body and its malfunctioning or impairments as givens; here the social constructionist critique is of the medical model of knowledge about the body through addressing the many variations that occur in how different cultures or historical eras make sense of the disease process (for a full debate on these different perspectives see Bury 1986 and Nicholson and McLaughlin's response 1987; see also Chapter 3).

Two key developments in social theory have been crucial to the emergence of this powerful perspective within medical sociology and anthropology. First, the contribution made by feminism when it sought to engage with Marxist structural perspectives in order to think about questions of patriarchy, rather than simply class, provided a different slant on the medical encounter. Second, were the insights into the structuring of a micro-politics of power which Foucault's (1973, 1979) work on the history of the clinic and, indeed, on the body provides. It is to an examination of these that we now turn.

The Social Construction of Health and Illness: The Feminist Contribution

A key contribution to the progress of the sociology of medicine was made by the anti-psychiatry school when it problematised the issue of *mental* health and illness. The most famous proponent of anti-psychiatry perspectives, Laing, reframed the illness category 'madness' through his suggestion that this was a sane response to an oppressive world (see Laing and Esterson 1973). In his view, the categories of psychiatry, generated through the medical encounter, were identity labels rather than 'scientific' descriptions of 'medical conditions' – and these were often used to silence those who failed to fit into a capitalist society by discrediting their voices.

Drawing strength from this perspective, while simultaneously criticising it for its lack of gender awareness, the radical feminist Phylllis Chesler (1972) argued that psychiatry and medicine have silenced *women's* voices in particular, since women are far heavier consumers of mental health services than men. Thus, she argued, diagnostic categories such as 'hysteria', categories that evolved in and through medical encounters, tied madness very closely with women and cut the ground away from their anger over the social conditions which flowed from patriarchal relations of power. Similarly, the diagnosis of depression, with its medicalised associations of emotional instability, helplessness, passivity, and low self-esteem, represented an extreme version of traditional or hegemonic femininity. In other words, Chesler argued, the psychiatric consultation created a Catch-22 situation for women in that they could be pathologised for being both too feminine (depressed) *and* for getting angry (hysterical) by resisting the accommodating role expected of women since the late nineteenth century (see also Showalter 1987; Usher 1991).

Chesler's work, though seemingly radical, remained focused on the structural framing of medical encounters, however, and told us little about the patient's (or doctor's!) experience, agency or identity. Indeed, 1970s feminists such as Chesler were later accused of reducing the very real mental suffering of women living within oppressive conditions to a set of psychiatric labels (Busfield 1996; Usher 1991). Nonetheless, this perspective did raise important questions about the social construction of medical knowledge and health identities through the process of identification. It made us ask, for example, whether women are *labelled* mad by psychiatrists within the context of the medical encounter, or *driven* mad by the inequalities which make up their everyday lives?

Labelling theory of the 1960s had suggested that the stigma attached to mental illness arose through particular social definitions being attached to behaviour, rather than being inherent properties of that behaviour itself, with the consequence being that when people took on such labels, any stigma was that much harder to remove. One answer to the problem identified above was, therefore, to suggest that, when women seek help from psychiatrists for the mental health problems which result from social and material disadvantage, their conditions are interpreted within a medical framework and that it is this which leaves them pathologised and stigmatised (Busfield 1996).

However, this structural account does not in itself explain how the power of psychiatry operates at the level of the individual within the medical encounter. Identifying the specialism's diagnostic categories as labels, and questioning the status of medical knowledge, tells us nothing, for example, about *the experience* of madness. Nor does it tell us how macro-level structures, such as patriarchy, actually impact upon particular bodies and minds – and indeed how individuals inhabit, respond to or resist these conditions.

To begin to explore some of these questions, questions which are central to the concerns of this volume, we have to turn to poststructuralism and the contribution of Foucault. Only by using these theoretical approaches can we get a more specific account of the precise ways in which power operates in the encounters that take place between doctor and patient.

The Social Construction of Health and Illness: The Contribution of Foucault

Doctor-patient interaction exposes what Foucault (1973, 1979) described as a micro-politics of power operating in local social contexts to produce particular health identities. According to Foucault, the power of the state operated rather like blood flowing not just through the main arteries, but circulating throughout the entire body via capillaries. In this way, institutional power is deployed at highly localised sites, such as the doctor's surgery, the hospital, the clinic, and through the actions of community health workers. Drawing our attention to the local effects of power, Foucault explained that it is not exercised overtly. Rather, power takes effect by securing the consent of those who participate in the system.

The pertinence of a Foucauldian position for understanding the relationship between the body, health and identity is particularly evident when we examine new trends in the contemporary provision of healthcare in western societies. The lay patient who simply puts themselves in the hands of the doctor has been somewhat displaced by the informed consumer of healthcare who monitors their own diet and exercise patterns (see Chapter 4). In such circumstances, Foucault would argue, the medical model is not so much being imposed upon the individual, through the structuring of the medical encounter. Rather, it is produced by the individual; that is, they willingly take it upon themselves by participating in a particular system of thought and practice. Indeed they may quite literally appropriate and internalise a whole regime via the choices they make, for example, about their diet. When Foucault talked about 'docile bodies' (1979), this is the kind of circumstance that he had in mind. He would argue that the body and indeed the self, or subjectivity, are produced within discourse, that is, within a particular set of ideas and associated practices. And, it is in the medical encounters between doctors and patients that discourses of health, illness and identity are primarily reproduced.

Prior's account of discourse provides a clear depiction of the issues involved. For him, discourse is,

> not merely a narrow set of linguistic practices which reports on the world, but is composed of a whole assemblage of activities, events, objects, settings and epistemological precepts. The discourse of pathology, for example, is constructed not merely out of statements about diseases, cells and tissues, but out of the whole network of activities and events in which pathologists become involved, together with the laboratory and the other settings within which they work and in which they analyse the objects of their attention (Prior 1989:3).

This capillary model is highly relevant to the concerns of this volume. It not only allows us to generate some account of how the individual becomes enmeshed within wider structural systems of power relations, but also attends to the processual nature of everyday individual experience and identity practices. As such, it can be used to investigate identification, that endlessly incomplete dialectic of ascription, appropriation and avoidance of particular social identities (Jenkins 1996). What Foucault's account eschews is the idea that certain institutions or individuals contain 'power', as if it were an enduring object or immutable property which will inevitably cause those who encounter it to respond in ways which suit the interests of others. Rather, medical power is seen as discursive. It is a form of power which operates within an 'assemblage of activities, events, objects, settings and epistemological precepts' (Prior 1989:3). As we go on to argue in Chapter 3, however, it is an approach which nonetheless maintains a distance from the choices and actions of embodied individuals.

Drawing on a Foucauldian perspective, Armstrong provides a graphic description of the structuring of the medical encounter as follows:

> Look at the lines of medical surveillance: 'What is your complaint?' 'How do you feel?' 'Please tell me your troubles'. See the routine clinical techniques: the

rash displayed, the hand applied to the abdomen, the stethoscope placed gently on the chest. This is the stuff of power. Trivial perhaps but repetitive, strategies to which the whole population at times must yield ... the stethoscope is an important instrument of power. Yet who can object to its technical necessity? Who challenge the 'value-free' nature of the whispering breath sounds it reports? Yet at each and every application it establishes, confirms and repro-duces the passivity, solidity and individuality of the silent body it surveys (Armstrong 1987:70).

These are, however, the given scripts of those who identify as 'doctor' and 'patient', rather than the more strategic exchanges of specific individuals who are engaged in a particular medical encounter. Thus, in contrast to both Talcott Parsons and the medical sociologists who work from Marxist perspec-tives, who understand power as something 'possessed' by the doctor, as if it were an object of some kind, Foucault offers instead a processual and more organic model of power. This allows us to understand its operation in medical settings, even where it is not routinely apparent in an overt or indeed violent form. His model is grounded in the idea of the panopticon, a form of prison within which inmates' cells are exposed to the gaze of the warder who occu-pies a central watchtower. The body of the prisoner is never touched directly within this system, and yet the gaze of the warder has a profound effect upon the body in that the prisoner knows they are potentially exposed to their view at all times.

Compared with a functionalist account of medical practice or a Marxist inspired political economy of healthcare, where the patient is rendered help-less in the face of class, ethnicity and gender-based inequalities, Foucault's conception of the workings of structures of power is far subtler – and more useful for our purposes. Existing within the *relationship* between the doctor and their patient, it is pervasive and mobile, rather than tied up in individuals who 'exercise it'. In this way, as Lupton argues:

> power in the context of the medical encounter is not a unitary entity, but a strategic relation which is diffuse and invisible. Power is not necessarily a subjugating force aimed at domination which itself is vulnerable to re-sistance, but rather is closer to the idea of form of social organization by which social order and conformity are maintained by voluntary means (Lupton 1994:111).

This perspective has implications for contemporary calls for patient empower-ment or for a more holistic approach to patients' needs in that, paradoxically, the more the patient participates, or gives of themselves, the more far reaching and powerful the medical gaze becomes.

Agency, Health and Illness

In considering theoretical perspectives towards health and illness within sociology and anthropology this chapter has so far focused exclusively on structural issues and we have already travelled some considerable distance. Beginning with the concern to map the patterning of illness in relation to social variables we have arrived at a point where the concepts of 'health' and 'illness' work as identifiers and are themselves to be scrutinised as social constructions, arising in and out of the different kinds of medical encounters that people have. And it is here that the theoretical contribution of more agency-centred perspectives make their mark, by expanding our understanding of the social processes and everyday interactions through which medical knowledge is constructed and health identities are taken on. These assume that concepts of health and illness, rather than being fixed and objective descriptions of somatic states, take on a fluidity of meaning within different sets of social relations and vary in and between the different social contexts of everyday life.

Helman's (1986) classic account of the lay understandings of colds and fevers showed, for example, how shared medical knowledge and health identities are negotiated and produced in the encounters between doctors and their patients. People living in an English suburban community drew on a folk model of illness that, traditionally, distinguished between chills, colds and fevers in relation to body temperature. However with the emergence of 'germ theory', a theory that provides such a powerful and causal explanation of illness, patients began to seek treatment from their GP whereas, previously, such illnesses would have been treated at home by self-medication. Thus, in the increasingly busy context of the consultation room, and despite their bio-medical knowledge that such conditions are self-limiting and not at all life threatening, as Helman showed, 'the language and concepts used by GPs in consultations with patients suffering from Fevers/Colds/Chills was in the idiom of the folk model, not the biomedical one' (1986:228). GPs told their patients that they had picked up a germ or caught a virus and prescribed antibiotics to 'cure' them, despite knowing that many such treatments 'cannot be fully justified in scientific, biomedical terms' (Helman 1986:229).

More recently, a study carried out by Coupland and Coupland (1994) of a geriatric clinic in South Wales shows how doctors and their elderly patients negotiate the often negative association between old age and poor health through the conversations that take place in the consultation room. Older people's own assessment of their 'health' status was often made in relation to their age, which they saw as an inevitable process of decline and deterioration. Such a view is at odds with modern gerontological medicine and the doctors worked hard to counter the inevitability of this association. Thus, for example, when one patient commented that he could hardly walk and was afraid to go out, the doctor laughed it off, saying that it 'must be the season' and 'you know everybody's feeling ill' (1994:119). By reframing the creaks and pains of old age in a normative light the doctor encouraged the elderly patient to take on the identity of a fit, rather than frail, old person and to downplay the age/health relationship (see Chapter 7).

Through practices such as these it is possible to begin to see how ideas of illness and of cure, and people's responses to them, are culturally framed while also remaining open to different interpretations in practice. But the importance of such agency-centred studies does not simply lie in what they reveal about the cultural relativity of medical knowledge. What they also demonstrate are the social *processes* involved in the ongoing construction of 'health' and 'illness' and the negotiations that take place around particular health identities during medical encounters. We shall have cause throughout the rest of this volume to return to such studies so it is sufficient here to note the ways in which such perspectives enable us to explore in detail the fine-grained interactions through which people come to understand matters of health and illness and to take on, reject or negotiate different kinds of health identities. In this sense, then, such agency-focused social constructionist studies provide an important counterpoint to the broader sweep of more structural accounts.

However, that said, what neither of these approaches effectively engage with is the experience of illness as a *bodily* as well as a social process and how this might work to shape health identities. In this final section, then, we turn to some recent work that, in our view, begins to make this connection more explicit and provides the groundwork for our emphasis on embodiment which, as Chapter 3 explores, is core to our investigation of the relationship between the body, health and identity.

Structure, Agency and the Body

In Williams' (2003) discussion of the relationship between class and health, we find a useful example of the links to be made between the macro-level of social structure and the micro-level of experience. According to Williams, and indeed Marmot (2001), it is not simply the material effects of inequality which undermine health, but the unequal distribution of resources. In other words, health suffers not just because basic resources are lacking, but also as a result of an environment where some people have a great deal more than others. This is something which impacts very directly upon issues of identity and Williams concerns himself with the social, psychological and emotional deprivation associated with class-based social inequalities.

Though acknowledging the importance of brute material deprivation in undermining health, he also shows how poor living conditions can undermine people's self-esteem and breed feelings of anxiety, fear, anger or resentment. His analysis of individuals' experiences of illness takes account, therefore, of a whole range of factors: the effects of neo-liberalism; the promotion of a market-orientated society; the demise of the welfare state and the resulting loss of social cohesion; post-Fordist conditions of work where casualised shifting labour forces migrate in an unstable fashion globally; and the psychosocial effects of an unequal distribution of resources. For Williams, relative deprivation impacts upon health both directly, through poor diet and living conditions, and also indirectly by producing stress-related changes which potentially undermine the immune system and induce unhealthy behaviours such as smoking or drug and alcohol abuse. For Williams, then, the embodied, emotional self is the place where agency and structure intersect through the social relationships and encounters that people have with one another.

Such an approach opens up the possibility of literally reanimating structure in numerous fully embodied ways and Williams cites examples of other work which give pointers as to how this project might be carried out, empirically. When Brown and Harris (1989) conducted their study of depression among women who stayed at home with young children, they took account of provoking agents, such as severe life events and long-term difficulties; and vulnerability factors, such as the lack of close confiding relationships. What their analysis gets at is the inter-relationship of everyday routinised sources of stress and a more free-floating and persistent layer of difficulties associated with an individual's personal motives, commitments, plans and purposes. Impacting upon one another, they can orient individuals to the demands of their present and future lives in ways which put their health at risk. Similarly, Watson's (2000) work on male embodiment tackles the inter-relationship between health promotion messages which stress the need to take personal responsibility for health, and what is expected of men, both structurally and ideologically, in terms of the work and leisure activities they undertake. What this allows Watson to pick up on is a problematic tension for men in their everyday lives between, on the one hand, the risk-taking associated with macho embodied masculinity and, on the other, structural factors such as government health promotion policies which make men aware of the need for a healthy diet and exercise regime. In practice, 'unhealthy' choices are its outcome. Such an example, says Williams, 'point[s] to a subtle and sophisticated form of socially pliable biology which accords emotional modes of being a central role in linking one existential-phenomenologically embodied agent with wider structures of power' (2003:52).

Conclusion

The psychosocial perspective outlined by Williams enables connections to be made, then, between social structures, individual agency and the body. This represents a relatively new departure within medical sociology and anthropology. As noted, hitherto the materiality of the experiencing body has been somewhat sidelined in attempts to *problematise* biological accounts of the body offered by the medical model and so progress the social constructionist agenda. It is therefore a timely reminder that, notwithstanding the contingent and culturally relative character of concepts of health and illness we need, nonetheless, to understand, *sociologically*, the role played by the material body in the formation of health identities.

Moreover, if as Fitzpatrick (2001) has observed there is an ever increasing anxiety and fear about illness in contemporary western society, we need to understand why that has occurred. That we are all now proto-patients and reflexive body minders (see Chapter 4) underscores for us the pressing need for theoretical approaches that can grasp the subtleties of the interconnections between structural and institutional processes and individual agency in the social construction of health identities and to explore the contexts within which these meet.

As social scientists we need, therefore, to interrogate the shifts which have been occurring in healthcare practices by asking rather different kinds of questions than in the past, questions that make us consider how, precisely, we know when we are ill? Thus, rather than reflecting the separation of health and illness from other aspects of social life, as this book unfolds, we shall reintegrate health, illness and social identity into the context of the ongoing everyday lives of individuals and, in so doing, explore the triangular relationship that exists between the body, self and society (Hockey and James 2003). In other words, we shall view the self, whether in sickness or in health, as actively inhabiting a body, a body which in everyday life is both shaped by and gives shape to particular sets of social structures.

3

Towards Embodiment

As the previous chapters have indicated, the connections to be made between social structures, individual agency and the body are critical to an understanding of why it is that the onset of illness may be accompanied not only by a changed social status but, more fundamentally, by an altered identity and sense of self. However, as suggested, the experience of the changing materiality of the physical body has traditionally been sidelined within medical sociology and anthropology. Instead, as we noted, the body has been viewed as a static object, something external to and apart from the individual, a perspective which potentially reproduces, rather than problematises, the abstracted and reductionist bio-medical model of the body (see Chapter 4). In our view, such a conceptualisation is inadequate since, as Benton argues, 'it is necessary to think of illness as affecting "persons" who *are* necessarily organically embodied [and] who also have psychological and social relational attributes which are causally implicated both in the aetiology and prognosis of disease' (1991:5).

Thus, although we go on to explore the cultural relativity of concepts of health and illness throughout this volume, including the many different ways in which 'disease' is socially constructed, in order to explain more accurately how it is that we come to know that we are ill, we also have to engage with the material fact of body changes; this too has a key part to play. In this chapter, then, we review a literature which outlines the possibilities that the concept of embodiment opens up for us in this respect, and consider how this helps us think about the body as both a living and a lived experience.

Models of the Body

Though not a new concept, embodiment has been underplayed as a theoretical and methodological resource within medical sociology and anthropo-

logy. In the urgent desire to dispense with the determinism of a universalising, medicalised view of the body, theorists have, for example, often concen-
trated on revealing its cultural relativity, and socially constructed character.
By exposing the existence of other models of the body, they could point to the
implications that this has for both health treatments and patient compliance.

It has been shown, for example, that the western view of the body as a container is associated with the idea of an individuated self which resides within
the boundaries of the flesh (Shildrick 2002). This container body has machine-
like properties, displaying the mechanical qualities of a system of plumbing
(Helman 1990:21–2), a perspective stemming from the development of medical
knowledge. The body was sub-divided by medical professionals into bounded
organs – the liver, the heart, the bowels and the lungs – or discrete systems,
such as the cardiovascular, endocrine or immune. Around each of these separable entities, specialisms developed, each one part and parcel of system of
healthcare within which the doctor – whether consultant or GP – was sovereign. Within this system the patient was treated as an individual undergoing a
temporary state of 'deviance', as a result of mechanical failure, but soon to be
returned to normal functioning.

Such mechanistic models of the body are still common as revealed by the
participants in Watson's (2000) study of men's health perspectives. One interviewee, for example, advanced a theory that the body is best not interfered
with since, like the cars which were his hobby, 'every time you do something
to make an improvement, it has an equal and an opposite effect. It messes
something else up' (2000:99). Similarly, when Martin (1987) interviewed
American women about their experiences of menstruation, childbirth and the
menopause, she highlighted their machine-like models of reproductive functioning. The use of terms such as 'labour' and the idea of the uterus as an
involuntary muscle that propels the baby forward, she argued, derive from a
root metaphor of 'production' which reflects a society organised around
industrialisation under capitalism. This cultural metaphor, she suggests, interestingly pervades both bio-medical expertise and lay understandings of the
body, thereby demonstrating the ways in which pregnancy and childbirth
within western societies have become increasingly medicalised.

However, even though in societies such as the UK, bio-medical models of
the body still predominate, there is, nonetheless, considerable diversity in the
ways in which the body is understood in everyday life. Boyle (1970, cited in
Helman 1990:15) reveals, for example, that 14.9% of his sample of 234 patients
envisaged the heart filling the thoracic cavity, 58.8% conceptualised the
stomach as an organ which took up the entire abdomen, from groin to waist,
48.7% believed that the kidneys were sited low down in the groin and 45.5%
imagined the liver to lie in the lower abdomen, just above the pelvis. And, in a
more recent study of decision-making about the disposal and memorialisation

of the remains of a close relative, Hockey, Kelleher and Prendergast (n.d.) show how a young man from Sunderland described the cause of his grand-mother's death in terms of a model of the body which he, as a plumber, could comprehend:

> obviously she had a lot of problems but she got a blockage, all her food backed up and obviously just stopped her from breathing and then she just, just stopped really ...

During the last 25 years, however, other models of the body and its manage-ment have begun to proliferate in the west, as notions of medicalised health-care have transcended the boundaries of the clinic to permeate the media, the workplace, the leisure venue and the home. 'Illness' is no longer a condition which can be bracketed within medicine (see De Swaan 1990). The container body – in sickness and in health – is now also the property, and indeed the responsibility, of the individual (see also Chapter 4). Moreover, this 'new' body is something which claims attention at all times, and not just when its normal functioning ceases. It requires constant vigilance and monitoring to maintain its healthy functioning. Indeed, so powerful is this imperative that, for the first time perhaps, the health of the 'male' body has begun to occupy the consciousness of *men*, rather than simply their wives and mothers (Daykin and Naidoo 1995).

Certainly, in Watson's (2000) study of men's perceptions of the male body, interviewees articulated quite explicit objectifications of the healthy body. It belonged to an individual who was 'just the right weight for his height. He wouldn't smoke or drink too much. He would have regular exercise, regular amounts of sleep and health food' (2000:76). His unhealthy counterpart was also envisaged in considerable detail, even down to exact height – 'five feet four inches' – and precise weight – 'fifteen stone'. This was an unequivocally stigmatised body: 'Totally gross!' said the 31-year-old male warehouse dis-patcher (Watson 2000:78).

All these examples, drawn from western social contexts, reveal, therefore, the social experience of the western body. It is a body that is bounded, indi-vidualised and container-like and central to an individual's self-identity. Ethnographic work in non-western settings, however, reveals the cultural specificity of this experience by drawing our attention to profoundly different ways of conceptualising the body and its relationship to the self.

Becker, for example, describes a corporate or more diffuse sense of the body among Fijians where, as she argues, 'the cultivation of bodies ... represents the cumulative efforts of the collective' (1994:129). Unlike westerners who see body management and maintenance as an individual project that is central to the formation of identity, Fijians derive their identity from their relationships with other members of their community. It does not come from the identificatory potential of their *own* body. What is crucial to Fijians, for example, is the capacity to provide food for others, to notice who is well-fed and who is neglected; and to be seen to remedy this through nurturance. For Fijians, therefore, the body is not really an index for individualised identity, as it is in the West. Rather, as Becker says, 'a body encodes social meanings as concretized care, and as such exhibits the collective handiwork of its community's labouring on its form' (1994:129).

It is not surprising, then, that different views of the body will go hand in hand with different understandings, and arguably, different experiences of illness. In Craig's (2000) account of Vietnamese conceptions of health and illness, for example, he shows how people's activities and bodies are understood to be very closely connected within a system that understands the body in terms of a binary, humoural taxonomy. Here illnesses are classified as either 'hot' or 'cold' and have to be treated accordingly. Thus, a father, living in Hanoi, describes his sick child's condition in the following manner:

> Our child is hot, it has hot blood. It's its body's nature. Hot means you're a very weak eater. She craves water, drinks a lot of water. Because she's hot, she has constipation, and is very slow to develop, and is a bit small. Her mother had a caesarean, and had to take a lot of antibiotics. So because of the antibiotics, the mother became hot, and didn't have much milk, and the child absorbed the antibiotics from the milk, and also became hot. So we have to give her a lot of fruit, to cool her body down and it's easy to digest. We don't like to give her antibiotics, because she is hot enough already (Craig 2000).

Within Vietnam, the conceptual opposition between 'hot' and 'cold' is integral to the daily management of the body and is used to classify not only its condition, but also its care, with food – that which is placed inside the body – being seen as a key resource. Fever is hot and therefore cold foods, such as those containing Vitamin C, are needed to regulate the body and restore its balance. In cases of fever, antibiotics, which are classified as hot, might not be appropriate. But, these understandings of the body and its treatment are not uniform; they vary according to gender. Men should ideally be hot, while women should be cold. Thus, in the case above, after following a course of antibiotics the child's mother became too hot, and transferred this heat to her daughter via the antibiotics circulating in her breast milk. The father was understandably resistant, therefore, to exacerbating the 'heat' already in his child's body by giving her more (hot) antibiotics.

Such examples illustrate well, therefore, the social and cultural diversity of models of the body and the implications these have for treatment during health and illness episodes (see also Chapter 4). Yet, we would argue, if

social scientists are to make a more significant contribution to the understanding of health and well-being, this kind of social constructionist
approach is not sufficient; we need also to find some way of acknowledging the common *human* condition of embodiment itself. In sum, our argument is that social science has to engage, on the one hand, with beings who
have the capacity to perceive both themselves and their environments in
ways which may be radically divergent and who yet, on the other, also
share experiences that are grounded in a broadly similar materiality – the
fleshy, organic body. Only if we do this can we begin to understand fully
the relationship that undoubtedly exists between the body, health and
identity.

Why Embodiment?

The ethnographic examples above revealed the socially constructed character
of the body and from a hardline social constructionist perspective it could be
argued that it is, therefore, through these models of the body – rather than
simply our nerve endings – that we experience the changes in the body that
health and illness bring! However, as noted in Chapter 2, this volume is concerned to develop alternatives to such a wholly discursive position, which sees
the body simply as the product of sets of representations. As social scientists,
concerned with people's everyday lives, we have to be able to account for the
bodily *experience* of becoming ill. So, we would agree with Jackson that 'the
subjugation of the bodily to the semantic is empirically untenable' (cited in
Csordas 2002:243) since such a perspective fails to account for the body's
undeniable and changing *materiality*, both from day to day and across the life
course (see Chapters 1 and 7). Moreover, a purely discursive view of the body
cannot explain why, as Merleau-Ponty (1974) argued, if an individual at some
point loses their leg, then their embodied perceptions (of both themselves, of
their environment and of their relationships with others) is often radically
altered.

It becomes clear, then, that no matter how many alternative representations
of the body we might choose to explore, these sources of data cannot, in themselves, take us to the heart of what a broken leg might mean to a professional
footballer, an athlete or a climber. Simpson's (1998) autobiographical account
of crawling down crevasses, over glaciers and across moraines, after his leg
was badly fractured during a climb, provides a powerfully embodied account
of his own physiological and emotional experience and for us, as social scientists, the challenge is to develop a comparably insightful, theoretical perspective on patient suffering and agency that can move beyond the individual
account. To do this we need to explore, for example, how individuals who
have become ill or injured now perceive their own bodies and their social

environment; the effects that their changed body might have on the pattern of their everyday life with friends and family, their earning potential and emotional well-being; and the consequent changes in social and self-identity that might follow on from all of this.

But, to explore these kinds of interconnections, *from within human experience itself*, we need a concept such as embodiment that allows us to move beyond treating the body as an entity somehow divorced from the individual who inhabits that body. The concept of embodiment gives us access to what Csordas (1994, 2002) describes as the pre-objective body, one which resides within – not apart from – the flux and change of everyday life. Though seemingly abstract as an idea, this is, in fact, an essential part of the human condition that we can all immediately recognise. Indeed, it is something we all experience in our daily lives. As we suggested in Chapter 1, for example, we feel the silkiness of cat's fur as we stroke it, without being conscious of the act of stroking *per se*. We do not objectify this motor action at all unless, by accident, we reach out too far to stroke the cat and pull a muscle. It is the fact of embodiment – as pre-objective – which enables us to feel the cat's fur, without being conscious of the specific parts of our body that enable that feeling.

Thus, in contrast with the way in which the sociology of the body has hitherto attempted to reintroduce the materiality of something called 'the body', by trying to make sense of its integration into both cultural imagery and everyday social practices (see for example Synnott 1993; Nettleton and Watson 1998), medical sociology and anthropology must, instead, take the human condition of embodiment as its starting point if it is to get to grips with the experience of illness.

In brief, what the concept of embodiment facilitates is an understanding of the ways in which particular kinds of bodies are *produced* through experience; it does not simply assume their prior existence, as bodies that are shaped by different kinds of behaviours. Indeed, we would go further. We suggest, that it is only by adopting this perspective that the nature of body's materiality can be envisioned at all – that is, as a changing and unstable body across both time and space, what Merleau-Ponty describes as *indeterminate* (Merleau-Ponty, cited in Csordas 1994:5). After all, as we all know from our own experience the body is not an enduring entity that exists somehow independently of us and irrespective of what we do: if we eat contaminated food we get sick; if we slip on an icy patch, we can twist our ankles. We need therefore to be able to capture this experience in sociological accounts. To appreciate the significance of such a shift in perspective, and the new possibilities that it opens up for understanding health and illness, it is necessary, however, to first set this distinctive approach within the context of the existing sociology of the body.

Social Constructionism, Medical Sociology and the Body

Debates about the body feature as part of the criticism of the strong, or poststructuralist version of social constructionism within medical sociology (see Chapter 2). As noted, in this the primary focus is discursive inscriptions upon, and readings of the body's surface (see Fox 1993), while experiences deriving from the materiality of the body and its organs take second place. At its most extreme, the very experience of pain or malfunction, for example, becomes open to question within this paradigm – is it or is it not 'real'? This led Bury (1986), for one, to plead for some common sense to be brought into the relativist debate. As he argues, 'demonstrating the problematic character of medicine is not the same as demonstrating its dispensability' (1986:165). For him, as for us, the body has a materiality that cannot be disregarded. Old people may, for example, become *seen* as child-like in certain social contexts, but they are clearly not the same as babies (Hockey and James 1993).

That said, Armstrong (1981, 1983, 1987), a keen proponent of constructivist approaches, has nonetheless argued that the body is not just 'there for the taking'. In his view, medical knowledge is not simply a culturally and historically specific *description* of the body. Rather, its practitioners have had to 'discover' the body through their work and develop theories about its functioning. So Armstrong describes the 'construction' of models of the body by medical science, through its practitioners' active engagement with the body's surfaces and interiority:

> At first it seemed strange to me how the apparent obviousness of disease and its manifestations inside the body had eluded scientific discovery for so long. How had pre-Enlightenment generations failed to see clearly differentiated organs and tissues of the body? Or failed to link patient symptoms with the existence of localized pathological processes? Or failed to apply the most rudimentary diagnostic techniques of physical examination? My disbelief grew until it occurred to me that perhaps I was asking the wrong questions: the problem was not how something which is so obvious today had remained hidden for so long, but how the body had become so evident in the first place. In dissecting and examining bodies I had come to take for granted that what I saw was obvious. I thought that medical knowledge simply described the body ... (however) ... the relationship is more complex ... medical knowledge both describes and constructs the body as an invariate biological reality (Armstrong 1983:xi).

What Armstrong seems to be questioning is the way in which we come to 'know' the body as an object at all. Like other medical sociologists, his aim is to problematise systems of medical knowledge and to challenge the truth claim that anatomical knowledge, and its diagnostic categories, corresponds directly and unequivocally to the body. He argues, therefore, that these so-called 'objective' or 'scientific' ways of knowing the body are themselves a product of cultural and historical processes. As such, they are as much a *political* as a medical anatomy.

While acknowledging the significance of this, what we would append to Armstrong's position, however, is a reminder that these cultural and historical processes of 'discovering' the body do not unfold at some disembodied meta-level of society. Rather, they are the outcomes of human beings' embodied engagement with one another – in this case, doctors treating sick people – something Armstrong himself makes plain in his account of his own experience of carrying out dissection. Thus, although his contribution is not one we would dispute – as already intimated social constructionist accounts provide us with a great deal of insight by making strange the intimate experiences of bodies in sickness and in health – his approach, nonetheless, still leaves difficult questions about what is actually going on *at the level of the body*. These questions demand an answer.

For example, if we can only 'know' or 'construct' the body via particular disciplinary specialisms, as Armstrong seems to be arguing, then how can we explain the somatic experiences that individuals have during illness? What is happening among the bones and tissues which make up a body, happenings which individuals feel – including ourselves as the writers and the readers of texts such as this? Are the qualities of these events removed from direct access to us, as sociologists? Or must we – at some point – acknowledge that forces of nature (such as the bodily changes that occur through illness or death) 'act as constraints over what constructions are possible and what are not'? (Bury 1986:153). In sum: does the body's materiality simply influence the ways in which human beings come to represent and think about the body, as Armstrong and others suggest? Or, as phenomenologists such as Merleau-Ponty (1962), Leder (1990) and Csordas (1994, 2002) would argue, is the grounding of our perceptions of 'health' and 'illness' to be found in the experience of our own, embodied condition?

For us the latter position offers more scope and therefore, in agreement with Bury (1986), we would suggest that the body's materiality is more than just a sociological conundrum conjured up by social constructionism. Rather, its physical, material condition constitutes an invaluable starting point from which to understand, sociologically, the production of different models of 'the body' and experiences of illness. Sickness and injury *are* aspects of being incarnate which demand that we understand them, sociologically, since these have the capacity to profoundly shape our perceptual processes of ourselves and others.

Consider the following bodily processes: giving birth, waking up with a hangover, dropping a heavy object on one's foot, eating infected food. All of these, while normal, non life-threatening occurrences, nonetheless produce bodily crises which are experienced by individuals as anything but 'indirect', 'mediated' or 'constructed'! If only! Yet, the pain of childbirth may be forgotten once the child is born, while the sore foot remains a constant, nagging reminder of one's own foolishness; the sickness and headache associated with a hangover may initiate a process of self reflection – 'never again'! And, when these symptoms are due to eating infected food, on recovery we may view the experience with anger, leading, in extreme cases, to litigation against the food supplier. Thus, the world as viewed when one is in pain, or experiencing some physiological limitation, is often profoundly different to the one encountered from a position of well-being, or perhaps elation – for example, when the marathon runner's body is flooded with post-marathon endorphins. Somehow, then, as social scientists, we do need to make a connection between the bodily crisis of pain or sickness and the effects of our social knowledge about, or representations of, that body in pain – whether these come from medicine's neutral and scientific diagnostic categories, or the familial wisdom passed between grandmothers, mothers and daughters (Blaxter and Patterson 1982). It is to a consideration of how this connection is made that we now turn.

Experiencing the Body

Armstrong's account of his puzzlement over the body's elusiveness to the gaze of medical science, cited above, is instructive. Though providing the starting point for his own Foucauldian position, implicit in his enquiry about how medical knowledge comes about, are already some phenomenological questions. He asks, for example, about the ways in which 'the body had become so evident in the first place' (1983:xi). And, by his own account, this is related to his own embodied experience as a medical student who was required, as part of his medical training, to dissect the same 'object' – the body – that enabled his own being-in-the-world. A strange phenomenon indeed! Good's study, conducted among American medical students, similarly asks how illness comes to be constructed 'as an object of diagnostic and therapeutic activity within American clinical medicine' (1994:66). What interests Good, however, are the '"formative processes" through which illness is shaped as personal and social reality' (1994:66). And these, in his view, are not simply the passive outcome of being born into a particular belief system – in effect, a set of social constructions. Instead, he argues, they are the outcomes of embodied action. Tellingly, Good acknowledges, therefore, that although Foucault's concept of 'discursive practices' did put some sense of action back into systems of representation, his disciplinary background as a historian seems to have distanced him from the actual phenomenology of how particular social realities are produced. For Good, therefore, what Foucault offers is 'intentionality without a subject, strategy without a strategist' (Dreyfus and Rabinow 1982, cited in Good 1994:69).

What Good's study exposes is the experience-near activities through which trainee medical practitioners come to know the body in sickness and in health. For example, discussing the anatomy lab where dissection takes place, one student said:

> Emotionally a leg has such a different meaning after you get the skin off. It doesn't mean at all what it meant before. And now the skin, which is our way of relating to other people – I mean, touching skin is … getting close to people – how that is such a tiny part of what's going on, it's like the peel of an orange, it's just one tiny little aspect. And as soon as you get that off, you're in this whole other world (Good 1994:72).

That said, students (and indeed Good himself) found, however, that 'this whole other world' of the anatomy lab was not necessarily bounded off from their everyday world. Their perceptions of 'persons', encountered at home or in the street, might suddenly shift; they would find themselves disconcertingly surrounded by 'bodies' instead of people – i.e. legs without the skin on! This double-take experience implies that medical training is, therefore, in part, about creating distance between practitioners and patients, a process that, as Good (1994) concludes, provides one of western society's core arenas for dealing with moral issues to do with human suffering. In this sense, it is not coldly instrumental.

The importance of Good's study, therefore, is that it provides insight into the significance of embodiment for understanding cultural differences in perceptions of health, illness and the body. It also highlights the common failure by social constructionists to attend to the embodied processes through which ideas about illness and health are brought into being – whether they are those of the clinician or the patient. It is this failure to attend to embodiment which, we suggest, has undermined social scientists' capacity to explain how it is that we know that we are sick.

The Lived Reality of the Body

If we now turn to Shilling's work on the body (1993, 2005), we find a concern to build upon social constructionist perspectives with insights from phenomenological and structuration theories. Both of these, albeit in different ways, attempt to explore how social actors come to understand the structure of the social world they inhabit. While phenomenology makes embodied experience the grounding of culture, structuration theory seeks to overcome the duality of structure and agency by arguing that 'structure is both medium and outcome of the reproduction of practices' (Giddens 1979:5). In 1993, Shilling proposed, for example, that since 'the body is a biological *and* social phenomenon' (1993:118, emphasis added), it could helpfully be construed as 'unfinished' (see also Chapter 1). In other words, our bodies change and alter over time, whether this occurs through diet and exercise or by surgical intervention. The biology of our bodies is therefore not given or static but, instead, is 'partially formed by social factors' (1993:118). For Shilling this means that, within affluent western societies, the body is becoming increasingly a project through which individuals can express lifestyle choices or choose identity options; in this sense it is pre-eminently a reflexively constructed phenomenon. But, to illustrate how this works in practice Shilling offers us a personal example taken from his own everyday life:

> Having taken up running over a number of years in the belief that it will make me fitter and healthier, I then learn that the wear and tear of the exercise has permanently damaged my hips. I then adopt a low fat diet in order to safe guard my health, but hear that some of the additives used in margarine may be a contributory factor to heart disease (1993:202–3).

Here, then, the body is being shaped and altered, or finished, by the social. Shilling highlights the ways in which social *factors* – the running, the low fat diet – work to produce a particular kind of body, while also drawing on social *constructionist* theory to flag the potential diversity of systems for classifying the body. However, Shilling goes on to comment perceptively that 'just because scientific knowledge and technological developments increase the degree to which we are able to alter our bodies [this] does not mean that their biological constitution becomes unimportant' (1993:203).

It is, therefore, the way in which these different perspectives interact with one another that concerns Shilling. To see the body as biologically open to change as a result of social factors *and* to focus on systems of classification would, he argues, simply sustain a dualism between 'biology' and 'society'. Thus, what is required instead is work such as Connell's account of the gendering of the body (1987, cited in Shilling 1993:108–14). This addresses the ways in which conceptions of 'masculinity' and 'femininity', for example, *produce* more muscular male bodies as boys are encouraged into different forms of play and, later, patterns of exercise. These material changes to the body subsequently give substance to discourses that, in turn, naturalise gendered inequalities, which themselves come to be reproduced, for example, in the social organisation of domestic and paid work along gender lines.

What Shilling's analysis addresses, then, is the critical question frequently asked of radical discursive analyses – is there a 'real' body which has its own properties and which can be said to exist independently of discourse, of the ways in which we have been culturally socialised to think about the body? Is there what Evans and Lee (2002) describe as the 'lived reality' of the body? Some would answer yes. Thus, in her account of the 'disabled body', Thomas acknowledges the very many benefits that the social model of disability has achieved – the reframing of positive identities for disabled people through arguing that it is the social, political and economic environments in which people with disabilities have to live that are disabling (see Chapter 4). Nonetheless, she clings to the 'reality' of the disabled body itself. Citing the work of feminists such as Jenny Morris she argues that:

> *some* of the restrictions of activity experienced by disabled people *are* directly attributable to the body and would not disappear with the removal of all disablist social barriers ... the lived experience of disability involves struggling with both social barriers and the effects of illness (2002:69).

For Thomas, then, medical sociology and anthropology do have to engage with the 'reality of biological bodies', adopting an approach in which bodies are 'theorized as, at the same time, bio-socially produced and culturally constructed entities' (2002:76):

> significant impairments need to be seen as real differences from the 'usual' body, whilst simultaneously understood to be invested with meanings or representations that construct these differences in the socio-medical language of 'impairment', disfigurement and so forth (2002:76).

In asking about the 'reality' of the body and how we might incorporate this alongside accounts that see both health and identity as contingent and socially constructed (see Chapter 1), we therefore need to be able to view the body as having its own kind of agency (Lyon and Barbalet 1994). That is to say, we need to see the body as one among other social 'actors' within what might be called the 'ritual drama of illness', that is as an agent capable of having an effect (see Mayall 2002:21 and Chapter 6).

This is a perspective that Morgan (2002), for example, begins to explore in his thinking about pain. Pain, he says, has the capacity to question our own sense of embodiment through making us consciously aware of that which we normally take for granted – pain does something to us, by changing our awareness of our bodies. However, because humans are 'not like organisms which are directly subjected to nature' our relationship to the body in pain is mediated by our language and culture (2002:87). Thus, pain *is* organic, in the sense of being produced by the biology of the body and it does have an effect upon us as embodied individuals. However, that effect emerges out of both a changed experience of embodiment *and* the cultural contexts within which a person lives; it depends upon the repertoire of explanations that are available and acceptable to them, and the ways in which these enable their everyday social interactions and relationships. This chimes with Csordas' (1994) view, discussed in more detail below, that while the body is pre-objective, it is not pre-social; our perceptions, or objectifications, of our own bodily states of 'pain' or 'well-being' derive from the classificatory systems that are available to us.

As Bendelow (1996) has shown, for example, while some people living with chronic pain see their lives as dominated by pain and are unable to envisage a pain-free future, others are, by contrast, able to accommodate pain into their lives and remain hopeful about the future. And she showed in her study that social factors, such as class and gender, intervene to make a difference. Middle class patients, for instance, tended to be more hopeful about the future than those who lived in poor housing, with little social support. Men who had good jobs and higher income coped better than those who did not, while for women it was the existence of high levels of social support that made a difference. Thus, as Morgan argues, 'in this way, the experience of pain can be seen as the intersection or embodiment of bio-psychosocial processes which link the body and self to the social world' (2002:88). Here then we can begin to see the connections to be made between the body, health and identity.

Real Lived Bodies?

Such debates about the existence of an 'authentic' body, which exists outwith discourse, outside of the representations we make of it, have also been advanced by B.S. Turner (1992), who usefully differentiates between the body as object – 'korper' – and the body as the site of human experience, 'leib'. Hitherto, for the most part, medical sociology and anthropology have both been primarily concerned with the fleshy 'korper', exploring the different ways in which we come to know and conceptualise the biological and material entity called the 'body'. In so doing, therefore, they have inadvertently helped sustain a top-down sociological perspective on the body, gazing upon it and examining, for example, the language and the cognitive categories through which people (clinicians *and* sociologists!) describe it. They have also explored how power, in all its various forms, operates to produce or construct particular qualities of bodily experience, certain subjectivities and distinctive embodiments.

In addition, however, such theorising about the body has replicated and helped sustain the markedly dualistic relationship between physical and mental health and illness that pervades western healthcare systems. Reflecting post-Cartesian thought (see Chapter 1) western medical science, unlike other healing systems that will be explored later in this volume, has been heavily influenced by the mind/body split since at least the second half of the nineteenth century. This has meant that many of the 'bodily' symptoms of 'mental' illness – sleeplessness, loss of appetite and libido, lethargy – have been bracketed off, seen as somehow separate. It has also excluded the links between such illnesses and brain physiology. By the same token, the 'mental' pain which accompanies 'physical' illnesses, which are either life-threatening and/or stigmatising, is divided off from the 'bodily' conditions which inspire it, so putting emotional well-being at risk when such conditions become the sole focus for medical treatment.

Jackson's study of a New England pain centre shows, for example, that patients living with chronic pain are themselves taught by doctors to separate mind from matter by rehearsing the phrase: "before, my pain controlled me, now I control my pain' (1994:208). In Jackson's view, however, this strategy may not be helpful, or sustainable since, as she observes, 'one's selfhood and one's body combine with pain. And all the time pain is a major component of the new self, the new identity' (1994:209). And yet, as she notes, it is ironic that the only legitimate ways in which patients are allowed to express their pain is through, in effect, denying its phenomenological status as pre-objective. Since the experience of pain can only be communicated to others through words, it is always objectified. This she argues is,

> why chronic pain sufferers report feeling profoundly misunderstood by non-sufferers, and profoundly understood by fellow sufferers. They are exiles in the province of pain, and they find the everyday-world language inadequate for communicating about their experiences there. And yet because they are unwilling sojourners, they continue to turn periodically to that very same everyday-world language to avail themselves of its promised rationality, order, explanation and control (1994:224).

Yet within other disciplines mind/body distinctions have already been problematised and indeed dissolved. The neurologist, Damasio (1994), for example, offers an integrated model of brain function which refuses not only the dualism of body and mind, but also the related distinction between reason and emotion. He argues that:

> the body, as represented in the brain, may constitute the indispensable frame of reference for the neural processes that we experience as the mind; [that] our very organism rather than some external reality is used as the ground reference for the constructions we make of the world around us and for the construction

of the ever-present sense of subjectivity that is part and parcel of our experiences (1994:xviii).

Human beings, in Damasio's view, are organisms which 'interact[s] with the environment as an ensemble: the interaction is neither of the body alone nor of the brain alone' (1994:xix). The western mind/body split is, therefore, a duality which social scientists also need to go on problematising, rather than reproducing and, in the next section, we focus on the experiential and embodied self as one of the ways to do this.

Towards a Theory of Embodiment

As indicated above, phenomenological approaches to the body that stress embodiment have been cited as one response to the limitations of social constructionism within medical sociology and anthropology, summed up by Csordas, as follows: 'social reality is "inscribed in the body" and … our analyses are forms of "reading the body"' (2002:242). Like other theorists discussed in this book, Csordas argues that adopting such purely constructionist approaches does not allow us to get at the experiencing body since they 'study the body and its transformations while still taking embodiment for granted' (1994:6). Remaining outside the body, trapped at the level of language, and looking down upon it, such a position is, for Csordas, untenable because it cannot provide us with any in-depth of understanding of how health and illness are actually experienced. Lyon and Barbalet put it this way:

> …[t]he body is a subject of (and subject to) social power. But it is not a passive recipient of society's mould, and therefore external to it. The human capacity for social agency, to collectively and individually contribute to making the social world, comes precisely from the person's lived experience of embodiment. Persons do not simply experience their bodies as external objects of their possession or even as an intermediate environment that surrounds their being. Persons experience themselves *in* and *as* their bodies (1994:54).

How then can we grasp and begin to explain the experience of embodiment? How can we understand the process of illness and recovery which begins, for example, with the moment that a heavy object crushes our toe and ends – perhaps provisionally – with a belief that the damage is 'cured'? For Csordas (2002) the solution lies in exploring what he calls the phenomenology of the transformative process.

In his view, all human beings have an embodied consciousness which is engaged with the world and, though it is not pre-social, it is pre-objective or pre-abstract. That is to say, we experience and understand the world *first* through our bodily engagement with it:

> our lives are not always lived in objectified bodies, for our bodies are not origi-
> nally objects to us. They are instead the ground of perceptual processes that *end*
> in objectification (Csordas 1994:7).

Viewing the body as the existential ground of culture, Csordas therefore treats it 'not as an object that is "good to think", but as a subject that is "necessary to be"' (2002:241). He suggests that we think about embodiment and the body in terms of 'being-in-the-world', an idea that allows us to engage with the 'exis-tential immediacy' of the body – how it feels and is experienced – rather than with the body as an objectified representation (1994:10). To answer our ques-tion – how is that we know we are ill – such a perspective is, therefore, extremely useful since it points to an underlying connection between the body and its health experiences, and self and social identity.

Drawing on the work of Merleau-Ponty, Csordas posits that, for human beings, objects are 'produced' out of a series of embodied perceptual and reflective processes. Thus, for example, if we stand on a mountain top, our fellow beings are perceived, in an elementary sense, as ant-like. It is only through a reflective process – thinking about what we have seen – that we come to 'objectify' them as human beings who are similar to us. Thus, humans, as embodied, spatially mobile beings, 'see' the world of objects in any number of indeterminate ways. 'Reality' – such as it is – only comes into being through the process of objectifying our embodied experiences as participants in the social world.

Working from within this framework, Csordas is concerned to challenge those theories of religious healing that are more discursive or purely represen-tational, since, in his view, these attempt to account for healing as an outcome of the 'persuasive' manipulation of symbols (2002:2). This neglects the experi-ential nature of healing since the body is regarded as simply the place where religious symbols take effect. For Csordas, however, healing, *as people experi-ence it*, is not just about 'the elimination of a thing' in the body (2002:3). Rather, it is about personal transformation – and, he argues, if we really want to understand what happens to health status, emotional well-being and social identity during any healing process – or indeed any illness episode – then it is this experience that we have somehow to grasp.

What Csordas' approach opens up, therefore, is a useful *circular* and thus dynamic perspective on 'the body' that enables us to take account of what Honneth and Joas call the 'unchanging precondition of human changeable-ness' (1988, cited in Shilling 1993:101). If our embodied, perceptual processes and experiences are the starting point from which we create for ourselves the object which we call 'the body', then it can take one of many forms. Or indeed, several of many forms, as our body changes over time or in response to the onset of disease. Moreover, as embodied beings who shift location between social spaces, we objectify our bodies in a variety of ways in everyday life: as something soft, vulnerable and exposed on a darkened city street; as something large and even ungainly when in conversation with a child; as something mechanical yet potentially shameful on a doctor's examination table.

B.S. Turner's notion, cited above, that the body is both possessed as an object (*korper*) *and* also lived (*leib*), is thus congruent with this phenomenological perspective that aims to capture the reality of the lived body. It draws attention not only to the embodied nature of human life, but also to the capacity of human beings to objectify their experiences. In this sense, though *korper* and *leib* are analytically separable, the embodied processes of objectification, described above, point to their inextricable connection and constant mutual reinforcement.

The phenomenological approach advocated by Csordas is not, however, simply another version of the argument that human beings appraise or interpret what they perceive within the world around them. Its distinctiveness lies in its grounding directly in bodily experience. And its usefulness for the concerns of this volume lies in its ability to question what kind of 'object' the sick body represents to people, in particular contexts and at particular times. It allows us to explore how individuals experience the changes and transformations that the body undergoes, as sickness strikes or old age creeps up, and what outcome all of this has for their health identities.

The Phenomenon of the Lived Body

By way of illustration of the potential usefulness of this approach we can turn to consider some examples from medical sociology and anthropology. In a very early medical sociology study of French people, Herzlich (1973), for instance, already identified that different kinds of understandings of illness varied along class lines, with each class viewing the health of the body in rather different ways. Manual workers, she suggested, saw health as instrumental, defining it as the absence of illness or in terms of their ability/inability to function. Amongst the middle classes, however, health was a more encompassing concept related to feelings of well-being. From a phenomenological perspective, Herzlich's study is revealing, however, of more than just the different conceptions of health which she foregrounds. The concepts that these different classes of French people use are surely premised on their rather different experiences of embodiment, different ways of being-in-the-world? The 'manual' worker's body, as the term implies, is quite literally a tool of his/her trade. The body's health and full functioning is a necessary, rather than simply a sufficient, condition of everyday life. The loss of a leg to a builder has, therefore, more immediate consequences for personal and social identity than it might, say, for someone working at a desk job.

Thus, as Leder (1990) argues, the object which we 'know' our body to be makes itself felt within our consciousness only at certain moments – when we are ill; when we feel concerned about our appearance; when sensations of pleasure are occurring. However, what this suggests, then, is that it may be difficult to access the processes whereby the body – or bodies – emerge. In Kingsolver's (1998) fictional account of how the Congolese body was perceived by a young American girl, we get a glimpse, though, of how this might take place through our social interactions in everyday life.

Ruth May, Kingsolver's character, is the young daughter of an American missionary who brings his entire family to Africa in the early 1960s. Newly arrived in the village of Kilanga, Ruth May notes how a neighbour who lost her legs in a fire continues to look after her husband and seven or eight children, saying, 'Nobody bats their eye when she scoots by on her hands and goes on down to her field or the river to wash clothes' (1998:60). Ruth May herself has a disabled sister, but this little girl attracts interest only on account of her skin colour, not her different body:

> 'Nobody cares that she's bad on one whole side', says Ruth May, 'because they've all got their own handicap children or a mama with no feet, or their eye put out. When you take a look out the door, why, there goes somebody with something missing off of them and not even embarrassed of it. They'll wave a stump at you if they've got one, in friendly way' (1998:61).

Their blond hair and raging sunburn makes both the sisters a focus for the gaze of children and adults in the village, however, and it is they who are transformed into 'freaks of nature' (1998:61). Thus, Ruth May becomes aware that her customary objectifications of the body no longer hold up in this context, and it is her mother who pinpoints why:

> here they have to use their bodies like we use *things* at home – like your clothes or your garden tools or something. Where you'd be wearing out the knees of your trousers, sir, they just have to go ahead and wear out their *knees* (1998:62, original emphasis).

Powerfully attuned to their embodied difference, the two children come to see, through these interactions, the social and cultural value which particular bodies represent in terms of identity; and they also experience the stigma attracted by bodies which deviate from the kinds of objectifications which are central to western thought and practice.

Indeed, as Urla and Terry (1995) argue, in western societies, differences between bodies have long provided indicators of social conformity and deviance. However, that the western model of the body not only reveals but also *contains* the self, as noted earlier, means that the onset of bodily illness may begin to unravel this meshing of body, agency and self. Shildrick (1997) shows, for example, that without a leg or a breast, we become 'other' to those around us; and the world we then objectify, from our new embodied position, begins to shift on its axis. We see and experience it differently. However, as long as we remain healthy and intact, we hear nothing from our object bodies. They are silent. Indeed, as Leder (1990) observes, their functioning is not usually a matter for the conscious mind: when the fingers grasp a knife and a fork, what we sense are the forms, textures and positions of those items of cutlery, not the hand we are using for this purpose.

Such examples underscore, therefore, the ways in which a focus on embodiment can enable us to explore how experiences of health and illness inform identity through the changing materiality of the body. They begin to show that a focus on embodiment does allow us to transcend both biological and social constructionist approaches to health, illness and identity. But exactly how we might understand, sociologically, the ways in which 'the body', whether sick or well, emerges out of the experience of human embodiment, and the implications that this has for self and social identity, is still in need of some further explanation. It is this to which we now turn.

Embodiment and Society

In Shilling's (2005) view a purely phenomenological approach tends to remain at the level of the experiencing body, without providing an adequate account of how 'society', in a broader sense, both impacts upon and is generated by the embodied individual. Thus, while phenomenology grounds the reader in the body, it provides an inadequate account of 'how the body is also receptive to, and able to be constrained by, society, or [of]... analyzing the outcomes of interaction between the body's agentic capacities and societal structures' (Shilling 2005:60). It therefore leaves something to be desired in terms of explaining, for example, the relationship between agency and structure – or the ways in which embodied perceptual processes of feeling ill mesh with larger scale 'structures' such as the National Health Service as we, as sick individuals, seek out help from doctors. Neither can a purely phenomenological account explain the power of an animistic religion whose adherents believe that the life-souls of young children are likely to wander off or be stolen, an event that brings illness (Fadiman 1997) (see Chapter 7).

In his later work, therefore, Shilling (2005) develops what he calls 'corporeal realism', in order to draw out the distinctive insights of social constructionism, phenomenology and structuration theory and to build a bridge between them. For him, corporeal realism highlights the emergent properties of both the body *and* social structure. Neither are to be considered as given and, Shilling argues, just as objectifications of the body cannot exhaust its potential meanings, so conventional conceptions of 'structure' also reify it in unhelpful ways.

Such a view resonates with Jenkins' (2002:78) discussion of 'structure'. He argues that, if social scientists are reliant on the reified presence of something 'out there' called structure as a way of explaining human behaviour, then we have to be able to demonstrate that it exists – and we can't. Nor can we explain how 'structure' might, in practice, connect with the everyday choices and actions of human beings. And if the something 'out there', broadly recognised by sociologists as 'structure', is, therefore, but an analytic device for making sense of what people choose to do, then it cannot, in itself, effect anything at all – apart from our understanding of the social world.

What Jenkins (2002:81–3) then points towards, however, is the possibility of something which does lie beyond the sum of society's individual members, albeit remaining part of the knowable world of everyday life. In other words it does not disappear into the abstractions of 'structure'. What he is referring to are the capacities of human beings to imaginatively transcend the here and now of the material moment; to identify with other people within groups; to draw on shared symbolic systems such as language; to participate in the dynamics of group interactions; and to agree upon a stable time-space called 'the present'.

This notion of 'the immanent "more-ness" of collectivity revealed in the practices of everyday life' is instructive (2002:81) for our focus on embodiment for what it draws attention to is how both 'structure' and 'the body' are processes which emerge out of the embodied acts, everyday interactions and the experiences of individuals. Together these make up what we know as everyday social life and is therefore pertinent to our understanding of the ways in which health identities are brought into being. In this way, then, the concept of embodiment is more than simply a way to discuss lay experiences of illness; it also reminds us that embodiment is the precondition not only for human *being*, but also for the social, political and economic environments which are the context of human life in whatever its form. In the following section we illustrate this by exploring, in some detail, the ways in which ideas of risk have led to the emergence of new forms of embodiment, new kinds of bodies and new health identities within contemporary western society.

Bodies and Risk

As Chapter 4 will explore in detail, western societies are now objectifying bodies in ways which are new and distinctive. While until recently biomedicine 'individuated' the organs of the body, making these its focus of attention individuals now regard their *whole* bodies anxiously. Thus, our experience of embodiment has changed: we have begun to scrutinise our bodies more carefully and, the more carefully we look, the more conscious we are of the changes our bodies undergo; and as we worry about these changes, so the nature of our embodied experience also changes.

In this sense, illness is no longer contained within the boundaries of a sick population and a sense of risk now problematises the experience of embodiment for many westerners. Yet, the notion of 'health risk' itself has become fractured in public discourses (Gabe 1995:3). There is the concern with environmental risk which embrace *bodies*, as populations – for example, the threat posed by nuclear waste and other forms of environmental pollution. But there are also individualised risky practices which are seen to belong to the person and to have implications for *their* particular body. Recent advertisements for pharmaceuticals to help lower cholesterol make this clear. One advert warns that:

> If you have diabetes it is recommended that you pay particular attention to lowering your risk of having a heart attack. High cholesterol puts you at an increased risk of heart disease and therefore managing your cholesterol level may help reduce this risk. (Independent 8/10/04)

Another, directs its attention to women in particular:

> Because I'd turned 55, my risk of heart attack was increasing. I had a chat with my pharmacist who said my risk could be as much as 1 in 7 ... Could your risk be as high as 1 in 7? If you're a woman 55 or over with an additional risk factor such as family history of early heart disease, if you smoke, or are overweight, then it may well be. (Advert for Zocor Heart-pro, Independent 12/10/04)

Are the new risks to health and identity therefore to be perceived as an outcome of industrialisation under the conditions of capitalism; or are they the result of the adoption of unhealthy lifestyles by individuals? Those with vested interests in such debates range from governments and global corporations, through to campaigning groups and individuals who are either sick, or feel their health to be under threat. It is within this context, therefore, that different objectifications of the contemporary western body can emerge, and indeed, at the level of everyday social relationships and interactions, different bodies and experiences of embodiment can have different rhetorical power, as the examples to follow demonstrate.

We begin with K. Lane's (1995) account of Australian women's desires for a birth without technological, chemical or surgical intervention. Their model of the body is framed in terms of 'the natural', a concept which, in their terms, is congruent with the traditional western notion of the container body in that it is seen as an entity over which they, as individuals, have rights. For their professional carers, too, their bodies are 'containers'. However, here the 'natural' metaphor gives ground to the 'machine' metaphor (see Martin 1987; Watson 2000) and, in this view the body 'is always ready to fail, even in ostensibly low-risk cases' (1995:57). This medical view therefore underpins particular notions of 'risk' but is one which is often entirely at odds with women's own concerns and embodied experiences. Lane sums up the medical objectification of the body as follows: 'In the medical model, birthing is conceptualized as a set of discrete, internal, muscular and chemical reactions unrelated to external (social, historical and personal) factors' (1995:62). This, she says, leads logically to the idea that it requires an external agent – the doctor and/or medical interventions - to correct the internal malfunction (see also Harvey 1997). Thus, the broad concept of 'risk' mobilises concerns that materialise in particular treatment choices and funding policies.

Yet in its breadth, the concept of 'risk' both encompasses *and* obscures the competing objectifications of the labouring body offered by women and their doctors. From the perspective offered by cultural phenomenology described above, it could be argued, for example, that this mechanical model of the body, rather than simply being a reflection of increasing medicalisation (Illich 1976 and see Chapter 4), arises, instead, out of the embodied perceptions of doctors who have been taught to view the birthing environment as one which they must take responsibility for, or indeed exercise mastery over. Thus, although the relative 'riskiness' of low-level medical intervention birth in a birth centre, or family home, when compared with high medical intervention hospital birth, is very difficult to ascertain, blanket medical risk criteria are imposed. This, in turn, obscures women's own embodied perceptions of the ways in which the birthing environment impacts upon their bodily functions and the process of labour. Thus, Lane's research among Australian women shows that women's subjugated bodily perceptions are literally produced intersubjectively, within the embodied experiences of all those involved in the medical encounter.

The emergence of the body – and bodies – as aspects of contested models and discourses, is also evident in the case of mass childhood immunisation (MCR) where, once more, a phenomenological perspective focused on embodiment can bring additional insight. Here, we find distinctions made between bodies 'at risk', through their exposure to particular environments, and the body as something which the individual makes vulnerable, by virtue of their 'risky' behaviour. However, immunisation campaigns are built upon epidemiological foundations that base their assessments of risk upon populations of bodies – they make the 'spaces between people' their focus, rather than the individual (Rogers and Pilgrim 1995:75). Thus, just as obstetricians have an externalised perception of birth as a process within which they must intervene, so, Rogers and Pilgrim argue, 'epidemiologists may treat the question of infection risk as if it is merely a mathematical or technical puzzle and lose sight of the citizen's view of their task' (1995:74).

In the promotional literature produced for the MCR, however, the benefits of immunisation for populations are sidelined. Instead, the protection afforded to the individual is highlighted – along with the possibility of distressing illness, or even death, for those who are not inoculated. Thus, when some parents refuse the admonitions of health promoters, who aim to secure the health of populations by inoculating as many individuals as possible, they are signing up to a notion of risk as something which the individual may, but may not, incur. In highlighting these different responses, what Rogers and Pilgrim are drawing attention to, therefore, are the different embodiments of risk perception among different categories of people – epidemiologists, health promoters, primary care workers and parents.

Of course, as they point out, the dilemma exists not just at the level of relationships between different groups, such as GPs and parents, but also within those individuals whose professional take on the world, as epidemiologists, involves a 'population' focus. Their embodied experiences as parents themselves may be far more individualistic. And, if, following Csordas, we consider embodiment as the pre-abstract, rather than precultural position from which objectification takes place, then it is also noteworthy that the perceptions of epidemiologists, for example, materialise within the context of scientific knowledge – whereas those of some of the parents interviewed by Rogers and Pilgrim are informed by concepts such as 'intuition', 'maternal instinct' or 'fate' or alternative forms of medical knowledge such as homeopathy.

Conclusion

What this chapter has set out to do is to problematise notions of the body as either the grounding for a variety of forms of cultural elaboration, or the product of discursive strategies which materialise the body through systems of representation. Instead, as we have argued, health, illness and identity are aspects of embodied human life which emerge out of our engagement within a cultural world. As we move from states of indeterminacy to objectification, the body, our body and other bodies materialise; but they do so in ways which are intrinsic to their environments, to the agendas of those involved and to the issues of power and inequality which unfold via different kinds of body-based rhetoric. Having therefore offered a way forward to dealing with the problem of the body and its role in the relationship between health and identity, we turn in the next chapter to examine more closely the problem of illness itself.

4

The Problem of Illness

Given our focus in previous chapters on embodiment and its role in the identification of the body's health status and in any individual's experiences of bodily changes, it might seem that bio-medical accounts of illness are to be distanced from the analysis presented in this volume. If bio-medicine, and the medical model of health that it sustains, has as its core an objective body of knowledge, generated through scientific principles, then health knowledge that is derived primarily through sensory and experientially-based accounts of the body would seem to stand in direct opposition to it. However, as this chapter explores, while such a binary opposition may be appealing in its capacity to provoke challenges to our thinking – and indeed is often a rallying call for those in western societies who wish to promote the use of alternative or complementary medicine – in practice there is a great deal of slippage between the kinds of medical knowledge that doctors have and employ and that which individuals acquire and use as a basis for their lay understandings of the changing health status of their bodies. In the practical articulation of both these kinds of knowledge, processes of bodily negotiation take place. They are processes brought to light in the 'problem' that illness represents. This chapter unravels therefore, the complexities of the negotiations that take place around the conceptualisation of 'illness' among lay and health practitioners alike.

Defining Illness

According to the World Health Organisation (WHO), as set out in its constitution of 1948, health is 'a state of complete physical, mental and social well-being and not merely the absence of disease or infirmity' (http://www.who.int/about/en). From this definition, therefore, it is already apparent that bio-medical science is understood to play only one part in definitions of health, with the social context of people's everyday lives also regarded as an important contributor to the state of individual well-being. It is not surprising, therefore, to see set out in the aims of the UN Millenium Declaration (2000), which was endorsed by 189 countries, a range of targets to be met by 2015. These comprise a heady mix of social, educational, economic and health goals that are complexly interdependent. One example is the aim, between 1990 and 2015, to halve the proportion of people living on less than a dollar a day. This is clearly linked to the need to halve the proportion of people who suffer the health and disease consequences of poverty brought about hunger – for example, malnutrition and high rates of infant mortality. Similarly, the many social factors involved in reducing the threat to world health posed by the spread of HIV and AIDS are acknowledged through the twin objectives of increasing condom use and encouraging the school attendance of young people.

These examples suggest, therefore, that definitions of health and illness are rather slippery – hunger is not a 'disease' or an 'infirmity' and yet it can have catastrophic health outcomes. And causes of ill-health are even more difficult to locate. As Armstrong (1981) argues, although one cause of lung cancer may be smoking, the social factors that encourage people to take up and continue to smoke are also causally implicated. This suggests therefore that while 'disease' can be objectified through the medical model as the pathological, organic changes that occur within the body (Seale *et al* 2001:27), concepts of health, and of what Frankenberg (1992) terms 'illth' – the state of ill-being or disease – have to be located more firmly within the social context.

From within sociology, it was Friedson (1970) who was one of the first to allude to the problem that illness represents by arguing, through a critique of the medical model, that doctors and patients might not share the same views about the body and its ills. Indeed, he went so far as to suggest that they had rather radically different world views. According to Friedson, the doctor perceives the body from a 'disease' perspective, as an entity susceptible to attack by viruses, organic pathologies and other malfunctions which can be 'scientifically' examined independent of the social context. Patients on the other hand, Friedson argued, view the body through the lens of their own changing somatic experiences. This 'illness' perspective thus represents a rather different kind of account than the disease focus of bio-medicine, tied as it is to the individual and to their particular embodied experience in the world. Thus one of the 'problems' of illness, Friedson argued, is that, unlike 'disease', it cannot be objectified in medical terms and is not therefore amenable to the 'scientific' gaze. It was left to Cassell (1976) to suggest later that 'illness' represents what a person experiences when they decide to go to the doctor, and 'disease' is what they return home with and for Kleinman (1978) to argue that clinicians need to understand the subjective meanings that individuals attribute to 'disease' in order to negotiate effective compliance with treatment.

For Frankenberg (1980), however, even these distinctions are insufficient for they do not really get to grips, sociologically speaking, with the cultural contextualisation of the somatic experiences that people have. Frankenberg argued, therefore, for the introduction of a third term – that of sickness. Through the idea of 'sickness', he suggested, we can get closer to embodied experiences of illness. For Frankenberg this meant, however, not just focusing on the subjective experience of organic bodily change but, instead, understanding such change as integral to what he saw as a wider, culturally located performance. In his view there is always a network of social relationships that shape people's subjective experiences of an illness; it is these that combine to produce what 'sickness' means to any individual. Young puts it this way: 'sickness is ... a process for socializing disease and illness' (1982:270).

In exploring the relationship between the body, health and identity, Frankenberg sees the idea of 'sickness' as a useful mediating term which allows us to engage with the 'total social process in which disease is inserted' (1980:199). That is to say, sickness, as a culturally and historically situated performance, involves any number of social actors, together with the array of local cultural symbols and ritual practices through which illness is managed by patients, by doctors, by families and by communities. As Young (1982) observes:

> sickness is ... the process through which worrisome behavioral and biological signs, particularly ones originating in disease, are given socially recognizable meanings i.e. they are made into symptoms and socially significant outcomes. Every culture has its rules for translating signs into symptoms, for linking symptomatologies to etiologies and interventions and for using the evidence provided by interventions to confirm translations and legitimize outcomes ... The path a person follows from translation to socially significant outcome constitutes his sickness (1982:270).

As Young goes on to note, in cultures that have pluralistic systems of medicine this means, therefore, that the same set of physical signs can come to indicate more than one 'sickness', since people may consult different practitioners and be prescribed different kinds of treatments. And, in western societies, although bio-medical science would seem to offer a dominant and universal system for the translation and treatment of the symptoms of disease, 'sickness' may nonetheless vary as a result of individuals' different socioeconomic positions and personal circumstances (see Chapter 2).

By problematising disease/illness/sickness in this way, perspectives such as these therefore underscore the distinctiveness of the sociological account.

Medical science concerns itself with the discovery of 'objective', generalisable evidence, albeit as the outcome of debate (Harari 2001). By contrast, anthropological and sociological approaches *anticipate* diversity in the ways in which the diseased body is experienced and negotiated within different social contexts, both by the individual themselves and those around them, whether lay or professional. It is this which provides the starting point for explorations of locally-sited and embodied systems of thought and practice. Thus, as this chapter demonstrates, our focus on embodiment and on the socially constructed character of illness and sickness inevitably leads to a whole string of questions about the relationship between the body, health and identity. Who is ill and who is well? What are seen as the causes of illness? How are they to be treated? And, perhaps more fundamentally, can sickness (as opposed to disease) be objectified in medical terms at all, or can it only be accessed through the embodied experiences of those identified as 'ill'? We begin by focusing on the question: who is ill?

Who is Ill?

In her vivid portrayal of the everyday lives and experiences of schizophrenics living in Montreal City, Knowles (2000) reveals the myriad ways in which their everyday social encounters – in the clinic, at the welfare office, within the homeless shelter and on the street – come together in the social production of madness. She tells a story of how, following the closure of local asylums and psychiatric wards, there has been a shift from public to private responsibility for the mad, under the guise of community care. This shift has become a key part of each person's 'terrifying descent into madness, homelessness, joblessness, loneliness and dependence on cocktails of legal/illegal drugs' (2000:1). The harrowing accounts of lives lived in transit – panhandling on the street by day and sleeping in hostels by night, lives dulled by medication and made worse by poverty and social exclusion – reveal beyond doubt that, for Knowles, madness has to be understood as 'socially scripted as well as being an individual experience' (2000:161). It is not only a clinical condition.

What Knowles describes for us are some of the problems involved in understanding the disordered mind, reflecting and refracting as it does a whole range of disordered *social* arrangements and living conditions with which the mad have to contend. These are the kinds of conditions that might drive anyone mad and they permeate the very architecture of our cities. Poverty, homelessness and joblessness mark the lives of many schizophrenics, forcing them to live on the street, to spend their days in cafes and shopping malls and to eat at soup kitchens. Such places not only 'expose them to the public gaze' but also 'to situations where their vulnerability and insecurity is heightened'

(2001:150). This compounds the perceived danger and risk posed by the mad to those of us who are not, and contributes further to their social isolation and stigmatisation. As Knowles argues, 'consigning [the mad] to the crevices of the city', rather than providing appropriate services and facilities targeted to protect them, does little to assuage public fear of the potential risk and danger involved in encounters with the mad (2000:150). What it does instead is simply to confirm many people's prejudices and so compound the problems of being mad.

However, though focusing primarily on the structural conditions which exacerbate madness, Knowles is not offering us a solely materialist explanation, nor indeed intending to soften the impact of its organic, despairing reality through her focus on the social context; rather, the opposite. Through detailing these harrowing stories, what she underscores is the importance of mundane and embodied everyday social encounters to the shaping of the health and illness experiences that we all have. Encounters with conventional medical professionals or alternative practitioners, with the words of homely advice given to us by our kith and kin, with the health warnings issued via state bureaucracies or private sector advertisements, all have a part to play in the ways in which, as individuals, we are enabled – or not – to negotiate the complex and varied path between experiences of illness and those of well-being. Indeed, as the early work by Zola (1973) showed, for example, it is through our everyday social interactions with family, friends or colleagues that we may first become made aware – through their worried comments about our appearance or their lay assessment of the symptoms – that our changed bodily feelings might be significant enough to constitute a state of sickness that warrants attention from a doctor. Being sick is not, therefore, simply or only a somatic state; instead, the sickness of the ill body (or mind) has to be understood within the total social context of people's everyday embodied experiences.

Thus, in a rather different example, we can see how social space can work to facilitate personal empowerment, rather than its opposite, with the body's health identity being negotiated more positively. During interviews with elderly women and men about their changed uses of public and domestic space after the death of their partners (see Hockey *et al* 2001), Mavis, a widow, described the pervasive loneliness among those in her age group now living alone: 'I know we all ... spend a hell of a lot more time alone in our homes, and we all say, we've lost our friends. Whereas before you went out in a foursome'. However, despite this, one of the avenues for contact which Mavis had discovered was the support groups she attended for her various chronic health conditions. Rather than simply seeing these as just part of her illness and its treatment, she made these visits an occasion for socialising, particularly by giving other people lifts in her car since she was unusual in being able to drive. Though admitting that some of the content could be 'boring', she went on to say:

> I go to the Diabetic meeting ... and Boots' Ladies ... I've been a couple of times ... er, I quite like them because it's educational ... is about why you're have(ing) vetting and screening, you know, and things like that ... and then there's the Dystonia meetings for these facial spasms ... I'm going to that Dystonia (meeting) because I haven't been for six months but I know another lady who has neck troubles and I've got her number. I gave her a lift home once. I shall phone her before next Wednesday and see if she wants a lift there because her husband used to take her and bring her ... (n.d.).

Similarly, although Mavis was able to manage her diabetes through careful eating, she strongly disliked having meals alone and would therefore seek opportunities to help friends in ways which involved them coming to her home at meal-times.

For Mavis, then, illness was not something she denied, unlike many other older people who will often resist confessing to ill-health to avoid membership of the negatively perceived social category 'elderly' (Hockey and James 1993; and see Chapter 7). Instead, Mavis saw that the kinds of chronic illness that accompany old age can in some instances be used as a passport to social participation and inclusion, rather than exclusion. For her illness provided a pretext for socialising, rather than the grounds for social exclusion. During the interview Mavis said:

> I'm just waiting for an 80 year old friend to phone me to take her home from the doctors' ... She's getting the taxi there and she's got ulcers on her legs and by the time she's got the bus to her house, the bandages all slip off the wound she's just had dressed. So I said, 'Right, on Friday ... when you've finished, phone me and I'll come and take you home. I'll take you for your pension and I'll take you shopping' ... bring her to my house for lunch ... 'and then I will take you home' (n.d.).

Thus, as Mavis negotiates the various chronic illnesses that beset her body she both resists and yet welcomes their power as identifiers. For Mavis, her sickness facilitates social life, neatly destabilising for us the oppositional relationship between 'health' and 'illness' and the Parsonian model of the 'sick role' (see Chapter 2). Mavis makes us ask, therefore, not just about what constitutes 'health' and 'illness' and whether their relationship with one another is self evident, but also whether the lines that we might wish to draw between them shift according to the social spaces and times within which they are located and how far, as individuals, we can exercise agency in the ways in which those lines are drawn.

Both the examples above therefore provide powerful illustrations of the ways in which social structures, social spaces and social interactions help construct and reconstruct our ideas of illness, while also highlighting the importance of agency in accounting for the ways in which sickness comes to be defined and health identities are produced and taken on. This more nuanced account of the complexities involved in being sick thus contrasts powerfully with Talcott Parsons' conception of illness as form of social deviance whose presence or absence is simply legitimated by the doctor (see Chapter 2).

A third example – Ablon's (1986) now classic study of Samoan burns victims – complicates things further, however, by exploring the role of the body itself – the agentic body or body as an agent – in the problem of illness. This not only makes us re-examine the hegemony of the medical model by acknowledging the importance of the social context, but also reconsider the ways in which the body is produced within the social context, as the last chapter described. Rather than being regarded as a given stable entity that becomes diseased, as noted, what a focus on embodiment does is to allow us to see how the materiality of the body is experienced differently by people during illness episodes and thus also the varied *social* contributions that the changed materiality of the body can make to our health identities. This is, however, neither a simple nor a necessarily causal relationship.

Following a fire that devastated a church social hall on the West Coast of America, in which many American and Samoan guests were badly injured, Ablon (1986) compared the reactions of Samoan burn patients with those of Americans and found great differences between them. The Samoans, in contrast to the Americans, complained relatively little about experiencing pain although, on the face of it, having comparable injuries. In seeking an explanation for this Ablon argued that the Samoans' 'undemonstrative acceptance of pain, death and calamities' was sustained by a view that whatever happens, 'life must, after all, go on' (1986:177). Her data suggested that so supportive was Samoan culture that it precluded 'many of the emotional problems that are observed routinely in association with severely injured and bereaved burn patients' (1986:180).

However, besides revealing socio-cultural variations in response to disease – this study was one of the first indicators that medically-based, naturalistic accounts of the body might benefit from a sociological input – what is important about this example is what it reveals about the part played by the body in relation to health identities. The Samoans' bodies were badly burned and, undoubtedly, they bore the traces of this in much the same way as any other body does – the bodies were scarred, disfigured and in need of multiple skin grafts. And yet, as burns patients, the Samoans maintained what Ablon describes as an outward stoicism and a flat affect which was continually remarked upon by the doctors treating them. While it is, of course, not possible to 'know' someone else's pain, its intensity can be easily guessed at. For the Samoans, however, the body's pain was something not to be dwelt on or even remarked in terms of how they saw themselves or, indeed, in Frankenberg's terms, performed this sickness episode. As an expression of God's will, the fire was simply something to be accepted – life moves on and the body, albeit changed, recovers.

What these three rather different examples suggest, therefore, is that one of the 'problems' of illness lies in the various factors which come into play when we try to explain our somatic states to ourselves or to classify and understand another's illness. As social scientists we might look, for example, to explain illness through reference to the structure of the social context and the extent to which some individuals, but not others, receive medical attention; we might consider the extent to which possibilities for agency and choice are made available so that, like Mavis above, individuals can 'choose' the illnesses which they wish to have and the ways in which they 'perform' them; or we might look at the body itself and consider the extent to which the limitations of the flesh enable or prevent certain outcomes in the illness process and the ways in which experiences of embodiment can vary. Illness, we quickly realise, is therefore neither objective nor fixed.

Similarly, neither are the conditions and experiences of illness invariant in relation to the presence or absence of disease. Indeed, recognition of what actually constitutes disease may itself be part of the problem of illness as our earlier example of AIDS/HIV suggested (see Chapter 1; see also Chapter 7 for a discussion of health and illness across the life course). We need therefore to understand the kinds of authority, power and efficacy that inform medically diagnostic decisions; the ways in which these understandings shape medical treatment and interventions; how these are experienced by individuals; and the health identities which result from them. Only then might we begin to grasp who is ill or who is well. However, before looking at the implications of these social constructionist perspectives in more detail, we consider questions of causality for these, too, are part of the problem of illness.

Why Me?

As a starting point for our discussion we turn first to a classic anthropological text – the study of Azande witchcraft (Evans-Pritchard 1937) which, though clearly dealing with medical matters, as Young argues, is not usually regarded as an example of medical anthropology. Alongside other work, such as Turner (1969), it is seen instead

as belonging to the anthropologies of religion, comparative modes of thinking, witchcraft, ritual and symbol, culture and psychology and so on. That is, we think of them as originating in problematics and analytical frameworks where sickness events are only vehicles for understanding other constellations of facts (Young 1982:259).

Young sees this as a function of the thorough externalisation of sickness experiences in such societies, which effectively reduces the body to a 'black box' that is not open for understanding. However, the reluctance to see this material as falling within the remit of 'medicine' can also be understood to reflect the hegemonic hold that the medical model has over our thinking for, as we shall see, the Azande example turns out to be highly instructive for thinking about the problem of illness.

Among the Azande of Southern Sudan, sickness or injury to the body was traditionally seen as one instance of misfortune, that is to say it was a misfortune that had a bodily consequence. While acknowledging, for example, that a wound was infected and required treatment, or that bodily injury was 'caused' by the collapse of a granary – their granaries were built on posts which were often eaten away by insects – the Azande derived little satisfaction from such explanations. Of more pressing concern was why a particular wound became infected *this* time, whereas earlier wounds had not; or why it was *this* man, rather than that man, who happened to be unfortunate enough to be standing under the granary. For the Azande these were the important questions that needed to be answered and causal explanations, using divination techniques, were sought in the social environment of the individual – and particularly in the scope for Azande witchcraft practices to cause harm. As Evans-Pritchard describes, accounting for the 'singularity of misfortune' enabled the Azande to explain what caused a person to become sick. That they were sick there was no doubt – but why had *they* fallen ill? For the Azande, then, the problem of illness lay in the way diseases claim particular victims and, for the Azande, witches were at the heart of the matter.

The question – why me – is not, of course, confined to Africa in the 1930s but remains one of the core problems of illness for us all. Not only might we pose this same question when faced with the onset of a serious illness but, like the Azande, even those wedded to the 'medical model' often feel the need to go beyond coping with the diagnosis and treatment of the disease or injury *per se*. Individuals may feel the need to contextualise their embodied experiences of being ill, to explain its disparate and particularised occurrence in their own body, both to themselves and for others. Why me?

Theorising about the 'causes' of disease constitutes what Kleinman (1978) has termed an explanatory model, a notion that embraces both lay and practitioner perspectives on disease. According to Helman (1986), the analysis of explanatory models provides us with four main locations for the causes of ill-health – that of the individual patient, the natural world, the social world and the supernatural. However, as he notes, although 'social and supernatural aetiologies tend to be a feature of non-western societies ... [and] natural or patient-centred explanations of illness are more common in the Western industrialized world ... the division is by no means absolute' (1984:75). Moreover, what all these models endeavour to achieve is, as Young (1982) observes, to allocate *responsibility* for disease through the very process of describing its aetiology and translating signs of 'sickness behaviour' into symptoms that can be explained.

Thus, Davison *et al*'s (1991, 1992) study of people's attitudes towards the prevention of heart disease in Wales reveals that individuals actively sought out ways to explain why I, rather than my neighbour, might succumb to heart disease and that they identified fate as a causal agent. Despite knowledge of the relationship between diets high in fat and coronary heart disease Davison *et al* show that many people did not adopt healthier eating practices. Instead they assessed the risks of whether they, rather than their neighbour, would be a candidate. Although acknowledging that they were in part responsible and were making lifestyle choices, they also believed that chance had a part to play: after all, not all people who eat fatty food get heart disease. A strong sense of fatalism, including ideas about the 'will of God' and reaching one's 'allotted life-span', were invoked as explanatory models for the onset of heart disease in particular individuals (see also Keane 1997).

Elsewhere, the social, rather than supernatural, world may itself be seen as the source of sickness through practices such as witchcraft, the evil eye, Voodoo and sorcery. However, although Helman observes that 'blaming other people for one's ill-health is a common feature of smaller-scale societies, where inter-personal conflicts are frequent', more complex societies also have recourse to this explanatory model (1984:78). Increasingly, for example, in industrial societies workplace stress, and more recently workplace bullying, are being acknowledged as legitimate 'causes' of sickness (see Karasek and Theorell 1990). De Swaan, similarly, points towards the extension of the categories of 'health' and 'illness' to include a range of *social* contradictions such as the dilemmas of personnel selection, absences from work and the allocation of social housing; 'the(ir) reduction to a medical problem', he argues, 'is a derivative application of medical knowledge; medical expertise is used as a cover for conflict management' (1990:68).

For bio-medical scientists, on the other hand, it is the natural world that provides the 'causes' of disease, with a pool of micro-organisms, parasites and environmental pollutants to blame for the onset of illness. However, although the meta-narrative of religion may provide fewer westerners with guidance as to how to make sense of affliction, the medical model which bio-medicine promotes as an explanatory system also often fails to satisfy. As Geertz describes, in his early work on religion and the problems of suffering and evil,

> the strange opacity of certain empirical events, the dumb senselessness of intense or inexorable pain, and the enigmatic unaccountability of gross iniquity all raise the uncomfortable suspicion that the world, and hence man's (sic) life in the world, has no genuine order at all – no empirical regularity, no emotional form, no moral coherence (1966:23).

However, although it is possible to separate out such different locations of causality analytically, as Helman does, people's own embodied experiences of coming to terms with their illness may, on a day-to-day basis, involve them drawing on a variety of explanatory models. For example, as Segar describes, although in Ciskei, South Africa, villagers are well aware of the connection between poverty and ill-health and also attribute many illnesses to natural causes, '*imimoya emdaka* is a phrase often used to explain the underlying causes of serious illness or death' (1997:1593). Literally translated as 'dirty winds', these are the evil spirits, sent by jealous people, that can cause specific illnesses to take hold of individuals. For the Ciskei, this helps explain the inexplicable injustice of illness in a society where material differentiation and poverty prevent them from otherwise exercising much control over their life circumstances.

Lay beliefs about the causality of disease provide therefore, as Young suggests, a way of exculpating the sick by transferring accountability

> onto some agency beyond the sick person's will ... [which may] be in some sense external to the sick person (a witch or a virus, perhaps), within his own body (a morbid, physiological process, for example), or, most often a combination of both (1976:78).

Different lay perspectives about the causes of illness are not therefore mutually exclusive, nor confined to any particular social or cultural context for, together, they represent a range of different avenues of explanation and paths of resort which people may use to answer the question: why me? Thus, even in the context of western medical science while a 'disease' may be identified by the doctor as being caused by a germ or virus, this explanation may not, for the individual, satisfactorily explain its occurrence within their particular body. In such cases 'fate' or 'God's will' remain useful explanatory models. For example, a 66-year-old woman in Bucharest who gave birth to a baby through assisted reproductive technology in January 2005 was challenged about the moral issues involved, and those pertaining to the child's future welfare and best interests. She responded by mixing explanatory models, arguing that it was God's will that the technology had succeeded after nine years of failure.

And indeed, the seeming fickleness of the body's flesh to succumb to or resist disease, *willy nilly* and *despite* the adoption of health promoting practices, may be increasing, rather than decreasing, the potency and significance which these kinds of lay explanations of illness have, particularly in western societies. Despite the great advances made in bio-medical knowledge about the causes of disease, accountability remains elusive. We may still need to explain: why me.

Staying Healthy?

It is a strange irony that as medical science penetrates deeper and deeper into the cellular structure of the body, furthering understanding of the disease process, and as screening practices can now identify patterns in genetic susceptibility to future disease, so the control that individuals have over illness appears *less*, rather than more certain. Indeed, as Fitzpatrick (2001) notes, in the context of western societies the threat which illness represents for our bodies and identities seems to loom ever larger. It is, however, a widespread concern which flies in the face of the statistical evidence that, in the case of Britain for example, 'infant mortality rates amongst the poorest families today is similar to that of the richest in the 1970s' and 'a boy born in Britain today can expect to live until he is 75, a girl until over 80', figures which represent an increase of over ten years life expectancy since the second world war (2001:2–5). In some of the poorest regions of the world, Malawi and Zambia for example, life expectancy is almost half of that, just 37.8 years and 32.7 years respectively (Source: United Nations Human Development Index 2004).

Notwithstanding such evidence, however, within the affluent west the worried well are being pressed into action to avoid the causes of illness through amending their diets and taking up rigorous exercise regimes. Thus, within the pages of the popular press, particularly women's magazines, can be found countless words of advice about the measures that individuals might take to avoid 'causing' illness (see Chapter 5). Many of these can be located, if not in the sphere of the supernatural, certainly in the *supra*natural. We are exhorted to 'protect [our] arteries with apple cider vinegar,' 'hit that headache with peppermint' to take 'meditation – not medication' for insomnia and, as we age and our bones begin to creak, to help our bodies 'create new cartilage' (Advert for Rodale Books 2004).

In addition, the western health promotion industry appears to be requiring that individuals *do* begin to exercise more and more control over their bodies to avert the onset of illness. Thus, although a victim-blaming approach to tackling the causes of ill-health might recently have been found wanting by

Governments, with more recognition now being given by the WHO to the social and economic factors involved in disease (Parish 1995), nonetheless individuals still find themselves confronted with the suggestion that they can – indeed should? – take personal responsibility for their health. This means, therefore, that increasingly individuals may not be able to escape some culpability for 'illness'. Within affluent western societies, for instance, ill-health is increasingly being linked with poor lifestyle choices – for example, smoking, obesity, alcohol and drug addiction. This means that if the achievement of individualism is taken as the mark of social personhood (Hockey and James 1993), then people may be held accountable for – or indeed are seen to be the cause of – their own sickness.

Recent examples in the UK, Australia and Canada of heavy smokers being refused surgical intervention for heart disease unless they stop smoking (see for example, *Toronto Star* 4th November 2003) some weeks prior to surgery represent instances of the reallocation of blame, away from society and onto the individual. Similarly, concerns about the poor outcomes of surgery for overweight people have led one UK health trust to consider rationing hip and knee replacements. If implemented, only those willing to lose weight will be given a place on waiting lists. Thus, although the 'cause' of heart disease is acknowledged within bio-medicine as due to the narrowing of the arteries within the patient's body – and in Young's terms, could therefore be seen as external to and beyond the patient's will – within contemporary consumer society this may be an indication that it is no longer considered to be a *sufficient* explanatory model for hard-pressed health services. Instead, the smoker's own embodied mistreatment of their body is also regarded as a key causal agent of the material changes that have taken place, changes for which patients have to take responsibility:

> smokers … consume valuable health-care resources, de la Rocha [the Canadian surgeon] says. If society is going to spend thousands of dollars to treat them, it's only fair to ask that they 'take the first step' and quit their risky habit (*Toronto Star* 4th November 2003).

Here, then, any exculpation of the sick is refused. In Young's (1976) terms, such people transgress the legitimated and socially prescribed conditions of behaviour that, in western consumer culture, are demanded of our relationship with our bodies. These are described by Featherstone in the following terms:

> Self preservation depends upon the preservation of the body within a culture in which the body is the passport to all that is good in life. Health, youth, beauty, sex, fitness are the positive attributes which body care can achieve and pre-

serve. With appearance taken as a reflex of the self the penalties of bodily neglect are a lowering of one's acceptability as a person, as well as an indication of laziness, low self-esteem and even moral failure (1991:186).

Thus, although as Keane (1997:182) notes, many of the people she interviewed about the necessity of adopting healthy eating practices thought that 'it was counterproductive to "think too much" about one's diet' and the effects it might have upon health, there has, nonetheless, been a progressive medicalisation (Illich 1976) and moralisation of more and more areas of human activity. Eating food, taking exercise, watching television or having sex, or indeed simple routines of personal care all appear, now, to be activities that potentially have a health or illness dimension. In an article entitled 'How toxic is your bathroom' the risk that 'your daily beauty regime could be taking years off your life' are outlined through an analysis of the chemical cocktail that may result from using a mix of different personal care products from hair shampoo to toothpaste:

> Absorbed into the body, they can be stored in fatty tissue or organs such as the liver, kidney, reproductive organs and brain ... scientists are finding industrial plasticizers such as phthalates in urine, preservatives known as parabens in breast tumour tissue, and antibacterials such as Tricolosan and fragrance chemicals like the hormone-disrupting musk xylene in human breast milk (*The Independent* 24th October 2005).

And so, as more and more of what we do in western societies becomes classified as good or bad for our health, the more closely we are encouraged to monitor and regulate our own behaviour within the constraints of these newly medicalised frameworks for living. We are all doctors now! But, as Armstrong (1995) notes, the outcome of this anxious scanning of our bodies for early signs of illness is that we are all, also, proto-patients.

While staying healthy may therefore be increasingly politicised as a matter of personal choice and responsibility, it is clear, nonetheless, that structural and cultural factors continue to be important, particularly as regards to the epidemiology of disease and its treatment (see Chapter 2). While in 2003 in western Europe the prevalence rates of HIV for people aged between 15 and 49 years ranged between 0.1% and 0.7%, in Malawi it was 14.2% and in Swaziland the figure was as high as 38.8% (Source: United Nations Health Index 2004). Given the limited healthcare resources in many African countries, combined with the high cost of anti-viral drugs, the possibility of 'choosing' to stay healthy takes on a rather different meaning in these contexts. And, similarly, in the debates over the post-code lottery for healthcare in the UK, it becomes clear that health is not necessarily a lifestyle issue. A recent report, entitled 'Cancer patients are dying because they are poor', revealed that the poorest women in Britain have a 5% reduced rate of surviving breast cancer when compared to the richest, and that 'for cancer of the larynx, survival rates for the most affluent men are 17.2 per cent higher than the poorest', differences in part attributable to inequalities in the provision of services and access to drugs (*The Independent* 10th March 2004).

Illness as a Problem of Identity

The mapping of both a tainted morality onto a newly defined and newly stigmatised 'sick' body in western societies – whether it is the heavy smoker, the overweight toddler, the painfully thin catwalk model or the overworked and overstressed city banker – is, however, nothing new. Rather, it appears to be an enduring cultural aspect of the way in which, in western societies at least, disease and illness can become regarded as potentially stigmatising aspects of a person's social identity. The existence of plague hospitals and leper colonies can, for example, be charted as far back as the twelfth century (Porter 2002; Lane 2001). Here the unclean, those who bodies showed very visible signs of disease through swellings, sores and ulcerations, were confined in places apart. Stigmatised by their bodies, they were punished further by exclusion from mainstream society since such disfiguring and disabling diseases were held to be God-given, a sure sign of divine retribution for past misdeeds.

This was particularly the case with respect to sexually transmitted diseases. In England, from at least the 1580s, it was believed that only the morally corrupt would contract syphilis. Regarded as a punishment from God for personal promiscuity, by the mid-eighteenth century, it was commonly believed that 'sexual intercourse with a virgin would cure a man of syphilis', the virgin's purity presumably providing a kind of symbolic moral cleansing (J. Lane 2001:152). Very much regarded as a 'secret disease', sufferers might receive treatment in a hospital, such as Lock Hospital in London; however, they were admitted only once 'so that the hospital could not be seen to be encouraging immorality' (J. Lane 2001:153).

This kind of discrediting of social identity is what Goffman (1968) depicts in his account of stigma. For Goffman, stigmatisation arises through what he calls 'the abominations of the body' and when these physical differences become regarded by others as 'undesired differentness' (1968:14–15). Such bodily differences have to be carefully managed, Goffman argued, lest they spoil a person's social identity. However, this linking of social morality with bodily sickness, combined often with the attribution of blame, is neither inevitable nor universal. In many cultures bodily differences *per se* do not bring with them such stigmas for, as Douglas (1966) notes, conceptions of what constitutes difference will vary between cultures (see Chapter 3).

Following Douglas (1966), then, the physical differences wrought upon the body by sickness or disease might better be understood as bodily anomalies, as representing 'matter out of place' that different cultures deal with in different kinds of ways.

For example, the extent to which – and ways in which – disease or disabilities impact on identity and concepts of personhood varies. According to Helander (1995), in Southern Somalia, disability is regarded as incurable illness and 'there [is] no clear border between what we call disease and disability' (1995:73). Rarely are individuals regarded as belonging to an all-embracing category of 'disabled people'. Instead,

> a person missing an arm is often talked of and addressed as *gacanley* or *gacamey*, 'armless'. Someone with a limp may be nicknamed *jees*, 'limpy'. Similarly, deaf people are labeled *dhegoole*, 'without ears', and the blind *indhoole*, 'without eyes' (1995:75).

Lacking a collective identity, people with disabilities are not set apart, their bodily difference being seen instead as a mark of their individual personhood. In a culture that sees 'persons as entities that are somehow in a continuous state of flux', Helander argues that changing and changed bodies present little in the way of an anomaly (1995:78). This contrasts powerfully with western bio-medical models of the stable body (see Chapter 3). In southern Somalia, only to those who are mentally ill, or who suffer from severe and incapacitating disabilities that render them immobile, would the diagnosis 'incurable' be given and stigmatisation and social exclusion follow.

Similarly, among the Punan Bah of Borneo, as living representatives of ancestors, all people 'whether they be of limited intelligence or suffering from mental illness or bodily impairment' are included in society, participating as far as they are able and being cared for when they no longer can (Nicholaisen 1995:53). Even those with leprosy or other contagious or infectious diseases are not secluded, although they will eat from different utensils. Thus, it is only those who are regarded as non-humans, such as witches, who will be excluded from participating fully in society. While such people may be socially marginal, or indeed be suffering from a mental illness, this is not necessarily or always the case.

Such examples therefore serve to underscore the social model of disability that argues for disability as a social construction, arising in and out of oppressive and discriminatory practices towards those who have different kinds of bodies and abilities (see Oliver 1990, 1996). Cross-cultural material not only highlights the cultural relativity of concepts of bodily difference, thereby breaking any necessary or universal connection between the body and attitudes towards it, but also reveals the *social* nature of the barriers that may prevent people with disabilities from participating fully in society. Unlike many western societies where people with disabilities may experience a range of social problems – from difficulties in accessing public buildings through to more outright discriminatory practices which disadvantage them in relation to employment – within these more traditional communities few people are excluded from participating, as far as they are able, in everyday social and community life. In this sense, the disabilities of their bodies have become aspects of the body to be negotiated, rather than embodied barriers to social participation. Lonsdale (1990) describes, for example, some of the strategies through which Westerners who are disabled might seek to *resist* the imposition of stigmatising identities. However these can carry their own costs, as in the case of women who choose the more feminine, graceful mobility afforded by a wheelchair over the awkward shuffling motion of walking supported by crutches.

As this brief discussion of the social aspects of disability suggests, therefore, one of the problems of illness lies in the particularity of the process of embodiment itself. The ways in which ideas about health inform bodily perceptions and the ways in such understandings of the body's health status shape the health identities that we inhabit or indeed ascribe to others, become part of our everyday bodily negotiations. These constitute the everyday cultural performances of sickness and combine to define the problem that is illness. That is to say, unless we understand illness as a physical, cultural and social process of identification that unfolds in daily life we cannot explain, for example, why it is that some people might not comply with forms of medical treatment offered to them, despite their identification as 'ill'; or, conversely, why our friend Mavis, above, so readily embraces such a variety of different illnesses. It is clear that we need to look carefully at what health identity 'choices' signal and at the processes of identification that they involve.

The Problem of Illness and the Problem of Identification

Research that explores people's accounts of their 'health' and 'illness' experiences underscores the contribution of the social constructionist agenda within medical sociology and anthropology if we are to understand illness as a process of identification (see Chapter 7). However, as suggested at the outset of this volume (see Chapter 1) the conferring of identity as 'well' or 'ill' is not simply a matter of labelling the self or another. It is the outcome of the dynamic interplay between the structures within which we, as embodied beings, are positioned and our agency, as individuals both engaged in, and moving between, particular social contexts. Thus, 'becoming sick' and 'getting better' are socially interactive, bodily processes of negotiation that unfold over time.

James (1993), for instance, shows that the rather different ways in which the health status of sick children was identified by parents were not simply a reflection of the material conditions of the disease. In large part, it was also a function of the kinds of treatment offered by doctors and the ways in which this delivered. The children had been diagnosed with a variety of common childhood complaints, including asthma and eczema, all of which required specialist medical treatments. However, the kinds of healthcare that the families had received differed, leading parents to conceive of the health identities of their children in rather different ways. Those parents whose children had asthma, for example, portrayed their children as 'differently normal', playing down the significance which asthma made to their children's everyday lives and to family life more generally. On the whole, they felt satisfied with the healthcare their children had received. Their children having been diagnosed as 'different' by medical professionals and as in need of special treatment regimes, the parents worked hard to ensure that 'having asthma' made as little impact as possible on their children's lives. Parents of children with eczema, however, were less positive about the treatment their children had received, eczema being regarded by many health professionals as a common childhood complaint and something that children will grow out of. Having received little affirmation from the medical profession of the 'difference' eczema made to their children's lives, these parents had often battled hard to get expert help. Such experiences helped shape their views of their children's health status – they thought of their children as 'normally different', as having a health identity that deserved, but rarely received, sufficient specialist attention.

In this example, then, we can see the ways in which 'health identities' can emerge out of the interactions that take place in medical encounters between doctors and patients. However, unlike the static model of the Parsonian sick role (see Chapter 2), where the doctor and patient are seen as having fixed and unequal access to authority and power, what this example reveals is not only the continuous nature of processes of identification, but also the subtle negotiations that take place around the body to permit a more flexible response.

Kleinman's (1980) extensive and detailed analysis of the healthcare systems in Taipei, Taiwan offers additional insight into this process. In Taipei there are three overlapping spheres of knowledge to which people have recourse when seeking medical treatment – the popular, the folk sector and the professional. Traditional Chinese medicine sits comfortably alongside folk medicine and western bio-medicine and people seek treatment across this range using a combination of different frames of reference and different patterns of resort (1980:188–9). In that, healing is often a family business, a variety of different healing traditions may be available to patients in any one location and there-fore patients can exercise a degree of agency, taking different ailments to different practitioners for diagnosis and, hopefully, cure.

However, what is interesting to consider is how this choice is made within a context of marked medical pluralism. To consult with a shaman is, for example, one choice available to people and that shamans offer divination for a range of different problems, including financial ones, suggests that shamans are seen as dealing generally with matters of misfortune, illness being just one kind. In Kleinman's words, they are 'indigenous crisis intervention experts' (1980:2). Although shamans would not treat serious illness – such patients would be referred elsewhere – they offer treatment for more common ailments. As effective communicators, often with strong personalities, shamans enter a trance state to receive God's words, for it is God, not the shaman, who has the power to cure. Divination of the cause of illness is achieved through a shamanic ritual that may involve the shaman undergoing a variety of bodily mortifications – treading on hot coals, lacerating the body, sitting on nails – whilst in dialogue with the patient about their troubles. The cure prescribed may often involve using Chinese herbs and making amends to the spirit world.

Kleinman's case study of a man with depression who visited a shaman is revealing of the embodied experience of illness and of cure and shows how the process of embodiment is critical in the negotiation of illness between the patient and his shamanic practitioner. After spending several hours with his family at the shaman's shrine, talking, laughing and joking with him about his business and family problems, Kleinman observes that 'this profoundly depressed man looked so much better when he left that I could not recall any case that I had treated or observed when the treatment had such a noticeable and immediate effect' (1980:219).

Whether the 'cure' lasted is not the most interesting issue. Instead what Kleinman points to is the implications of the choice of shamanic treatment. In Chinese society, where depression is heavily stigmatised, admitting feeling depressed would have brought shame to the man and his family. By consulting a shaman, one who speaks with the voice of God, the man achieved some legitimation of his condition – a form of esculpation. Being 'God's will' the man was free from blame and was able to both accept the diagnosis and to begin the cure. As Kleinman notes, by contrast, other people in Taipei who attend the outpatient clinics offered by western medicine will not readily accept such a diagnosis from the doctor. In this case, then,

> therapeutic success was achieved by the insight this indigenous practitioner
> had into the kinds of culturally constituted concerns that were likely to be

causing problems for the client and his family during this sickness episode (Kleinman 1980:222).

Thus, following Kleinman (1978), we have to regard any clinical consultation as a process of negotiation between two world views, between lay and professional explanatory models of illness (see also Chapters 5 and 6). The 'illness' is presented by the patient, both verbally and non-verbally, a performance of symptoms and signs which the clinician translates into named pathologies before prescribing a treatment regime. Health identities are, in this sense, the product of medical encounters. They are socially constructed through, not only the conversations about illness that take place within the clinic, but also through the framing of gender, class and ethnicity-based identities that both the doctor and patient bring to their conversations.

Strong (1994) demonstrates, for example, in two rather different types of medical encounters, how this process of identification occurs through the shifting dynamic of power that, simultaneously, enables the authority of the doctor and the moral status of the patient. Comparing clinics in the UK with those in the US Strong argues that, in the context of the UK national health service system, the doctor's authority comes with the job; it is ascribed and not open to question. Patients exercise very little power both within the encounter itself and also in relation to diagnosis decisions (but see Chapter 6). In the US, by contrast, because doctors have to recruit and keep their private patients, they are much more in the business of selling their skills as individuals. They have to win their patients' confidence. In this context, the clinician's authority is much more negotiable. Patients may vote with their feet – and wallets – if they do not like what they hear. However, the cash nexus that binds US doctors to their patients means that in cases of charity, American doctors feel much freer to be critical and judgemental about the moral status of their clients. Unlike their UK counterparts, they offered little in the way of sympathy and understanding to patients. US patients in the charity baby clinic were therefore obliged to perform a lot of 'character-work' in order to overcome the assumption that, through attending the clinic, they had 'already proved their incompetence as mothers' and were 'apriori, stupid, lazy, incompetent and unloving' (Strong 1994:35).

Conclusion: The Problem of Embodiment in the Problem of Illness

The above examples suggest, therefore, that medical encounters work to shape identity through the negotiations about illness that take place between doctors and their patients. However, in our view, this predominantly social constructionist perspective is not a sufficient explanation of the 'problems' that illness makes for our health identities. We have also to consider what part the body itself plays in this process of identification and therefore to also consider what additional insights a focus on embodiment might bring to our understanding of this process.

Returning to the Taipei case study, discussed above, provides us with some clues. Although not discussed by Kleinman directly, embodiment clearly has a role to play in the kind of decision-making people in Taipei make about where to seek treatment. The body's symptoms dictate the patterns of resort which people choose to follow, Kleinman suggests. Thus, for example, in cases of acute, non-serious illness people self-treat and then adopt popular remedies, before seeking help from either a western or a Chinese-style practitioner. Those with chronic or recurrent conditions will, by contrast, seek out both western and Chinese medicine, while also continuing to use popular remedies. This suggests, therefore, that these rather different experiences of embodiment – acute illness episodes as opposed to the relentless drag of chronic illness – might have a part to play in the decision-making process. Indeed, evidence about the treatment choices made by people in western societies, between orthodox medicine and complementary techniques, suggests that people who are consulting alternative practitioners for the first time often do so because other treatments have failed. That is, because they still *feel* unwell, they seek alternative kinds of treatment (Sharma 1994).

Similarly, the emergence of 'new' diseases also reveals the importance of embodiment for the problem of illness. Initially dismissed by orthodox bio-medical practitioners as Yuppie flu, chronic fatigue syndrome (CFS) was later reluctantly identified as a disease category through the persistent presentation of embodied suffering by individuals. Symptoms first dismissed as psychosomatic, that is all in the mind of the patient, were later granted the status of 'real' embodied experiences. Somewhat ironically, though, as Seale *et al* observe, CFS has, as yet, failed to produce any physical 'scientific evidence of disturbances to cell function which might explain the chronic fatigue' (2001:131)!

Thus, in some senses the problem of illness remains elusive, despite this chapter's intensive engagement with this as an issue. Defining what illness is involves further exploration of the ways in which illness is constituted and understood as an embodied experience. This is the task of the following chapters.

5

Representing the Body's Health and Identity

For those of us living in the modern industrialised societies of the west, the technological advances of medical science, combined with improvements in public health, would seem to have increased our control over the uncertainties and problems that illness brings to our sense of self and identity, for the brute experiences of death and disease are now a more distant experiential reality for the majority of westerners. In Norway, ranked at the top of the human development index, life expectancy at birth has increased from 74.4 years in 1970–5 to 78.9 years in 2000–5, with comparable figures for the US of 71.5 and 77.1 years and, for the UK, 72.0 and 78.2 years (Human Development Index 2004). And many of the diseases that threaten the lives of people living in poorer countries such as tuberculosis (TB) are no longer common killers for westerners – just five cases of TB per 100,000 of the population were reported in Norway in 2002 compared, for example, to 734 per 100,000 in Cambodia (Human Development Index 2004).

Such encouraging developments in western societies seem curiously at odds, therefore, with the seemingly constant presence of health-related news and information in the pages of their press, on radio, on television and on the now infinite array of health-related websites that are to be found on the World Wide Web. As noted in Chapter 4, it is as if, despite increasing life expectancy, westerners have become more, rather than less anxious, about their health as, time and again, different media sites promise the reader, writer or listener an opportunity for 'making sense of illness'.

The task of this chapter is, therefore, to explore further the conundrum identified in Chapter 4, here through a consideration of the different ways in which the body's potential for health and for illness is *represented* and the import that this has for health identities. Is it, as Geertz (1966) said of the symbols which make up a cultural system such as religion, that these representations provide models which give meaning to experience by both 'shaping themselves to it and shaping it to themselves' (1966:8)? In other words, does the process of representing health and illness provide a source of health information and advice about health statuses that works, at the same time, to represent health as a problematic *for* identity and therefore as something for which solutions must be sought? Is it the case, therefore, that despite – or perhaps *because* – people in industrialised societies are, on the whole, living longer and healthier lives that the prospect of suffering has become a powerful source of biographical disruption, a new threat which must be actively managed?

Work on the biographical disruption precipitated by illness (Bury 1982; Williams 1984), and the related generation of illness narratives (Kleinman 1988; Bury 2001) suggests, for example, that the less familiar death and disease become, the more these need to be guarded against and, importantly, to be made sense of, through seeking out information that can enable understanding to be achieved and solutions to be found for the practical difficulties they may cause. Thus, for example, the historically shifting media images of the encounter between patient and doctor – as in classic UK television series, such as *Dr Finlay's Casebook* or, more recently, *Casualty* and *Hotby City*, – provides a representational culture that enhances the repertoire of resources through which health, illness and the body are objectified. Thus, for UK viewers, at different times, the doctor has been made to represent benevolent paternalism, as in *Dr Finlay's Casebook*, the 1960s series representing a 1920s Scottish GP practice, and the under-resourcing of service provision in Accident and Emergency departments, as in the series *Casualty*, screened from 1986 onwards. Such images help inform patients' expectations of both the scope and limitations of healthcare provision as well as the resilience and vulnerability of the sick or injured body – as this chapter goes on to demonstrate.

However, in the developing world, where sickness and ill health *are* still a constant feature of everyday life, it remains no less important for those who are sick that they, or their carers, can also seek out information that might enable them to comprehend the causes of illness and to find ways of dealing with the problems that ill health brings. Here, though, it may not be to the mass media or the Internet that people turn; instead it may be to the more traditional, and often more personalised, representations of illness that can be provided by a healer or diviner. However, this process, like the scanning of the Internet, also involves the search for information that will help the uncertainties of illness to be managed (see White 2005).

As Geertz observed, then, it may be that 'the problem ... is ... not how to avoid suffering but how to suffer, how to make of physical pain, personal loss, worldly defeat, or the helpless contemplation of others' agony something bearable, supportable – something, we say, sufferable' (1966:19). Whether in the media or a diviner's account, we can consider the extent to which representations of health and illness, like religious symbols, therefore provide people with a kind of

> cosmic guarantee not only for their ability to comprehend the world, but also, comprehending it, to give a precision to their feeling, a definition to their emotions which enables them, morosely or joyfully, grimly or cavalierly, to endure it (1966:19).

Such questions permeate this chapter as we ask how representations of health and illness might work to render human beings' inevitable vulnerability to suffering more bearable, whether they be passed over the garden wall in neighbourly chat, gleaned from a healer or posted and read on the Internet. First, however, we need to set out the theoretical context for our discussion.

Re-presenting Representations

Hall's definition of representation provides a useful starting point when he writes that,

> representation is the process by which members of a culture use language (broadly defined as any system which deploys signs, any signifying system) to produce meaning. Already this definition carries the important premise that things – objects, people, events, in the world – do not have in themselves any fixed, final or true meaning. It is us – in society with human cultures – who make things mean, who signify (Hall 1997 cited in King and Watson 2005:6).

But, as Hall points out, because this process of meaning-making or representing is always located in particular historical moments and particular spaces it has to be understood as a set of situated practices or, in Foucault's (1972) terms, a discourse. Framed in this way, for our purposes, the concept of discourse becomes a useful shorthand for thinking about the ongoing production of health knowledge as a systematic set of representations, whether this is through the images that appear on television screens, adverts in magazines, newspaper articles, healer's divinations or the 'old wives tales' that are related across the generations as sources of advice and understanding. But the concept of discourse, in relation to representations of health and illness, is the more encompassing, since it also provides a way of engaging with issues of power. If representations are to be regarded as fundamentally situated in the social practices of everyday life, then we need to explain how it is that particular discourses predominate – as the way things are, as how life is – at any point in time. We also need to be able to consider questions of social change and how particular hegemonic discourses might come to be disrupted, amended or even over-turned. In doing this, therefore, we can acknowledge Foucault's observation that the power that specific representations might have over our thinking is not simply a matter of coercion or control; rather, the power of discourse can be productive since 'power is a field within which relationships are constituted' (McGowen 1994:96):

> For Foucault the central question is always: what permits some things to be said and not others. By this he does not simply mean what preconceptions shape our knowledge, but what existing power arrangements constitute the conditions under which something can be said (McGowen 1994:97).

However, turning now more specifically to representations of health and illness as one kind of discourse, and linking this to the notion of embodiment that is core to this volume – the being-a-body in the world that is already socially informed – immediately a Foucauldian formulation of discourse becomes problematic for our understanding of health and illness experiences. We can no longer see representations as 'out there' and as having an effect upon us and upon our understanding of ourselves as 'well' or 'ill', however subtle, persuasive or creative their play upon our senses. Instead, if, as we are arguing in the volume, embodiment is a core aspect of identity, then we have to explore the complexity of the interactions between different kinds of representations and the embodied experiences of health and illness that make some discourses more persuasive to us than others. Indeed, as we shall see, this embodied engagement with representations of health and illness is one important aspect of the ongoing negotiations that we make with and to our bodies as they undergo change across the life course (see Chapter 7). In this sense, therefore, representations of health, illness and bodily experience contribute to an ongoing dialogic process of identification through which we negotiate our bodies and get to know whether we are ill or well. And, ironically, the stories that we begin to tell ourselves about the illnesses that we experience or observe in others may, as we shall see, come to constitute new discourses or sources of representational authority; they may become the narratives and representations that others will consult in the future when they, too, seek out health information of particular kinds.

For example, in the parallel circumstance of the ageing, rather than sick body, Hepworth (2000) explores the role of fictional representations of later life, arguing that these can *complement* academic/medical accounts. They demonstrate the diversity and richness of embodied, subjective experience and point out the 'differences between the perspectives of insiders and outsiders on ageing and death' (2000:4). And, in terms of how engagement with representations such as these might shape individuals' conceptions and experiences of health and illness, Hepworth's view of reading is insightful. He describes this as 'a process of symbolic interaction where the reader has some freedom to interpret the text according to his or her own ideas, emotions and consciousness of self' (2000:5). In this chapter, then, we examine a range of representations, seeking, as Hepworth says, to find out how culture shapes our 'personal ideas' (2000:3) about embodied experiences such as ageing, health and illness. In addition, we investigate those imaginative processes through which, via different forms of representation, individuals engage with embodied experiences that others are currently undergoing or which they may fear will happen to them. As Hepworth argues, '[u]ltimately, writing and reading are processes of emotional and intellectual interaction where symbols – words – are the currency. As readers we interact with the text in terms of our understanding of the words before us; and this understanding involves an interplay between shared meanings ... and our own personalised versions of them ...' (2000:6).

Elaborating upon this process, Lupton (1994) draws attention to the importance of metaphor in allowing imaginative identification such as this. Despite the powerful bodily sensations which can accompany illness – pain, fatigue, nausea, dizziness – these remain curiously private to the individual. Indeed as Scarry (1985) argues, pain resists language and therefore objectification, dividing individuals from one another, insofar as it makes it difficult both *not* to grasp one's own pain and to grasp that of someone else. What Lupton (1994) traces are the metaphoric systems through which illness has been represented, showing how medical metaphors of the body during the Early Modern period drew on architectural forms such as 'fortress' or 'house', so articulating a notion of the body as protected by culture against 'the incursions of untamed Nature' (1994:57). Once we enter the Modern industrialised period, mechanical metaphors begin to dominate – and Lupton notes the use of language such as 'recharging our batteries', 'blowing a fuse', becoming 'wound up', which draw from the more tangible domain of electrical equipment, clocks and plumbing to allow engagement with the body's private and invisible workings, the 'pump' of the heart, the 'pressure' of the blood (1994:59).

Part of this chapter's intention is, therefore, to show how the representation of medical knowledge as a stable and uncontested source of information about health and illness is achieved. In addition, however, as already indicated, it examines the ways in which alternative and potentially challenging conceptions and experiences of health and illness are represented. It does this by examining the ways in which not only bio-medicine, but other kinds of medical practices and lay accounts of health and illness, are represented in different mediums and by exploring the ways in which these different 'knowledges' about health and illness are produced and reproduced over time and across social space. Each kind of representation offers the individual different possibilities for engagement and, emerging from this, the possibility of different kinds of health identities.

Thus, whether in modern industrial societies or in the context of more traditional communities, the seeking out of explanations for and information about suffering is more than an act of cognition by which we try to make sense of any inexplicable body sensations that we might experience (see Chapter 4). As Reynolds Whyte so shrewdly observes, it also involves, quite literally the *making* of meaning, that is, the seeking out of very practical 'means to deal with life's uncertainties' by investing our somatic experiences with meanings that make some kind of sense to us (2005:246). What this chapter's focus on embodiment allows us to do, therefore, is to explore how this meaning-making takes place. Thus we examine the *process* of representing health and illness, rather than simply the content of representational forms (see King and Watson 2005 for an overview). Importantly this involves exploring the production and consumption of representations as a form of social practice that is integral to what Csordas terms the 'constant reconstitution of the self' (2002:59). As emotional, cognitive and material 'information' is made to intervene in the perceptual processes through which we encounter and respond to our embodied experiences of health, so our existing representations of health and the body are reconstituted. Thus, it is through this process of constantly re-orienting ourselves in the world, through ongoing processes of reflection, identification and objectification, that we get to know whether we are well or ill.

Wilkinson's (1988) work on children's illness experience and how children communicate – or represent – that bodily experience provides an initial illuminating illustration of this process. Given that young children's health status is usually legitimated by adults, then as Wilkinson shows, the ways in which children learn to 'represent' common illnesses to adults, and how it is consequently interpreted by them, are core to understanding children's illness episodes. In Wilkinson's view, children learn to take on the 'sick role' through a dynamic engagement with the representations adults offer them about 'how' to be sick (see also Chapters 6 and 7). What children learn are sets of situated bodily practices that enable their changing somatic states to be made meaningful, both for themselves and for those from whom remedy is being sought. An interesting outcome of this, however, is that children also learn how to *pretend* to be sick. These too are a set of situated body practices, listed by the children as: not doing 'what you normally do', 'sleeping in', 'by not eating your food', 'being quiet' and 'coffing down the loo and saying I've been sick' (1988:180).

As this example provocatively highlights for us, representations of health and illness are not therefore 'objective', pre-given and waiting simply to be decoded as markers of identity; rather they are 'an indefinite series of perspectival views' in relation to which 'the body takes up a position' as well, ill or just not quite right (Csordas 2002:86). In sum, therefore, rather than positing a top-down model of cognitive structures being imposed upon object bodies via different forms of representation, we have to explore, instead, the way in which embodied agents act to negotiate the body's health status as an aspect of social identity.

Representing the Hegemony of Bio-medicine

Notwithstanding this chapter's intent to focus on the wide variety of health and illness representations that are available, bio-medicine provides our point of departure for it is a key global discourse through which individuals get to know about their health or their illness, and through which health identities are taken on. Although itself the product of changing historical discourses – witness the shift from the bedside medicine of the eighteenth century, through the clinical medicine of the early nineteenth century to the twentieth century's focus on laboratory medicine (Seale *et al* 2001), bio-medicine is, nonetheless, a very powerful form of medical knowledge. Defined through its basis in the objective scientific principles of 'systematic observation of natural phenomena for the purpose of discovering laws governing those phenomena' bio-medicine differentiates itself from doctrines that embrace 'superstition, magic and the supernatural' (BMA cited in Seale *et al* 2001:15, see also Chapter 4).

Thus, for example, in Jerome K. Jerome's *Three Men in a Boat,* published in 1889, we find bio-medicine represented as an authoritative source of knowledge. The opening passage of the novel describes three young men who decide they need a short boating holiday to remedy their ailing health:

> We were all feeling seedy, and we were getting quite nervous about it. Harris said he felt such extraordinary fits of giddiness come over him at times, that he hardly knew what he was doing; and then George said that *he* had fits of giddiness too, and hardly knew what *he* was doing. With me, it was my liver that was out of order. I knew it was my liver that was out of order, because I had just been reading a patent liver-pill circular, in which were detailed various symptoms by which a man could tell when his liver was out of order. I had them all (Jerome [1889] 2004:1).

This discussion leads the narrator to recall visiting London's British Museum to read up on another 'slight ailment'. Like the liver-pill circular, the medical textbooks' lists of 'premonitory symptoms' persuade him that he not only has typhoid, St Vitus Dance, ague, Bright's Disease but also Cholera. He says: 'I plodded conscientiously through the twenty-six letters, and the only malady I could conclude I had not got was housemaid's knee' ([1889]2004:2). However, in this nineteenth century example, self diagnosis was not followed through in self medication or lifestyle change. Instead the narrator reports his symptoms to his 'medical man' whose expertise is then validated in a pre-scription which listed beefsteak, beer, a ten-mile walk every morning, an 11pm bedtime and the injunction: '... don't stuff up your head with things you don't understand' ([1889] 2004:4).

Albeit fictional, Jerome's 'medical man' responds in a way which under-scores the dominant status of 'official' bio-medical representations by warning against the narrator's attempt to make sense of them himself. Bio-medicine was becoming increasingly professionalised and the power and prestige of its practitioners was in ascendance at the end of the nineteenth century (Seale *et al* 2001). And by the end of the following century, when Oakley (1995) recorded interactions between pregnant women and doctors, a similarly joking response to the patient's expertise on the part of the doctors was firmly in evidence. When women claimed knowledge about the baby's weight, for example, flower and produce shows and women's ability at Guess-the-Weight-of-the-Cake competitions were referred to by the male doctors, these being regarded as the more traditional domains of *women's* expertise. In this way the patriarchal foundations of professionalised medical practice reproduce themselves.

By contrast, in the twenty-first century, our understanding of the ways in which the discourse of bio-medicine is encountered, interpreted and used by people who are seeking health advice or information, and the health identities that follow on, appears to offer a *challenge* to the hegemony of bio-medicine and its practitioners' medical expertise. Thus, for example, Cornwell's account of London East End life (1984, cited in Williams 2003:103) reveals, for example, the possibility of *normal* illness. In this context, health problems may not be represented by East Enders as illnesses, since 'illness, like hard work itself, is only to be *expected* (a normal part of life one might say) and not therefore to be moaned about' (2003:103). Such illnesses are not biographically disruptive, therefore, since they are encountered by people whose embodied expectation is of *ill-health* (see also Chapter 7).

What this indicates, therefore, is that localised lay narratives or folk theories can offer representations which challenge the hegemony of the bio-medical discourse and thereby disrupt the usual processes of health identification that bio-medicine enables. Highlighting the significance of people's embodied experiences of illness means, therefore, that representations of health – even bio-medical ones – have always to be seen as situated practices. Questions constantly have to be asked about who is representing what for whom.

Thus, Mogensen (2005) for example, describes how, in Uganda, people work happily with both traditional explanations of misfortune (see Chapter 4) and bio-medical representations of illness. Indeed, it is a combination that helps them to understand the full complexities of why they get sick by 'opening up different ways of linking events and trying out different things' (2005:242). In this sense, this is a very practical system of information gathering that is being used by embodied, sick individuals to help 'make a whole of a disrupted life' (2005:240). Although objectively the two systems of representation may seem incompatible, as Mogensen argues, it is important to look at 'what people do with biomedicine, when reaching out to act upon the world' rather than simply to ask what bio-medicine does to people (2005:237). Thus, while tablets may be taken to alleviate the symptoms of diarrhoea, if it keeps recurring, then this sickness is understood and explained within the larger *social* context through the allocation of blame and responsibility to the actions of specific individuals (see Chapter 4).

Elsewhere, Wenzel Geissler's (1998) account of how children in Luo, western Kenya, understand their intestinal worms also demonstrates how western and traditional sources of health knowledge can be meaningfully integrated into people's experiences and understandings. While the children's grandparents believe that worms 'digest' food eaten, and help distribute it about the body, their parents share this traditional belief, but with an openness to western bio-medical views of the worms as parasites. The children, however, have learnt to *integrate* both views. They differentiate between good and bad worms which inhabit different parts of the body, and between traditional medicine which appeases the good worms and western medicine which kills off the bad ones. Thus, in this context, a new representation of intestinal worms – here the bio-medical representation – has been integrated within the existing traditional system of health beliefs that, of course, is part of the wider cultural system through which children's everyday lives are managed.

As these different examples illustrate, therefore, the use and application of medical knowledge is not simply the province of medical practitioners, despite the traditional representation that it is through the interaction between doctor and patient that medical diagnoses transform the patient's 'illness' into a medically defined 'disease' (see Chapter 2). Indeed, now that health promotion strategies are everywhere placing new responsibilities upon the individual client or consumer of health services (see Chapter 4), 'patients' are increasingly enlisted as active consumers, rather than positioned as the objects of medical attention; and, precisely because they are consumers, they may conduct independent enquiries into sources of 'health information'.

As we shall see, therefore, health-related materials continue to accumulate in bookshops, health clinics, news stands and on the Internet, providing a wide array of knowledge for the consumer, much of which is located within the sphere of bio-medicine. Thus, for example, while reporting the Advertising Standards Authority's decision to insist that the French cosmetic giant L'Oreal withdraw a major advertising campaign which made false 'scientific' claims for its products, McCartney points out that 'the new hard sell is science', is a possible explanation for L'Oreal's over ambitious statements (*The Guardian* G2 18th August 2005). However, alongside the 'giant' institutional providers of health-care, both state and privately owned, we also need to take account of the many *personal* narratives of ill-health that can offer individuals more immediate sources of embodied recognition and identification through providing experiences against which they can compare and contrast their own somatic suffering. Thus such personal experiences also make powerful claims to truth and authenticity. Given the sheer variety and availability of sources of health information, ques-tions have to be raised, therefore, about their status and authority and about the different ways in which these health representations might engage embodied individuals, who seek out information.

To understand the power of any representation to influence thinking and practice, as we shall now go on to do, we therefore need to examine the bases of its truth claims. In addition, we need to consider how representations might intervene in the perceptual process through which individuals understand or objectify their experiences and understandings of illness, be it their own or that of someone else. In so doing, the chapter therefore develops the focus on embodiment by exploring how it is that an individual moves from a pre-abstract state of mental or physiological disturbance – a feeling of being unwell or not quite right – to some form of self 'diagnosis' and the taking on of a particular health identity through engaging with different kinds of health and illness representations.

Health 'Information'

In modern industrial societies visual and verbal representations of health and illness are multitudinous and are to be found in both elite as well as more pop-ulist genres (Lupton 2004). Among others, examples include: information which appears to have an immediate bio-medical source (e.g. cutting edge scientific reports of medical advances heralded on television and on the radio that offer new hope for sufferers, websites that provide advice and information, news reports about health policies and the role that medical institutions play in the promulgation of these); information which has a more tangential relationship with bio-medical sources (e.g. TV documentaries which describe developments in curative medicine, news stories about hopes for cures and dashed expectations of recovery, adverts for remedies and therapies); information which is grounded in personal experience (e.g. written and verbal narratives of personal experiences of serious illness, TV documentaries picturing personal tragedies and triumphs in relation to disease); and forms of entertainment which locate their narratives in medical settings (e.g. medical dramas about health and hospitals that provide us with 'factionalised' forms of entertainment).

As King and Watson observe 'it seems that we cannot escape a "daily diet" of health advice, or representations of therapy, illness and medicine, as long as we have access to any forms of media' (2005:2). Explanations for this proliferation are wide ranging – for example, from the power of drug companies to persuade us of the potency of their products and the freeing up of healthcare markets, through to the demands of post-modernity that has turned us all into reflexive and individualised consumers. Yet, as already identified (Mogensen 2005; Wenzel Geissler 1998) elsewhere we can find local belief systems remaining in place, despite the persuasiveness of global health promotion and advertising campaigns which are grounded in a bio-medical model of health and illness. In addition, in societies where the bio-medical system has come to dominate, other kinds of health knowledges, that were once decried as 'alternative' or 'fringe' medicine, are now more often being regarded as 'complementary' and indeed becoming mainstreamed. Is it the case, therefore, that in the risk society (Beck 1992), we may not necessarily trust the old authority invested in the notion that 'the doctor knows best'. Instead, are we actively seeking out other kinds of health-related information on our own behalf? Does this explain the proliferation of health representations? And, if it does, then clearly what this vast array of different representations also constitutes is a new discursive site within which the negotiation of identity is actively taking place.

As Hall argues, 'precisely because identities are constructed within, and not outside, discourse we need to understand them as produced in specific historical and institutional sites within specific discursive formations and practices, by specific enunciative strategies' (1996:4). Thus, as we shall see, whether they inform us how we might avoid illness, how we can identify or predict its occurrence, and how its effects can be treated or minimised, such representations are pervasive and persuasive sites of identification. Included are images of physical and mental health which, when linked with particular 'medical' products, offer the viewer or listener an escape from the inevitabilities of the human condition: loss and indeed mortality. Indeed, a kind of 'healthism' as Bunton *et al* argue, lends a health-related status to an ever-widening range of products: 'food and drink; myriad health promoting pills; private health; alternative medicine; exercise machines and videos; health insurance; membership of sport and health clubs; walking boots; running shoes; cosmetic surgery; shampoo (for "healthy looking hair"); sun oils; psychoanalysis; shell suits' (1995:2).

And yet, the process through which such health identities are forged is not a foregone conclusion for, as people encounter representations, they do so as socially-located individuals. Thus in an examination of health information campaigns in Egypt, S. Lane (1997) argues that, although the mini-drama format adopted for this health promotion was technically sophisticated, it

lacked a well-thought out, readily understood content and so failed to persuade. With an ethos that reflected social marketing, rather than the empowerment agenda of giving choice, these mini-dramas would, at first sight, seem
potentially effective for an audience with 60% illiteracy among women and
38% among men. However, what the Egyptians received were representations
of 'good health' which not only reflected the agendas of western funding
bodies, without whom these costly adverting films could not have been made,
but also told people what they already knew! These and other problems, such
as the overcrowding of the films with too many points of information reflected
not only a lack of pre-testing, Lane suggests, but also a reliance on uninformed
policy-makers' assumptions about which health issues are the most urgent,
and what health-seeking behaviours are most realistic among the Egyptian
population.

Similarly, in a study of the Malaria Radio Campaign targeted at the UK's
Pakistani populations who travel regularly to malarious countries, Doi (2005)
reveals that it reflected the assumptions, and indeed the prejudices, of the
dominant white population. As Doi's (2005) analysis of both the medium and
the message of the radio campaign shows, the campaign was ineffective
because although the adverts were broadcast by ethnic radio stations, the
radio itself was seen as a primitive medium, only half listened to and for short
periods of time. Cut off from their countries of origin, Pakistani interviewees
said they preferred the quality of the programmes they accessed via the satel-
lite channels on their televisions, finding more there that were relevant to
events in Pakistan. In addition, traditional music had been used to back the
adverts and this was seen to undermine the seriousness of their content,
rendering them offensively 'childish' or 'patronising', a representation felt to
reflect white western assumptions of superiority. Finally, the simple nature of
the information broadcast lent it little value for a population which saw itself
as already well informed about the risks of malaria.

Thus, whether in the context of western bio-medicine or indigenous knowledge systems worldwide, what these examples demonstrate is that key questions have to be asked about what constitutes 'health information', the
processes through which it is represented, by whom it is represented and for
what reasons and with what outcomes.

Encountering Representations of Health and Illness

Turning first to explore the role of discursive representations of health and
identity within the media, Seale's (2003) overview provides a useful
summary of the issues that need to be addressed. He argues that representations of health and illness are no more neutral than the role of media in
society. Questions always have to be asked about which stories get told and

why; about who has access to and control over the media; about the form in which stories are told as well as the messages they disseminate; about how they work and what they accomplish in terms of people's everyday lives. Taking the lead from media studies, attention must therefore be given to the social relations of production and reception, as well as to the analysis of the representational forms themselves.

Of particular interest for the concerns of this book, however, is the issue of audience reception. It is the question we have already raised with respect to the ways in which, as embodied individuals, people make sense of and engage with the representations they encounter and what they do with them. As Seale notes,

> Once considered passive recipients (or forgetters) of information, audience 'theory' developed during the 1980s towards a conceptualisation of audiences as much more active in relating to mediated messages. A reconceptualisation of the 'mass' audience towards a view of fragmented 'audiences', with varying motivations and competencies, has also emerged (2003:516).

Indeed, for Seale, there are a number of core areas to attend to when trying to understand how people engage with representations of health and illness of different kinds. Some people may 'seek health-promoting information as a part of rational risk profiling at fateful moments', while others may seek 'emotional stimulation' through dramatised accounts of illness such as films and docu-dramas (2003:517). However, people also 'receive' – or more properly engage with – such messages in different ways, actively resisting as well as aligning themselves with representations. In Seale's view, when people engage with representations of health and illness they have an 'imagined conversation with mediated ideas, and in an imagined community of other viewers, people "like me"' and in so doing they 'construct themselves' (2003:517). Or, in Csordas' terms, a 'person encounters representations of the body and ... has its being-in-the-world altered' (2002:261).

To illustrate the ways in which representations of the body's well-being are involved with such processes of bodily negotiation and identification this section focuses on the example of 'health', rather than illness for, in some senses, representations of the 'healthy body' are the more problematic. 'Health' is somehow a less tangible bodily state – how can health be defined other than negatively as the absence of disease? Disease and sickness usually have material and physical manifestations with which to engage and identify. And indeed, the difficulty of representing 'health' is revealed in the problems encountered by health promotion campaigners. They have to address a wide diversity of people who, as embodied beings, receive 'health promotion messages' from a variety of standpoints and perspectives. This may help explain therefore why Featherstone's observation that one of the prescriptions of twentieth century consumer society is the moral obligation to achieve young, healthy, fit and beautiful bodies – the kinds of 'idealised images of the human body which proliferate in advertising and the visual media' (1991:178) – appears to have failed to persuade people to change their behaviour at the start of the twenty-first century. Obese, rather than slim, bodies are fast becoming the norm in western consumer societies, with an estimated 24 million adults in the UK now reported to be overweight or obese (*The Independent* 16th November 2004). Thus, it is precisely because we are embodied beings who are already situated in the world, with particular kinds of bodies and experiences, that there is no necessary or deterministic translation from representation to social action. Even within one society such as the UK, the diversity of the social, economic and material environments within which individual, embodied life unfolds renders the outcome of engagement with representations of health highly unpredictable (Nettleton and Bunton 1995).

In their study of health promotion, Bunton *et al* (1995) begin to explore this issue in depth. They argue that, in the context of late modern public health, that has witnessed the shift from curative to preventive forms of medicine, there has been a greater emphasis placed on participative health and new forms of governance. Individuals are now charged with taking responsibility for their own health; they are expected to act rationally and to take account of the advice and warnings offered to them through the media:

> the contemporary citizen is increasingly attributed with responsibilities to ceaselessly maintain and improve her or his own health … To do this she or he is increasingly expected to take note of and act upon the recommendations of a whole range of 'experts' and 'advisers' located in a range of *diffuse* institutional and cultural sites (Bunton *et al* 1995:208).

Essentially linked to lifestyle, 'health' has become represented, in this sense, as another instance of consumer choice, something to be bought into – and indeed purchased – alongside other commodities. Thus, following Shilling (1993), conceivably we might choose to 'finish' our body project by adopting less healthy, as well as more healthy behaviours. However, drawing on Bourdieu's (1977) notion of the cultural 'habitus', Bunton *et al* (1995) criticise the individualised focus of health promotion campaigns. They argue that these fail to take account of the extent to which people's 'choices' about lifestyle are culturally circumscribed. And this is not simply a choice limited by economic resources; more fundamentally, it is *culturally* located. As their secondary analysis of the British General Household Data shows, class and gender are key factors in shaping not only whether people drink or smoke, but also the types of drink they consume and even the cigarettes brands they choose. In Bourdieu's (1984) terms these are markers of 'distinction' that reflect and refract class and gender affiliations.

This means, therefore, that the appeals to identity through 'lifestyle' choice, upon which many contemporary health promotion messages rest, are destined to fail since they are encountered by people whose culturally embodied practices may be very different from the new 'style' being offered to them. This is illustrated well in Pryce's (2005) historical analysis of the representations used in public health campaigns directed towards combating sexually transmitted diseases in the UK (STDs). He argues that the iconography of sexually transmitted diseases moved 'away from control over behaviour reinforced by stigma and social control' in the war and post-war periods and towards an emphasis on education and the individual 'negotiation of risk' by the 1970s and 80s (2005:181). It is this, he suggests, which helps explain the dramatic rise in STDs – chlamydia rates increased 14% between 2001 and 2002, syphilis rose by 67% in males and 33% in females and gonorrhoea was up by 8% in males and 10% in females during the same period (2005:180). In the post-AIDS context of the twenty-first century, Pryce argues that 'mass education campaigns are no longer appropriate, or are insufficiently nuanced with regard to the potential audiences' who are now encountering them (2005:180). With a new kind of bodily habitus that involves a widespread acceptance of erotic pleasure, the more individualised approach towards health education is failing to encourage people to regulate their behaviour since 'the observation of the body for signs and symptoms of diseases is [now] located in discourse where the body is the site of pleasure' rather than, as formerly, one of deviant behaviour where there was felt to be a need for collective moral restraint (2005:179).

It would appear, then, that government health campaigners might need to look more closely at the workings of the market place if they wish to succeed better. A rare study of the pharmaceutical industry by Bode (2002) provides evidence of this. Discussed in detail by Whyte *et al* (2002), Bode's study describes the *production* of lifestyle representations by drug companies in contexts where a recognition of the importance of the 'habitus' is readily apparent. Set in India, Bode's research shows that the 'ancient tradition of hand-made medicine is ... giving away to industrial production in modern laboratories' and that treatments are now being manufactured in the form of 'pills and capsules which can be precisely measured, as is the case for Western pharmaceuticals' (Whyte *et al* 2002:134–5). Thus, for example, an oral rehydration treatment that is derived from a traditional and highly efficacious tonic first made in 1907 has been redescribed by the drug company as a 'herbal polypharmaceutical drink'. Its effectiveness is promoted through appeals to a western 'scientific' discourse – for example, the advertising literature claims that it 'increases the Hb percent of blood', 'increases the Ca^{+2} in serum' and possesses an 'androgenic activity as shown by its role of indicting nitrogen balance' (Whyte *et al* 2002:135). However, at the same time, the promotional literature acknowledges the hidden dangers that people might be perceive to be lurking in modern medicines that are backed by western science. Thus the company also emphasises that these new pharmaceuticals are thoroughly Indian: they are described as natural and fortifying as well as curative, so embodying traditional Indian values. Thus, according to Bode's (2002) analysis, these

> Indigenous medicines satisfy the demands of the new Indian elite who combine modernity with adherence to Indian identity. A brochure shows a traditional sage sitting in a test tube while preparing herbs. The products share in the prestige of high technology but retain their naturalness (Whyte *et al* 2002:136).

What this example demonstrates, therefore, is drug companies' recognition of their customers as embodied individuals.

Other studies of drug promotion and advertising in less economically developed countries, discussed in detail by Whyte *et al* (2002), support the argument that drugs are not only widely promoted – about 25% of their cost is spent on promotional activities – but that claims about efficacy are likely to be tailored to fit in with local populist notions about illness and the body. Thus, although Whyte *et al* argue that it would be too simplistic to claim that drug companies make exaggerated or even fraudulent claims about their products, it is nonetheless the case that they 'manufacture not only medicines but also the meanings of medicines and the need for them', a need which, as they are well aware, presupposes socially located, embodied consumers (2002:144).

From these examples of how health information is promoted and marketed it is clear therefore that understanding the ways in which representations of health and illness become meaningful to us, involves more than simply considering the body we end up with through the health and illness practices we adopt. Importantly, the negotiation of health identities involves taking account of the body that we *start from* – and indeed act with. Bodies are not simply objective, material entities; critically, they are already socially informed and situated in significant ways.

Authoritative Representations

That in the developed world people readily turn to the media to source health-related information, in addition to or even instead of their doctor (but see Henwood *et al* 2003) means that we have to attend closely to the *form* in which advice and information is given, as well as to how it is received. Though representational sources are very varied, as noted above, Seale (2003) argues that the way information is given is never neutral:

> People do not make TV programmes or publish newspapers solely in order to provide the public with accurate health information. The entertainment agenda (and this applies to news and current affairs as much, probably, as it does to 'fictional' products) is more dominant, and scientists, medical care providers and health educators have increasingly come to recognise this (2003:519).

Indeed, as Karpf (1988) has noted, stylistic traditions govern the ways in which health-related news is reported – and these change over time. For example, as heart transplants have become a more routine surgical procedure, so their representation has changed, with the highly charged, emotional opposition between life and death diminishing as a theme. In relation to other illnesses, however, a life:death opposition remains an important meta-narrative in contemporary health representations within the news media. According to Seale (2003), this narrative sits alongside those that dramatise the dangers of modern life, its villains and its freaks, and the nature of victimhood. In addition health-related news often *personalises* health experiences, identifying both professional and lay heroes who step in at times of crisis.

Similar meta-narratives underpin fictional representations of illness. For example, in stories or film dramas, disabled characters are often used as the vehicles for telling a moral story and 'are regularly cast as victims, deviant, bitter, foolish, and in contexts of violence' (Wilde 2005:67, see also Shakespeare 1999). In television dramas and TV documentaries doctors are 'routinely presented as superhuman figures, the secular equivalent of clergy, and medicine is portrayed as the avenue by which miracles may be wrought' (Lupton 2004:57). Even humorous representations of healthcare practitioners in UK films and TV series from the 1950s onwards – *Doctor in the House, Carry On Nurse, Carry on Doctor, Carry on again Doctor* and *Carry on Matron* – derive their humour from the tension between the authority and status usually accorded to real-life practitioners and their foolish, caricatured stage and screen counterparts. And in relation to the status of the Internet as a source of information, comparable narratives can be identified, leading Seale (2005) to question the supposed empowerment that the Internet brings (but see below). In representations of gender and cancer, for example, he argues that there is scarcely any difference between the narratives to be found on the Internet and those in more conventional media. In both forms, women with cancer are represented as skilled emotional labourers, while men's stoic resistance works as a form of denial.

In our quest to explore the relationship between the body, health and identity and, given the consistency of these narrative practices over time and space, we therefore need to understand why they take the forms they do and what happens when, as embodied members of particular societies, we encounter these representations. Are they narratives which provide confirmation of health identities, both our own and those of other people, through the provision of authoritative information of different kinds? If so, to what extent might we, as lay observers, resist or challenge this hegemonic discourse of medical knowledge?

Turning first to the role of television, Karpf (1988) has argued for the media's role in sustaining the continued hegemony of medical authority. She observes that although the form may have changed the message remains: doctor knows best. These findings and the implicit critique embedded in Karpf's analysis has recently been challenged, however, by others such as Davin (2005). In her study of the American TV medical drama *ER,* she argues that audiences are not passive, cultural dopes to be manipulated by the media. In Davin's view, people do not necessarily regard medical dramas as 'truthful' and often question the 'realism' of *ER's* portrayal of everyday life in an American emergency department. Similarly, Macure (1994) observes the lack of realism in the British hospital drama *Casualty.* Being a junior hospital physician himself, he suggests that many doctors would leap at the chance to 'step out of their miserable circumstances into any one of the more comfortable environments that television has created' (*The Independent* 17th April 1994).

The series does nonetheless highlight some of the more troubled aspects of this work setting and Macure notes that the power of the media to persuade has meant that *Casualty* is regarded as a faithful representation of the NHS. As a result, he suggests, the 'series has stirred the ire of Government Ministers and won the approbation of many groups of health workers with its account of today's NHS':

> the patients no longer hang on their doctor's every word, being more likely to respond with abuse; the nurses are no longer decorative handmaidens, instead giving commonsense guidance to callow senior house officers; omnipotent consultants and matron have been supplanted by administrators (*The Independent* 17th April 1994).

More recently, *No Angels,* the British TV series about four nurses, was criticised by the Royal College of Nursing (RCN) for misrepresenting nurses and nursing work and, thereby, damaging the profession. According to the RCN, *No Angels* depicts nurses as 'sex mad ladettes who sleep with doctors and take drugs' (*The Independent* 16th February 2004). Its creator rebuffed the charge, however, arguing that not only was the series made through consultation with nurses but that it 'would be a wonderful recruitment advert for nursing'. With reference to the sanitised, even romantic British TV soaps which portray the drama of hospital life, he said:

> Are they saying *Holby City* or *Casualty* are good for recruitment? Those shows serve a purpose but are not fair representations of what the nurses' lot is like. After watching them, people might think that nursing is a nice, clean job full of handsome doctors. We do a better job of showing the reality of nursing. People will be able to enter the profession with their eyes wide open (*The Independent* 16th February 2004).

That fictional programmes produced ostensibly as entertainment can give rise to this kind of heated debate underscores their perceived power to persuade, particularly those offered through visual media. Indeed much traditional and popular research on media 'effects' would make such a claim. For example, in discussions about the relationship between viewing violence and violent behaviour *'correlations* between viewing and behaviour continue to be seen as evidence of *causality'* despite there being little evidence to support such a view (Buckingham 2000:129, emphasis in the original). However, as Davin argues in relation to the question of the 'effects' that hospital dramas such as *ER* have on the audience, 'while top-down transfer of knowledge, intentional or otherwise, does occur in *ER*, its audiences are by no means the proverbial blank slates waiting to be written on' (2005:28). Instead, as she shows, they are well versed in media use. They compare information contained in dramas with that in documentaries; they cross-check information from TV with that contained in newspaper articles; and they use their own and their friends' real-life experiences as anchor points: 'viewers compare television to reality, programme to programme, reality to television' (2005:36).

Thus, for example, although recognised as primarily entertainment, medical dramas were nonetheless regarded as fairly reliable sources of information about medical matters by Davin's informants: 'just under half ... reported acquiring data on physiology, symptoms, diseases, treatments, the practice of medicine' (Davin 2003:664). By contrast, documentaries which purport to engage critically with the latest development in medical research or technology were, paradoxically, regarded with some suspicion by viewers. Despite their high status and reputation for objectivity, when women were interviewed about their viewing habits, they

> repeatedly wondered about the 'off camera' and 'the editing', sometimes speculating as to what had (perhaps) been removed from the screen, and documentary images were said to be fragmentary and artificial (Davin 2003:668).

Those who acted on information gleaned from documentaries therefore verified the advice given, before acting on it. In dramas, on the other hand, the information provided about social issues and medical knowledge was felt to be of a kind which people might draw on later, should they have to enter an emergency ward themselves. This was despite interviewees' recognition that this information is built around the demands of the script.

One explanation of this paradox might be that documentaries create unsettling, 'dramatic' instabilities in those systems we feel most dependent upon. By contrast, when fictional representations depict interpersonal tensions around, for example, new discoveries in medical science, viewers, well versed in the narratives of soaps, are confident that such tensions will be resolved, somehow, in the course of the programme. And indeed, in presenting the ambition or the frailty of medical personnel on screen, their 'real life' status is underscored. Thus, the medical soap derives its appeal from a dramatic tension with customary expectations of such professionals and their conduct. The attraction of the documentary is less clear-cut, since it risks disrupting rather than confirming our certainties.

As these examples show, then, the ways in which representations are not only formed but also encountered by people in their everyday lives, and the experiences which they bring to them are critical to any analysis of the 'effects' or 'impact' of the media (Buckingham 2000). All the more reason, then, that in exploring representations as a site at which health identities are produced, that we work with the idea that it is embodied – rather than disembodied – individuals who encounter them.

Gabe and Bury's (1996) discussion of the shifts in media representation of tranquillisers over a period of 30 years exemplifies the importance of such an approach. Whereas in the 1960s the benzodiazepine family was welcomed as a new wonder-drug, media reporting from the mid-1970s onwards became highly critical, stressing the risks of tranquilliser addiction over the medical benefits to be gained. Through focusing on the personal stories of individual users, Gabe and Bury argue that the media 'helped provide a public and especially moral framework within which tranquilliser use could be interpreted and understood' (1996:79). However, while the media drew great attention to the risks associated with tranquilliser use, the ways in which such messages were received varied. As Gabe and Bury suggest, therefore, 'risk perception needs to be seen as an active process, shaped by personal beliefs, social circumstances and experience' (1996:79). In this case, risk was often managed, rather than avoided, even though media representations clearly played a part in people's ambivalence about the use of tranquillisers. They weighed 'the risks of use against the need for drug therapy to help them with their personal problems, on the basis of available knowledge and existing resources' (1996:91). Within the moralistic climate that developed around the addictive properties of tranquillisers, a range of responses could be seen: for some people, the drugs constituted a life-line while for others they were a standby.

Thus, as this example demonstrates, the material condition of the body, along with its habitual social and cultural orientations together constitute the embodied individual and are integral to the process of identification through which health identities are taken on, as described in Chapters 1 and 3. In this sense, the 'authority' of health and illness discourses is by no means guaranteed; representations are always open to re-representation by those who encounter them. It is therefore to a closer examination of the role that representations play in the relationship between the body, health and identity that we now, therefore, turn.

Self Presentation and Re-presentation

The importance of giving verbal account of embodied experiences was central to seventeenth and eighteenth century medicine. Physicians listened to the patient's story and developed treatment regimes in accordance with it (Lawrence 1994; Jewson 1976, cited in Bury 2001:265–6). However, as Bury notes, with the arrival of bio-medicine, 'the study and treatment of disease became separated from the individual and located within body systems only understood by experts' (2001:266). No longer was the patient's own account so necessary for diagnosis and treatment. However, more recently, both the decline in infectious diseases and the rise in chronic illness have meant that 'assessment of the quality of life, the impact of illness on carers and a renegotiation of the role of professional care all appear on the professional agenda', creating a new 'space for lay narratives to flourish' (2001:267). And lay narratives are not only important in underscoring the problems involved in defining illness (see Chapter 4), and in strategically enabling people to come to terms with illness (see Chapter 8); they are also critical to any understanding of the embodied experience of illness. That is to say, lay narratives enable people to represent their own somatic experiences to others.

In asking about the role of these lay accounts in the forging of health identities, Bury identifies three kinds of narratives: contingent, moral and core. According to Bury, contingent narratives present beliefs about the causes of illness and describe the unfolding of events in becoming sick. They testify to the practicalities of the day-to-day management of a disease or chronic illness, with the experience of illness being normalised in two ways: either emphasis is placed on 'pre-illness life-style and identity', or the contingencies of illness are described as integrated into a new way of living as a 'culturally competent person' (2001:273–4).

This evaluative dimension is most prominent in moral narratives 'as sufferers seek to account for and perhaps justify themselves in the altered relations of body, self and society brought about by illness' (Bury 2001:274). Commonly, this involves not only both presenting the self as morally virtuous and free from blame in relation to the onset of illness, but also seeing 'illness as a form of disruption that can be turned into self discovery and renewal' (2001:276).

For Bury, however, illness narratives do not simply operate in this way to represent the different changes to self-identity that the experience of illness can bring. Rather, people draw on a range of core narratives that enable them to locate their own personal story within a particular cultural genre – comic; ironic; epic; heroic; tragic; romantic and so on. No less in accounts told to doctors and researchers, than in popular women's magazines, the stories people tell of their illness experiences enable them to take up particular self-identities – as victim, as hero or as someone with a sense of humour who can overcome the debilitations that illness brings.

Such lay narratives therefore offer different representations of the experience of illness, so constituting a form of personal fieldwork in the illness arena that 'produces a kind of authority that is anchored to a large extent in subjective, sensuous experience' (Clifford and Marcus 1986:32) and in many societies, as we have already seen, such accounts form an integral part of traditional curative systems (see Chapter 4). For bio-medicine, however, now that the laboratory holds greater sway than the bedside as the site of diagnosis (Seale *et al* 2001:51), lay accounts that are grounded in personal experience may be in tension with kind of medical knowledge that is represented by the 'science' of bio-medicine.

A first example of the tension between the knowledge or truth claims of bio-medicine and the narratives of embodied, potentially suffering individuals can be found in Grue and Laerum's (2002) discussion of disabled Norwegian women's experience of motherhood. They argue that disabled women are trapped in a medicalised discourse of disability that means they are 'looked upon by professionals and lay people as receivers [of care] ... and not as carers' (2002:682). In that disabled women are not expected to have children, because they are themselves thought of as 'dependent' and as therefore not capable of rearing dependent children, taking on the identity of mother represents a particularly difficult challenge. Thus, for example, while being 'mother's little helper' is often regarded as being important for children's social and personal development in western societies, if – as was often the case – children *had* to help their disabled mother, this supposedly valued aspect of the socialisation process became redescribed as potentially problematic. Being disabled meant, therefore, that these women had to work extra hard to present themselves as 'normal', by putting on ideal performances of good mothering. As one woman commented:

> There are very few children who are as nicely dressed and well-kept as my children. I was the first parent to put name tags in my children's clothes when they started at nursery. Nobody should have a reason to criticise me (2002:677).

As Grue and Laerum's (2002) research shows, representations – whether of the self, by the self, or for the self by others – are therefore critical to the discourses through which processes of identification take place. As they argue, the women's 'main problems were other people's disbelief (disablism) and the social and material "framing" of motherhood in today's Norwegian society' (2002:682).

First explored in Goffman's (1968) classic study of stigma and the management of a spoiled identity, there is now wealth of literature exploring disability, identity and personal experience (for various overviews see, Oliver 1990; Corker and French 1999; Shakespeare 1997). Often with a focus on the constraints that debilitating illness and disability bring, this literature provides authoritative accounts of the disempowerment that these different experiences of embodiment entail.

However, the truth claims of sick or disabled people assume authoritative status not simply on the basis of 'subjective, sensuous experience' (Clifford and Marcus 1986:32). It also arises out of the embodied experiences of subjugation which, as disabled people, they are struggling to overcome. As V.W. Turner (1969:95) argued, individuals who fail to belong, or are either permanently or temporarily excluded from society's structures, attract to themselves 'the powers of the weak'. Among the Ndembu and Lamba of Zambia, for example, there were traditional cult associations, with therapeutic powers, whose members 'gained entry through common misfortune and debilitating circumstances' (1969:96).

Thus, for example, those doubly stigmatised by their sexuality and their illness – gay men dying of HIV/AIDS – have provided autobiographical accounts which contribute to what Small describes as 'changing patterns of social expressiveness and … a breakdown in monolithic narrative constructions of death and loss' (1998:216). He goes on to say that '[a]utobiographies present us with the small narratives that make up the overall of understanding of living and dying with AIDS' (1998:216). Made public through these accounts, particular experiences of illness and dying become core identifiers which unite people living with this condition and so transcend the individualisation otherwise introduced through both medicalisation and stigmatisation.

In light of examples such as this, it should come as no surprise that when we examine the Internet as a new site of and for representational practices, we discover that an alternative and more empowering avenue of identification has opened up for those who – through ill-health – are structurally weak. Although Leve (2005) humorously describes the dangers of self-*mis*diagnosis via the Internet, with its irresistible immediacy for individuals who are faced with extended anxiety-laden periods of waiting for the outcomes of conventional medical tests (*The Guardian* 26th July 2005), Thomas-Maclean (2004) notes its benefits. With the arrival of the Internet, there has been an increased public interest in narratives of illness, making a wealth of information available. Some illnesses have cornered the story-telling market:

> a recent search of a major internet bookseller returned 1054 texts related to breast cancer, including numerous autobiographies, while comparative searchers of 'prostate cancer' and 'colorectal cancer' returned only 300 and 71 hits, respectively (Thomas-Maclean 2004:164–7).

What, then, does this explosion of accessible health narratives tell us about processes of identification? While some would argue that, despite the detailed, sometimes graphic focus on quite specific bodily pathologies, the Internet enables people to become disembodied and thereby to wrest free from the body's identificatory capacity, others suggest that this disembodied empowerment becomes an avenue through which, paradoxically, the identificatory power of the body can be explored, examined, investigated and made sense of. In a similar vein, Small describes the highly 'embodied' nature of what is written in the pages of AIDS autobiographies, arguing that '[t]he body is not sequestrated in this discourse on dying. There appear to be no taboos. Further, the space between medical discourse and personal experience has been closed by assertive, metropolitan, patients who were not always patient' (1998:217).

Gillet (2003), for example, examined the personal Internet sites constructed by people with HIV/AIDS and discovered that these sites provided a range of opportunities for people to identify themselves in different ways. Thus, it was used as a 'strategy for self representation' through: the posting of autobiographical accounts of living with HIV; through the demonstration of expertise in its management; through various forms of self promotion that advocated a positive approach to having AIDS; and, interestingly, through the signalling of dissent (2003:612). In Gillet's view the Internet offers an 'open and democratic venue for people with HIV/AIDS who are seeking self representation and social change' in a context where, as embodied persons in real-life, they may have fewer opportunities for participation (2003:620; see also Bury 2001). As such, therefore, the Internet may enable people with HIV/AIDS to escape from the representations that other people may have of their bodily condition through being momentarily disembodied.

Hardey (2005) takes this idea further, describing how an individual's 'home page' provides a powerful identifier, replete with symbolic material which can embody their key values and interests. Using the case study of David, a man in his 40s whose parents had moved from Jamaica to the UK, Hardey presents material from David's website. This sets his long-term experience of depression within a life course context. Letters and reports on his 'case' by healthcare professionals and social workers are posted on the site. David says, 'White doctors don't understand black experience. Some of them thought "Give the man the drugs, he won't bother me and I've done what's expected". No therapy. No reality. No hope' (Hardey 2005:141). David uses his experience to develop a sustained challenge to bio-medical accounts of his condition and how best it might be treated, drawing on religion and his black identity as more fruitful resources in dealing with his health problem. As Hardey says, '[t]he writing and re-writing of his home page, therefore, provides a place where the author makes sense of life events and weaves together emotional and material transitions' (2005:142).

Conclusion

Throughout this chapter we have explored the importance of embodiment for understanding the ways in which representational practices enable links to be made between the body, health and identity. Examining a variety of representational forms, in different contexts, the chapter has highlighted the increasing global power that the bio-medical discourse has in terms of understandings of health and illness. Reaching out into the farthest corners of different communities worldwide, bio-medicine would appear to have a strong grip over health identities, as more and more aspects of life are being brought within its gaze. However, at the same time, this chapter has shown that challenges are increasingly being made to this hegemony of bio-medicine within our thinking about health and illness, challenges based on a reappraisal of the importance of embodiment and experience to the meanings that health and illness have in terms of ourselves and our identities. How this unfolds in the drama that is illness is the subject of the next chapter.

6

The Ritual Drama of Illness

If the previous chapter explored the ways in which individuals engaged with, resisted or supplanted the representations of health and illness they encounter, these were in no sense simply cognitive 'information-gathering' or classifying exercises. As we argued, embodiment constitutes the grounds and the conditions from which representations are encountered or produced and through which health identifications of different kinds take place. Through these active, perceptual processes, states of 'health' and 'illness', grounded in the body, are brought into being, objectified and subjected to scrutiny, treatment and management or disregard – whether by the person themself or other groups and individuals. Thus, as noted in Chapter 4, becoming sick is 'a total social process' (Frankenberg 1980:199). From the ways in which we get to know we are ill, to the ways in which others respond to our illness, to the encounters that we have with medical professionals of all kinds and the structural inequalities that contribute to our experience of sickness, the power of the social is evident. Our identities as 'well' or 'ill', and our experiences of these states of being, are shaped, in large part, by the varieties of environments within which we find ourselves, and the encounters and interactions that we have there.

However, despite the social constructionist bias of this stance, as we have also been keen to point out throughout this volume, the fact and experience of our embodiment has to be recognised, since it this which provides the existential grounding of our sociality. Our status as 'well' or 'ill' therefore has to be understood within the context of the materiality of the body, a body that changes over time, whether through the processes of ageing or of becoming sick.

In setting out to capture these embodied experiences of change over time, this chapter draws, therefore, on the concept of the ritual drama of illness as one way of documenting how it is that we come to know that we are sick

(Frankenberg 1980). It is an approach that incorporates aspects of Goffman's (1969) dramaturgical perspective on the presentation of self in everyday life, alongside Van Gennep's ([1909] 1960) and Talcott Parsons' (1951) conceptualisations of roles and rites of transition in order to investigate the totality of the embodied social processes through which illness comes to be known and health identities are taken on.

In adopting this perspective, the chapter therefore briefly revisits the book's earlier discussion of structure and agency for, as we shall see, these somewhat troubled concepts remain important in explaining the health identities that become available during illness episodes. At this time, as noted earlier, identities may have to be renegotiated, temporarily or more permanently. In this respect, Jenkins' observation that 'the materiality of identification … and its stratified deprivation or affluence' means that 'in any given context, some identities systematically enhance or diminish an individual's opportunities' proves useful (2004:50). The dramatic unfolding of illness, as we shall see, has possibilities for both, despite its more common representation as simply suffering.

Drawing on sociological and anthropological accounts of illness, and placing these alongside autobiographical material, this chapter therefore documents the ritual drama of illness as the *embodied process* through which we come to know that we are ill and reveals as Csordas argues, that 'ritual healing is a window onto larger cultural processes' (2002:141).

Illness as a Rite of Passage

In seeking to explain how society's members were able to make transitions between different identities, Van Gennep ([1909] 1960) developed a schema which provided a theoretical route through the complexity of earlier ethnographers' data on rites of passage (see Hockey 2002) and the robustness of his thinking about the significance of social transition is evident in a range of subsequent anthropological and sociological work which reflect similar ideas.

In Talcott Parsons' (1951) model of the sick role, for example, there is a parallel theoretical explanation of how individuals make transitions – here from one health-based identity to another. Parsons' (1951) focus, as noted in Chapter 2, was on the beliefs and practices that act to exclude those legitimately defined as 'sick' from society's dominant structures. The time-bounded move into and out of the sick role, he argued, acts to protect the smooth functioning of the wider society from its temporarily incompetent members who, in turn, are required to profit from a legitimate break from their duties and make as speedy a recovery as possible. Parsons' work therefore sets out some pointers with respect to the structural context within which changing health and illness identities are to be located.

In the work that built on Van Gennep's schema, on the other hand, though illness and healing rituals are also explored, these are not treated simply as structured technical processes. Rather, being regarded as a set of *ritual* practices, they are seen as meaningful acts which carry implications well beyond the immediacy of a condition such as infertility (Turner 1969), depression (Kleinman 1980) or epilepsy (Fadiman 1997). This point is made clear by Helman (1990) in his exploration of the role of ritual practices, cross culturally, within the management of illness. He describes them as repetitive yet without overt technical effect – and, by way of example, he differentiates between the routinised health practice of brushing teeth at night and a *ritual* practice such as always using a pink brush and uttering the same words prior to the act. While the former has specific functional goals, the latter orients the person in their bathroom towards symbolic ends, its meaning referring to questions or issues which transcend the actual teeth. Helman (1990) is, however, less interested in private rituals of this kind and focuses mainly on public rituals, particularly those which contain a blend of the technical and the symbolic. For example, as Helman describes, the physician's authority and expertise is symbolised in the white coat which serves the parallel technical purpose of protecting his or her everyday clothes from, for example, patients' body fluids.

However, despite the apparent usefulness of these kinds of approaches, as discussed in detail elsewhere (Hockey and James 2003), if we look closely at the rite of passage schema we find that it has little direct bearing upon the experience of transition or, for our purposes here, the ritual drama of illness as an *embodied* experience. While it *is* concerned explicitly with change, and recognises that the individuals who make up society *are* in a constant state of flux – being born and dying – the schema itself is focused primarily on how those individuals, changed as they are, can be unproblematically incorporated back into society, whether as one of its new members or as an ancestor. Indeed the well-being of society, rather than simply the sick person, lies at the core of much ritual practice according to this perspective. The schema is not, therefore, designed to capture experiences of transition *per se*. Instead, using the metaphor of a house with different rooms, Van Gennep is keen to show that individuals move from one 'room'– status or identity – to another. At the point of transition, people – and indeed society itself – are vulnerable; people are caught between two identities, betwixt and between the fixed points of social structure.

According to Van Gennep ([1909] 1960), what rituals therefore do – whether they are puberty rituals or those of healing – is not only deal with the uncertainty of transition; they also work to *produce* that change as normative, by engendering in those undergoing transition a sense of becoming someone different afterwards. Rites of passage, in this sense, are both educative and creative devices for managing the uncertainties about identity that change can cause. Like Parsons, however, Van Gennep's ([1909] 1960) primary concern was not the changed individual, but the effect such changes can have on society as a whole – and the need to explain how social order is maintained despite such changes.

The notion that an individual's illness can have wider social implications is an interesting one and is exemplified in classic anthropological accounts of rituals of healing, such as Beattie's (1960) study of the work of Bunyoro diviners in western Uganda. He shows that illness is the most common reason for seeking the services of a diviner and that sorcery, ghosts and spirits are often seen as the cause of sickness (see Chapter 4). In other words, social tensions, manifested in cults of sorcery or the actions of malicious spirits, are understood to be the underlying, but pressing, source of ill health. Turner (1964, cited in Helman 1990:210), similarly shows that rituals of healing among the Ndembu of Zambia are focused on the social causes of illness. These rituals are public and ensure that parties divided by social tensions articulate their grudges against one another and so, gradually, resolve their differences: 'sealing up the breaches in social relationships simultaneously with ridding the patient ... of his pathological symptoms' (1964, cited in Helman 1990:210). Rites of healing of this kind are, therefore, understood to be of communal, rather than individual, benefit.

However, though still concerned with the ways in which rituals work to 'heal' social rifts, the later elaborations of Van Gennep's schema do begin, nonetheless, to shift its focus somewhat, giving far greater theoretical attention than Van Gennep himself did to the changes that might be occurring for those undergoing a rite of passage. Turner (1969), for example, in his study of Ndembu society shows that, during the middle or liminal phase of a rite of passage, individuals are subjected to a process of symbolic and physical separation from the everyday social world through the removal of markers of their previous identities. Carried out by ritual specialists, tribal elders and healers, the initiation and puberty rites which V.W. Turner (1969) discusses involve physical 'stripping' such as the loss of previous forms of dress or, in more extreme cases, bodily refashioning – the cutting away of the foreskin, for example. Initiates will live together in isolated places of seclusion for shorter or longer periods of liminal time in places somehow set apart from mainstream society where they come together to form a kind of community, bound by the shared experience of communitas, rather than the constraints of social structure. During this time of transition individuals may also have to undergo tests of physical endurance that cause them to be humiliated or to experience bodily pain, as Richards (1956) describes in her classic account of Bemba girls' initiation rites.

In this formulation of rites of passage we can find, then, some important initial insights into illness as a form of ritual drama through its focus on the

social and structural conditions through which changes in identity are managed
– and, importantly, in the view of V.W. Turner (1969), *produced*. Froggatt (1997),
for example, used the schema of rites of passage to help explain the ways in
which hospices, in western industrial societies, enable people to experience a
'good' death and allow the social disruption caused by death to be managed.
Within a society where bio-medical definitions of the *moment* of death serve to
create an oppositional relationship between 'life' and 'death', the *process* of
'dying' is either denied (Glaser and Strauss 1968), or marginalised as the after-
math of social death (Mulkay 1993). Within this context, the Hospice Movement
has attempted to create a liminal period betwixt and between the categories 'life'
and 'death' so that, although within a hospice the imminence of death is recognised, either explicitly or implicitly, the social, emotional, physiological and
spiritual well-being of the individual remains a matter of urgency, just as it was
during their earlier life. As Froggatt (1997) identifies, concepts such as 'family'
and 'holism', which are central to the philosophy of the hospice movement, act
to create an atmosphere of communitas, akin to that of the liminal period of rite
of passage. Thus, although her study provides a relatively 'top-down' account
of the structural role of the hospice in transforming personal experiences and
making them manageable, it does reflect the significance of the ways in which
anthropologists such as V.W. Turner (1969) developed Van Gennep's ([1909]
1960) concept of liminality.

   Another study which, similarly, draws upon a rites of passage schema to
make sense of the organisation and operation of institutionalised health care
as a 'stage' within which the ritual drama of illness is enacted is Bellerby's
(1993) work on closed head injury survivors. What he suggests is that the accident which caused the injury, and the emergency surgery which follows it,
constitute a rite of separation. Of surgeons, for example, he says '[o]f all
medical specialisms, surgery is most inclined to view the presenting problem
as exclusively biomedical … where little if anything is learned of the patient as
a person and his or her experience of the condition before intervention'
(1993:172). Becoming victim to a grievous accident and undergoing surgery
therefore effectively sever an individual's ties with their previous identity.
Where they survive surgery, they are then likely to enter a liminal phase in
their illness experience, where they become 'a "novice" under the tuition of
nurses, occupational therapists, physiotherapists and others …' (Bellerby
1993:172). During this phase they are taught to recover memory, mobility,
speech and cognitive functioning. Like the initiands whose names and individual identities are subsumed within a categorical identity such as 'novice',
the closed head injury survivor *becomes* their 'illness' at this point. That is to
say, their prospects for attaining a future independent identity become the
status upon which who they are, as liminal beings, is predicated. In this case,
however, both Van Gennep's ([1909] 1960) third stage of incorporation and

Talcott Parsons' (1951) notion of a return to functional membership of the wider society, often fail to be realised. Indeed the closed head injury survivor may go on to assume a liminoid, rather than liminal identity, a concept which Turner (1974) developed as a way of classifying those who retain a permanent social position as an outsider – the shaman, the tramp, the artist. As Bellerby says, rather than returned to full health, 'the victims may be discharged to prolonged periods of chronic illness and impairment' (1993:174).

Such accounts effectively detail the ways in which changes in health status are managed within society, but provide scant explanation, however, of how that transition comes into being for the embodied individuals whose condition has been objectified as indeterminate. It tells us little about what such identity transitions might mean to the individuals who are undergoing them and how they manage that change. It is to a consideration of the usefulness of the rite of passage for exploring these kinds of issues that we now turn.

Illness as a Drama

As we have argued, anthropological studies such as those described above deepen the heuristic value of Van Gennep's ([1909] 1960) schema. What V.W. Turner's (1969) work, in particular, details is the healing efficacy of the transitional or liminal phase of a rite of passage, when individuals are betwixt and between, socially no longer who they were or who they will become. It is during this process that identity temporarily ceases to be particular to the individual. Typically, everyone going through the rite of passage shares the same identity of ritual liminar, that is, of someone defined as being in transition. As Turner (1969) noted, equality, rather than difference is therefore a key feature of the liminal period. Only following reincorporation into society do individuals once again assume the markers of social differentiation. Thus, although the liminal period is transformative for individuals in terms of their movement from one social status to another, even in Turner's account the sense of communitas experienced by ritual liminars during transition – the highs and lows produced by extreme bodily experiences – are depicted as essentially normative, for it is the restoration of social order itself that rites of passage are primarily thought to be about.

It is this point precisely which we find elaborated in Talcott Parsons' (1951) model of the sick role. This classic account of the medical encounter explores the ways in which illness is socially legitimated and the return to health managed both by and for the patient. In this model, the authority vested in the doctor presupposes a compliant patient and, through legitimating the patient's experience via the sick role, the doctor enables this potentially disruptive event to be contained and managed within what could be called an illness drama. However, as noted in Chapter 2, now that the pattern of illness has changed and chronic illness is more common, especially in industrialised societies, this model proves less useful for it presupposes cure and the restoration of people to an earlier state of health. This is problematic in two ways.

First it ignores the experiential learning that is part of any individual's sickness episode. This irrevocably changes an individual's embodied experience of themselves; in this sense, although bodies may recover a state of health, people's experience of their own embodiment can never be the same again. Not only do people have new knowledge about the ways in which their bodies work and feel, but this knowledge provides the basis from which future bodily symptoms of illness are understood and acted upon. As Goffman's (1968, 1969) work has shown, this can mean learning new and inventive ways, through the unfolding drama of everyday encounters, to present oneself to others. As embodied beings, we therefore remember not simply cognitively but with and through our bodies.

With respect to our senses, for example, Stewart (1999) reminds us that these are not simply organs which register the world around us, but sources of material memories: the smell of a particular cleaning fluid which evokes lying in a hospital bed whilst a ward cleaner worked around us; the sound of metal curtain hooks drawn hastily along steel runners which returns us to a death in an adjacent hospital bed; the feeling of thick starched sheets confining our body which directs us back to that same bed. As Stewart argues, '[w]e may apprehend the world by means of our senses, but the senses themselves are shaped and modified by experience and the body bears a somatic memory of its encounters with what is outside of it' (1999:19). When we take up our role within the ritual drama of illness, therefore, we enact it as embodied beings who sense the sights, sounds and smells of a medical setting in ways which transcend the here-and-now of any particular medical moment.

Second, Parsons' (1951) explication of the sick role cannot help us understand the experience of living with a chronic illness, where pain levels vary, skin lesions come and go, and aching shifts from joint to joint – and the body itself is in a continuous state of flux. Here *maintenance* of a fluctuating *status quo*, rather than restoration to some former state of well-being, becomes the only option when faced with the constant threat of bodily deterioration (Radley 1994:136). This kind of permanent 'sick role', therefore, raises rather different kinds of issues for the doctor-patient relationship by calling into question both power and authority. That the doctor can no longer cure, but simply manage an illness changes the nature of the professional authority they might assert over patients, and patients themselves often learn, through the unfolding drama of their illness, to become the experts in relation to their particular health condition.

For example, as Sharma's (1996) intensive study among UK users of complementary medicine shows, while bio-medicine might be first in patients' 'hierarchy of resort' (1996:235), its failure to remedy their condition satisfactorily, particularly when that condition is chronic, can lead to the use of alternatives. Indeed, what constitutes a satisfactory remedy is itself contestable. As Sharma (1996) notes, for example, while an external evaluation of a treatment's clinical effectiveness might judge a prescription as appropriate, the patient's *embodied* perception of its impact, and therefore its usefulness, may derive from its unwelcome side-effects. What Sharma emphasises, therefore, is that the use of complementary medicine can enhance a patient's autonomy and self confidence: after using it for rhinitis one woman in her study said that 'I make up my own mind about these things now. Now I feel I am in control of my life' (cited in Sharma 1996:238). Kelleher (1994) makes a similar point with respect to self-help groups, formed by or for people with chronic illnesses, again stressing the emancipatory outcome of responding to illness in a way which contrasts with bio-medicine's technical-instrumental approach to human suffering. Thus, although self-help groups in some senses complement bio-medical practice, by giving space to the experiential and emotional impacts of illness, Kelleher also views them as part of a new social movement which challenges bio-medicine *directly* by 'retain(ing) the possibility for seeing things differently, creating the opportunity for medicine to be challenged and interrogated' (1994:116). Herein lies the importance of grasping the embodied process of illness as an unfolding and processual transition between different kinds – and ways – of identification.

Embodiment within the Ritual Drama of Illness

Once health and illness are reformulated as embodied and ongoing experiences of change that impact upon our identities, as we have been doing throughout this volume, we then need to draw on rather particular kinds of theoretical resources. For example, if we wish to use a cross-culturally comparative approach, Helman's distinction between the public and private ritual is somewhat problematic, as is his notion that 'in Western society, diagnosis and treatment also take place in "ritual time" and "ritual space" – that is, at certain times, and in certain settings, carefully marked off from the rest of everyday life (such as a hospital clinic, or a doctor's office)' (1990:206). As we have already seen, (Chapters 4 and 5), the ongoing and everyday interplay between the body, health and identity can take place across a range of different social environments and can involve our friends and family, as much as the doctor, in generating our 'diagnosis'.

Thus, rather than relying on traditional anthropological conceptions of ritual's relationship with the sacred or set apart, as evidenced in the work of Van Gennep ([1909] 1960), here we turn to the concept of *ritualisation*, as used by Seremetakis (1991). This concept, in providing a critique of bounded models of ritual practice, draws attention to rituals which are situated 'within the flux and contingency of everyday events' (1991:47). Using the example of death, Seremetakis details the concept of ritualisation as follows:

> A treatment of mourning rituals which acknowledges the problematic nature of discrete beginnings and endings also assumes that there is never a full restoration of social stability; that death, its representation, its discourses, and its perfomative elaboration can haunt society and become an essential collective metaphor of social experience beyond the margins of ceremonial performance (1991:48).

Given our concern with the indeterminacy of embodied experience which at particular times and places becomes a focus for medical science or other healing authorities, but inevitably overspills the boundaries of such encounters, this perspective is promising. Indeed Seremetakis' (1991) depiction of death ritual's capacity to become a haunting collective metaphor for marginalised social experience is suggestive in light of our concern with the pervasiveness of the proto-patient who, everywhere and at all times, concerns themselves with their body's potential for sickness (see De Swaan 1990).

In the rest of this chapter, therefore, we are concerned to present examples of ritual dramas of illness which have both more, but also less, by way of 'discrete beginnings and endings' (Seremetakis 1991:48), the latter conception of ritual providing a valuable theoretical approach to exploring the experience of chronic illnesses in particular. And, in addition to problematising the notion of ritual as by definition bounded and set apart, we make metaphoric use of the concept of *drama* in order to demonstrate how ritual practices and roles come together in such a way as to enable the embodied perceptual processes which 'terminate' in 'health' or 'illness' to be brought into being. While such a dramaturgical approach echoes the ways Goffman (1969) was concerned to understand how individuals negotiate their everyday performances to present a 'self' to the world, we need to acknowledge, however, that there can be no drama without a plot. So returning to Chapter 5's discussion of illness narratives, here we show how their status as a purely personal account is somewhat misleading. Within the ritual drama of illness, issues of power and hierarchy, structure and agency emerge as key to the production of definitive perceptions.

Thus, Prout and Christensen (1996) draw on the idea of the 'cultural performance' of sickness (see Chapter 4) to show that knowledge about health and illness, and about associated patterns of authority, is acquired by children, gradually, in the course of their everyday relationships with adults. Through these social relationships and interactions, children get to know, for example, 'which different worrisome biological and behavioral signs and changes get a socially recognisable meaning which constitutes them as "symptoms"' and which do not (1996:35). In a later study, Christensen (1997) then goes on to show, for example, how children learn that taking someone's temperature indicates the possibility of a person moving from a state of wellness to that of illness. And, in addition, children learn to evaluate the seriousness of their own illness through noting the symbolic differences between illnesses that are treated by doctors, and those that are subjected to remedies provided by their mothers. For some children, as Wilkinson (1988:91) has described, such knowledge, and the power that it unleashes, becomes invaluable. It enables them to feign – or represent – illness in the most convincing way (see also Chapter 5).

As this example of children's socialisation into illness shows, therefore, within the ritual drama of illness, plots may involve negotiation between the members of social categories which stand in some kind of hierarchical power relationship to one another – in this case children and parents. But it is at the site of the body that the drama's tension can build, eventually finding a resolution of some kind, whether permanent or temporary, and one which may either reinforce, or disrupt, those relations of power. Thus, Christensen's (1997) study shows that, as well as the doctor, it is individuals identified as members of the more powerful social category of 'parent' who can provide accreditation for the illness status of children's bodily changes. However, that accreditation can subsequently become a resource which children themselves then put into play *vis-à-vis* members of another powerful social category, 'teachers'. A 'healthy' child wishing to stay at home, rather than go to school, is not empowered to make this choice themself. Yet their acquired ability to *feign* illness can represent a position of strength for children who aim to avoid school. They silently display what they have learned to objectify as symptoms – immobility, a slumped posture, downcast eyes and a pained expression (see also Wilkinson 1988).

In addition to identifying the ways in which power, and the structural institutions of medicine, have a part to play in the everyday ritual drama of illness, what these examples also highlight are the ways in which embodied actions themselves serve to engender perceptual processes – the child displays the cut to the adult's gaze and so discovers how to 'objectify' or categorise this break in their skin according to the way the adult perceives it (Christensen 1993; see also Chapter 7). This process can also be seen in the individual's culturally-informed engagement with their own body, that allows or forbids them to expose certain of its parts to a partner, a parent or a doctor. For example, a 25 year-old male participant in a study of heterosexuality within extended families in East Yorkshire (see Robinson *et al* 2004), described a family culture of openness about the emotional, embodied nature of sexual practice. When he discovered a growth on his foreskin he therefore 'presented' this change to his mother:

> I once got like a lump on the side of my foreskin which was like really raw, red and sore and I talked to mum about it … I could probably discuss anything with my mum, you know, if I got, I've never had a sexually transmitted disease as far as I'm aware … if I got something like that … I wouldn't have any shame in asking my mum.

The capacity of the parent, as an authority figure, to legitimate the occurrence of 'sickness' in their children is also reflected in the 'dramatic' encounter that takes place between the embodied patient and the high status consultant on the hospital ward round. As Davies (1995) has shown, here the role of the nurse is to 'position' or 'stage' that patient and their symptoms in such a way as to attract a diagnosis, in a Goffman-like presentation of the 'self' of the patient.

As can be seen from these examples, therefore, it is in fact the body's conditions of indeterminacy (see Chapter 3) that opens it up to this range of possible interpretations. Selective embodied actions can work to enable particular perceptions: the woman learns (how) to examine her breasts and find lumps which require investigation; the man, similarly, learns (how) to examine his testicles. It is this embodied perceptual process, therefore, that lies at the heart of the drama of illness that unfolds in every-day life.

However, its denouement is far from predictable. As Goudsmit (1994) notes, for example, when women choose to present aspects of their bodies to the gaze of the doctor, the resulting diagnosis may focus more on their psychological, than their physical, well-being. She refers to an example where three women 'presented' at casualty with breathlessness and panic symptoms. They were diagnosed as suffering from hysterical hyperventilation and received prescriptions for diazepam. Three days later they had all been re-admitted, the tranquilliser having done little to alleviate the diabetes which they were eventually discovered to be suffering from. The gender of the embodied individual can therefore influence the role which they come to play within the drama of illness. Here stereotypes and assumptions about women's vulnerability to mental instability (see Showalter 1987 and Chapter 2) lead to the body itself being perceived through the lens of these wider cultural beliefs.

Health Transitions and Transformations

Medical sociology has, of course, a long tradition of being concerned with 'lay experience' and 'folk models' (see Chapters 4 and 5), but the inclusion of these alternative perspectives does not, in itself, explain *how* changes in health identities come into being. Rather, they are in danger of providing simply an 'add-patient-and-stir' account – and this is precisely the point of our emphasis on embodiment. If we are to understand how, for example, a healed body or the return of peace of mind is achieved, we need to engage with the embodied grounding of particular cultural performances, exploring the perceptual processes which, through the ritual drama of illness, produce healing and indeed healed cultural objects.

To understand this aspect of the ritual drama of illness we need, therefore, to focus more directly on the experience of the *process* of status change, from well to ill or vice versa and, once again, we can draw upon the concept of rites of passage. Thus, despite the early theorists' foregrounding of structural change, which we have critiqued above, the insights into the relationship between transition and identity that they provided have, in many ways, proved foundational for understanding about what happens to identity during and after episodes of illness.

Radley (1996), for example, draws explicitly on the theoretical model of rites of passage when he asks how people make sense of the changes that surgery can bring to their everyday lives. What he shows, in his study of men undergoing coronary bypass surgery, is that they are able to transform a life experienced as sickness into one of health, with surgery providing the rite of passage. However, he argues that the transition that patients undergo during the 'experience' of surgery – the transition from ill health to better health through the removal of the threat of sudden death – is, paradoxically, not an experience of which they are at all aware. Of necessity, the operation itself takes place in a 'non-time' in terms of their own embodied experience, anaesthetics doing their job of temporarily eradicating the perceptual process. Patients have, therefore, to infer what that 'experience' was like from what they have been told and 'subsequently, from their own bodily feelings' (1996:118). And yet, this non-time – the time which the operation required which they do not remember as an embodied experience – is always understood, *and experienced*, by patients as a critical moment in their lives. It is a veritable turning point in terms of their health status. How then do they reach such a conclusion?

Drawing on Turner's (1974) elaboration of the liminal phase of a rite of passage, Radley finds useful parallels with the ways in which ritual initiands place themselves in the hands of the ritual specialists during a rite of passage. For example, for the heart patient:

the giving-over of responsibility for the patient's life to another person (someone who will open one's chest, take and modify one's heart) rendered the 'non-time' of the operation into something special. In consequence this had the effect of permeating all of the patients' actions that led up to this episode (1996:127).

Following the operation, like ritual liminars living in seclusion, the patients experience a sense of camaraderie through their interactions with one another:

> they had gone through something special together. Though they were alone in the hours after their operation, in the ward and in the weeks afterwards, they shared their experiences together (1996:132).

Indeed, for Radley (1996), it is not simply the success of such operations that accounts for the shared experiences of patients. In his view, these patients experience a transformation of self and identity akin to a religious experience such that 'being a *bypass patient* – having passed through that non-experience – had established a place from which to reconstruct one's view of life' (1996:134). And, for Radley, this is not simply a function of the kind of treatment heart patients receive; rather, as 'embodied beings, who in this case have submitted themselves to surgery and intensive care, ... their basis of judgment has been changed' (1996:136). Such transformations of the self and identity are, as Turner (1974) notes, a central feature of rites of passage.

In a related attempt to understand how rituals of healing take or make their effects upon the body and psyche of the sick person, Csordas (2002) conducted ethnographic work among native American Navajo. In order to understand ritual's efficacy he interviewed those who had undergone healing and so provides us with insight into their experience. Thus Sylvia, a 30-year-old Navajo woman, had developed shoulder and arm pain which, when treated with western bio-medicine, left her dependent upon a drug which inflamed the lining of her stomach. Coming from a family with a strong belief in traditional Navajo religion, she chose to undertake a healing ceremony in the belief that her continued suffering had a spiritual origin. In preparing for the ceremony it emerged that the death of Sylvia's father had weighed heavily upon her for the previous seven years. Witchcraft was not only identified as the cause of this death but also, by virtue of its capacity to linger within the family, the cause of Sylvia's pain. In response, the Navajo diagnostician prescribed an Evilway ceremony, which was preceded by a series of consultations involving the ritual extraction of 'objects' from Sylvia's shoulder and the healing of her pain. While western bio-medicine might have seen this as the finale of the ritual drama of illness, a full Evilway ceremony, led by a chanter, was still needed before the *channel* of the suffering – Sylvia's emotional attachment to her father's memory – could be broken. Sylvia describes her experience of being healed:

> the stuff you hold like they have the arrow-head and that stuff. Those are very powerful. All that comes with, you know, stories and behind that there's a meaning for all that ... I could feel it within me. I could feel a mixture of all that he was praying about. And I could feel it. You have to really understand, you know, why your ceremony is being conducted ... (Csordas 2002:156).

By gathering data which describe the subjective, embodied experience of being healed, studies such as Csordas' (2002) contribute, then, to our overall understanding of how a cultural performance such as the Evilway ceremony actually takes effect. As he notes, this contrasts strongly with the 1970s anthropological approach to rituals of healing that focused primarily upon the manipulation of symbols, making the agency, or 'symbolic mastery' (Bourdieu 1977) of those who *manipulate* more central to understanding, than the experience of those who are healed.

Like Csordas (2002), Draper's (2003) starting point is voices and experiences which are not customarily drawn upon in analyses of how rituals of transition achieve their effect. With a focus on the embodied experiences of pregnancy and labour, she sought out British *men's* accounts of how they made transitions to a new identity, or a new stage of their identity, as a father, when their own bodies seemed to remain unchanged. Thus, for example, one father, expecting his first child by a new partner, described himself, his partner and indeed their unborn child as *all* in transition, using the metaphor of being en voyage, betwixt and between. He said 'the baby's waiting until the time and we're all in the same boat' (2003:70). Overall, for the men Draper interviewed, pregnancy confirmation via the ultrasound scan, antenatal education and being present during labour and delivery, were all cited as the ways in which they, as men, experienced passage to a new or altered identity, as father. Though pregnancy, for men, is not an embodied experience, it is, Draper (2003) argues, via body-mediated-moments, such as seeing and displaying the unborn baby via the ultrasound scan, that men's passage to fatherhood was felt to occur.

Murphy's (1987) account of his own transition into a disabled identity through progressive paralysis, provides a comparable embodied account of the ways in which new health identities come to be taken on. However, the rite of passage involved in becoming disabled, whether through accident or illness, is often not completed since there may be no final rite of reincorporation for the individual. Indeed, death, rather than reintegration, may be the result of the onset of chronic and disabling illness. However, as Murphy (1995) recounts in a later analysis, disability may also be experienced by people as a state of permanent liminality, since the able-bodied world may not offer opportunities for full social participation.

Thus, in an evocative account that echoes V.W. Turner's (1974) analysis of the common identities, social isolation and confinement of ritual liminars, Murphy describes the experience of living as a disabled person:

> Our shared identities as disabled people override the old hierarchies of age. Education and occupation, and they wash out many sex-role barriers as well ... As liminal people, the disabled confront each other as whole individuals, unseparated by social distinctions ... Many seek one another's company, often through membership in disability organisations. There they find fellowship and refuge from a world that commonly relegates them to the margins (1995:156).

Unlike ritual liminars, however, where a symbolic death is followed by rebirth into society with a new social status, in Murphy's view, this may not occur for many disabled people: 'just as the bodies of the disabled are permanently impaired, so also is their standing as members of society (1995:156).

The disabled feminist academic, Morris (1991) provides a similarly personal account of how sudden changes in her body prompted a radical alteration in her identity. Climbing over a wall at the bottom of her garden to rescue a child stranded above a 20-foot-drop above a railway line, Morris fell and broke her back. She says of the point at which she lost mobility,

> I didn't realise it then, but by stepping over that wall I became someone whose physical condition others feared ... [i]n subtle and not so subtle ways a number of people conveyed to me that they felt my life was no longer worth living (1991:2).

She goes on to state that '[l]ittle did I realise that by becoming paralysed I had become fundamentally different and set apart from the non-disabled world' (1991:3). Yet Morris herself had already made plans to convert her home in preparation for using a wheelchair by the time the ambulance service had arrived at the scene of her accident. For her 'losing the use of my legs was not by any means a tragedy' (1991:3). In the changes wrought to her body through the fall from her garden wall, we see its intrinsic condition of indeterminacy intensifying (see Chapter 3). Perceptions of her now disabled body produced the competing 'objectifications' of both a tragically useless life *and* a challenge which adapted living arrangements could help her respond to effectively. What Morris' experiences most powerfully reveal, however, are the implications for her identity through a newfound sense of being 'fundamentally different and set apart' (1991:3).

By contrast, Svendsen's (2005) account of people who undergo genetic counselling for cancer depicts the transformation of self that occurs through the *removal* of uncertainty. Whatever the outcome, the individual achieves a new status through choosing, voluntarily, to undergo a rite of passage from ignorance to knowledge: 'when the fear of the future frames the present, scientific knowledge is seen as a means to reframe the present to extirpate fear' (2005:97). As she suggests:

> while from an existential point of view, the need to act and 'do something' is a struggle for control, the need to 'do something' also resonates with the cultural understanding that to seek counseling and articulate family histories … becomes a way of *acting* in order to *know* one's *being*. The anticipatory element of becoming survivors is at once an existential imperative and a process of becoming morally right persons (2005:101).

Though not explicitly framing the process of counselling in terms of rites of passage, Svendsen's analysis of the outcome of the drama that is involved in this pursuit of knowledge about cancer risk mirrors that of a rite of passage. In phrases that parallel those of V.W. Turner, she argues that:

> new contexts for understanding identity and social relationships are created. In this sense, knowledge becomes irreversible. The interpretive moves of counselees move them into new frameworks for understanding their lives and obligations in social relationships (2005:119).

The Drama Unfolds

The accounts presented in the previous section provide us, then, with rich and detailed micro-level accounts of the social interactions and the symbolism that accompanies different kinds of health transitions. There remains, however, a need to explore the concept of agency and how this might be experienced and expressed by the person undergoing transitions into and out of illness. In classic accounts of a rite of passage, things happen to the initiand; whilst experiencing a lot, they may, in fact, initiate very little. Instead, individuals undergoing transition seem to assume a passive role in a ritual drama that unfolds around them. It is one that is being orchestrated on their behalf by those in power over them, an approach that contrasts strongly with the more agency-centred account embraced by dramaturgical perspectives that have their roots in Goffman's work.

Sinclair, for example, describes the rituals of the hospital ward round in this manner. Curtains are drawn around the patient's bed, creating what he calls a 'temporary dramatic space' (1997:215). For him the metaphor of theatricality and drama precisely match his own experience of medical training. He talks particularly about the notion of 'presentation', arguing that medical students learn to 'present' the patient and their complaint to the consultant during ward rounds. Nowhere does the patient themselves contribute to the drama. Indeed, it is the illness, rather than the patient, which is ascribed the agentic capacity to 'present' itself to the doctor as an unusual bodily change or crisis.

Once we begin to listen to the voice of the person experiencing the ritual drama of illness, however, as we did in the previous section, then we are working with data capable of providing more insight into the patient and their bodies as agentic entities. One source here are personal narratives, presented by the individual themself – and it is noteworthy that the publication of such narratives by individuals who have undergone serious health problems is on the increase. Not only is this happening in the popular press (see for example, Watt 1996; Bauby 1998; Diamond 1998; Ed Guyat's weekday column in *The Guardian* newspaper on living with paralysis; and Rebecca Atkinson's column on living with increasing visual impairment in *The Guardian Weekend*), examples can also be found among the predominantly 'scientific' articles contained in medical journals. For example, Brooks (1990) describes his experience of living a life supported by home ventilation:

> It was August 1989 when I was first connected to Fifi, my Cape Cuirass pump. We make a slightly daft couple – she, short and squat, and me, long, very thin and absurdly decked out, like a gangly stork, in a blue jacket ventilation outfit. The pair of us are joined in mock matrimony by a length of black hosepipe. Fifi huffs and puffs away all night long while I sleep, content in the knowledge that she will take sole care of the business of breathing. As in so many happy relationships, the male sleeps while the female does all the hard work. We have been sleeping together for about six months. From our very first night she made a quite startling difference to my life. When I was first introduced to Fifi, I did not believe I could ever get used to the noisy machine and the fancy dress. However, just one night converted me to the joys and thrills of home ventilation (1990:96)

These sources all provide embodied accounts of how a change in health status is undertaken or managed and provoke a series of questions. To what extent, for example, does the individual contribute to – or resist – the new identities that may accompany the body's changed health status? Does the process of medicalisation (Illich 1976) always pose a threat to people's identity and sense of well-being, by making health concerns central within people's thinking and experiences? Or might the onset of illness facilitate new kinds of possibilities that are empowering? Asking such questions about the ways in which the drama of illness unfolds means looking once again, therefore, at the relationship between structure, agency and the body (see Chapter 2), but this time teasing out the intricacies of the experiential meanings of the transitions people make between health and ill-health. These are not necessarily predetermined, either by the body's changing materiality or the demands of the social contexts within which the embodied individual is located. One way to capture this, then, is to explore further the narratives people provide about their illness. These we now examine.

Illness Narratives

If we are to work with illness narratives, whether provided by the individual or gathered by the social scientist, we need to recognise, however, that these are not simply transparent descriptions and reflections upon what has occurred (see also Chapter 5). A useful reminder of this is the theoretical perspective offered in Bury's (1982) interrogation of the concept of illness as a biographical disruption. He shows how modern medicine does not simply come to dominate the lives of people living with chronic and disabling conditions through making them subject to new, medicalised identities. Instead, medical categories offer a way for people to manage their transition into chronic illness, enabling them to give explanations and account to others for their altered state. Later, Bury (1991) developed this idea further, exploring the different ways in which people engage with the process of becoming ill; the ways they cope, the strategic actions they take. As he suggests, the adjustments they make to how they live their lives can mean that the onset of chronic illness or disability may broaden or enhance, rather than disrupt their biographies, as we saw in the case of Jane Thomlinson (Chapter 1). Similarly, it was after Jenny Morris became paralysed that she developed her earlier involvement with the trade union and labour movement, and the feminist movement, to become a disability activist. What this work draws attention to, therefore, is the idea that the transition to ill-health, and possibly to a new identity, is not simply determined by biology; nor are people always rendered passive in the face of the structural difficulties and changes that chronic illness can bring in terms of employment and changed family relationships.

Denny's (1996) research, for example, based on in-depth interviews with ten women undergoing private IVF treatment, draws upon a small sample of infertility narratives. These stand testimony to individuals' scope for repairing biographical disruption through revealing the various ways in which women came to experience themselves as agents, rather than victims. They provide a vivid account of how identity categories, such as 'parent' or 'childless', figure within women's experiences of not being able to conceive – and of their seeking IVF treatment. As these data indicate, passage towards a new, desired identity of 'parent' takes place across the months during which women are trying to conceive and bears many of the hallmarks of a classic rite of passage. It has, for example, clearly bounded stages, defined both by the medical profession and the demands of the science involved; and, indeed, it is designed to change identities, to transform women from childlessness to parenthood. In addition, the process of embarking on IVF also involves transitions which evoke Parsons' (1951) sick role model, except here, as in other examples, there is no guarantee of a return to 'health' and power can shift from the hands of doctors into those of women who become their own experts.

Although for a few women IVF provides the rite of passage to motherhood, for many more there may be no endpoint, in terms of achieving a 'take home baby', or even a successfully implanted embryo. Why then, Denny (1996) asks, do women begin a journey that may have no end-point and which locks them into repeated cycles of failure and self-blame? While radical feminists present IVF as another example of the patriarchal medical profession taking over women's reproductive lives, by not only deciding who will get treatment but also riding on the back of pro-natalist ideologies which make women feel less than adult if they have no children, Denny suggests that this approach is too simplistic. Instead she looks to women themselves for an explanation as to why they willingly submit to highly invasive and 'dramatic' procedures with no guarantee of success. Although some women saw themselves as victims of a society that expects women to be mothers, and a science that persuades them that this might be possible, others, by contrast, saw IVF as empowering. These were women who felt able 'to control their treatment' (1996:221):

> They define themselves as 'infertile', albeit in society that expects marriage to lead to reproduction, and they decide on the medical solutions to their infertility. They initiate treatment, they withdraw either temporarily or permanently and they move from one clinic to another if dissatisfied (1996:221).

For Denny, this does not represent an instance of false consciousness, of women colluding with men against their own interests. Instead, the women she interviewed felt that the IVF rite of passage to a *potential* pregnancy 'gave them back control, as infertility meant a loss of control' (1996:216). As one woman said, 'your body is letting you down' and what IVF offers is 'the right to exercise reproductive choice in deciding to use every means available in order to have a child' (1996:217).

Denny's study, therefore, enables us to focus in detail on the ways in which, as embodied individuals, people undergoing dramatic health transitions can, nonetheless, exercise a degree of agency in terms of the identities that they take on. It recalls Davis' work with women who 'knowledgeably choose to have cosmetic surgery' (1995:169). Although aware of the dangers, women see cosmetic surgery as empowering and do not feel themselves victims of the male gaze or of a patriarchal society that commodifies women's beauty. Instead, they see cosmetic surgery as enabling them to achieve a new body that is, not necessarily beautiful, but is just like anyone else's. And through this rite of passage to a new body women have new experiences of embodiment that enable a changed sense of themselves. Even when operations fail to produce the desired results, women experienced an empowering sense of personal agency as a result of having made a decision and taken control of their bodies. Caroline, for example, one of Davis' interviewees, had endured three failed breast enlargement operations yet 'whereas she previously presents herself as the hapless victim of fate, she now portrays herself as an agent in interaction with her circumstances' (1995:143).

Strategies of Narration

The twin examples of IVF and cosmetic surgery outlined above provide illustration of the agentic experiences of people undergoing health transitions of different kinds. However, in some senses, these transitions can be seen as matters of personal choice, unlike the onset of sudden illness that may dramatically, and radically, alter an individual's embodied experiences and sense of self. To what extent does the notion of rite of passage enable us to engage with issues of agency with respect to these kinds of health transitions? In answering this we consider illness narratives as a key resource for the active negotiation of the body (see Chapters 1 and 3), and ask about their role in the ritual drama of illness.

We begin with Frank's (1995) account of illness narratives. For Frank, the importance of exploring sub-genres within the stories people tell of their illnesses is that it enables us to see the process of embodied meaning-making that people undertake during their illness experiences. This allows us a way to understand a little more about the nature of that experience in terms, for example, of feelings of loss, hope, or confusion. However, although each story told is individual, according to Frank (1995), people do draw on the types of narrative that are culturally available to them, weaving them together into a unique account of their own experiences. He identified three narrative types that people alternate between.

First is the restitution narrative which charts a passage across three themes – from health through to sickness and a return to future well-being. In such accounts, which reflect a medicalised focus on cure, illness is transitory and has the potential to be overcome. By contrast, the chaos narrative, as the name suggests, dwells on the idea that life will never get better and is characterised by a loss of control, feelings of futility and impotence in the face of illness. The third narrative is the quest narrative, one which suggests that the experience of illness may be therapeutic and even transformative. However, since these narrative types are all culturally available, people may switch between them in any one story of illness, as Thomas-Maclean (2004) demonstrates in her analysis of the stories women tell about having breast cancer. Although women choose to present a version of the 'restitution' narrative, as a way of minimising the bodily changes that having breast cancer may have wrought, at points in their stories, the narrative also often becomes one of chaos, reflecting the chaos of the women's lives at that time.

However, the women's narratives that Thomas-Maclean (2004) analyses do not just provide evidence of the ways in which women interpret their new experiences of embodiment, to and for themselves. Buried within them are also the practical negotiations women have to make with their bodies, day in day out, as they change over time, the strategies they adopt in the presentation of a new kind of self. Thus for example, one woman, who chose to have a mastectomy, rather than a lumpectomy, reasoned that 'the way my breasts were developed, with all the little bumps and lumps that are in them it was better to do the whole thing' (2004:1652). For her, the body's changing irregularities had to be continually negotiated, so that rather than living in and with such a body, she decided on full surgery. Another woman also expressed the ways in which the changing nature of the body had to be continually negotiated:

> If there is unusual things that happen, and there has been, because I have had a couple of surgeries since then [surgery for breast cancer], they had to take my gall bladder out because it had collapsed. And I didn't know if I had gotten cancer in that area, if it had spread. Then you wonder, is it cancer …. But I don't dwell on it. But then I've been lucky because I've been tested a lot too (Thomas-Maclean 2004:1653).

Through these narratives, then, women exercised agency, restoring order and meaning to embodied life events which otherwise threatened to profoundly disrupt their identities.

Experiencing the Ritual Drama of Illness

As shown above, narratives of illness can reveal the agency that individuals can have in relation to the experience of illness, through the negotiations they make, as much with their own bodies, as with the medical professionals who are treating them. Unlike the model of transition presented in traditional accounts of rites of passage, where it is suggested that a new identity is imposed by society, accounts such as these therefore position the individual as a social actor, navigating a path through the drama of illness that is transforming their identity in different ways. But, as indicated above, it is the growing autobiographical, rather than social scientific literature on health and illness that most privileges the agentic experience of the ritual drama of health.

For example, Ben Watt, one half of the 90s pop group *Everything But the Girl*, produced an autobiography in which he detailed the experience of having a very serious condition which destroyed most of his digestive system. Perhaps crucially it was a condition which was not easy to diagnose or to treat – he could not simply give himself over to the hands of the medical experts for an 'account' of his illness. Instead, he generated his own narrative. Clearly his identity was massively transformed. He describes not only his consternation at his body no longer behaving itself – but the resulting helplessness from being hospitalised:

> At first I couldn't understand why doctors weren't called every time I was in pain. The staff nurses were kind and the student nurses young and keen to help, but both were untrained in diagnosis and when I'd call one of them with my call button they could offer no answers and I would get fractious and upset. Nobody told me that, except in times of emergency, the doctors only came round twice a day – and that only they could take big decisions. I had to learn the pace of the days (1996:12).

In many ways his adult status was escaping him – he felt both old and child-like at the same time. Treatments such as the catheter for urination and difficulties in focusing his eyes made him feel 'old, incapable, incontinent' (1996:71), and at times he is quite explicit about the experience of a changed identity. Watched by student nurses as he was being sick he said:

> Kneeling there by the basin, I felt I was adapting already, like a creature moving from the sea to the land, evolving a new identity. And I was sealing myself away. My sense of time and space was shrinking. The invisible thread that had been tying me to home and the desperate desire to get out had slackened (1996:18).

Eventually he recovers and goes on holiday in America with his girlfriend, but his identity, as read off his body, is clearly altered. He wears a new pair of size 'small' shorts and describes looking at himself in the driving mirror:

> My scars wouldn't change colour, not even the little ones on my wrists and chest. They stayed white, like marker flags on a playing-field. In the driving mirror I noticed how I now have crow's feet in the corners of my eyes and the skin hangs looser on my cheeks even though the sun had tightened them up like a hazelnut. My face was like a new friend (1996:176).

In Watt's account are all the features of a rite of passage. He finds himself removed from normal time and space through his illness, an experience that disorients him and he has to learn to live life at a new pace. He experiences his body differently and, at times, feels humiliated by that difference as he is no longer in control of his bodily functions. He also describes the slow emergence of a new self through this changing body experientially, as a process of adaptation. He was learning, as it were, to inhabit a changed body. But, what we see in his account of his own 'reincorporation' into society is not just his restoration to health or the taking on of a new social identity. Watt's experience is, quite literally, an account of a new embodiment, a new perceptual process; his face, he says, was not the face he knew. It was that of another person, a new friend.

Alongside Watt's narrative, then, we can place the proliferating range of health and illness narratives which provide personal perspectives on the ritual drama of illness. Newton (1984), for example, produced an account of what felt to her to be incarceration in a nursing home in her 70s, following her sister's failure to be able to look after her. She describes being given the verdict that she should not return to her home by her GP, rather than her sister, prefaced by the words 'We've decided that it would be best for you …'. She says, 'they might at least have given me a small voice in their decision to wrap up my life forever' (1984:280).

What this account suggests, therefore, is that the ritual drama of illness often produces a sense of helplessness among patients. However, this is not necessarily generated through bodily incapacity, but can be the result of structural and institutional practices which act to disempower the individual socially. As Newton says of the effects of her GPs decision, 'You are no longer an average human being, alive with joys and doubts and fears … [f]rom today you are a Patient' (1984:280). Clearly then, the ritual drama of illness is unequivocally social in nature, the implications of its outcome for embodied identity being potentially profound.

Conclusion

This chapter began by highlighting the lacunae in the concept of rites of passages as a theoretical resource to account for the transition into and out of illness, suggesting that it fails to take account of patients' experiences and to acknowledge their embodied agency. This raises the question of whether individuals who are sick can and do exercise agency in the face of the changing materiality of the body which, inevitably, they have negotiate. Indeed, is it, perhaps, this undermining of agency that reflects or compounds the structural disempowerment associated with literally being (a) patient during the ritual drama of illness that is enacted around the individual on their behalf?

However, once we turn to the narrative literature on sickness and illness, what we discover are individuals who, in narrating their experiences, achieve a variety of accomplishments through that process, in terms of representing their experiences, to themselves and others, as stories told. In that our evidence, as social scientists, tends to be qualitative, interview material such as Denny's (1996) and Davis' (1995), which provide *accounts* of women exercising agency, it needs to be read as an additional example of the narrative reconstruction of embodied experiences which engender changes in health status and identity. We also see, however, that what these autobiographical narratives can do is enable individuals to participate in the ritual drama of illness; this time not simply as patients, but as embodied individuals who are coming to understand the illness events that are happening to and with their bodies.

7

A Medicalised Life Course?

Through the concept of the negotiated body, which we have been developing in this book, we can begin to see the ambiguities of 'health' and 'illness' as not simply a form of problematic blurring which renders them relatively meaningless as ways of categorising embodied experiences. On the contrary, the difficulties of predicting and recognising both our own health status, and that of others, are an integral part of everyday interactions and social practices that, as we saw in the last chapter, can find some resolution through the ritual drama of illness. However, the ambiguity or indeterminacy of bodily and mental states and their intrinsic instability as physiological processes yield new perspectives on the relationship between health, illness and identity when we consider them within the broader context of the life course – the task of this chapter. As we shall see, it is a context which brings another set of questions to the surface. For example, how does medicine deal with the radical transformations that the human mind and body undergo during the process of ageing? Do 'birth' and 'death' mark ultimate bodily boundaries to the life course, or are these points of transition negotiable? How do people at different points in the life course experience the well and ill body? And, how might our identities have to be renegotiated in the course of life, as we come to terms with the physical changes that ageing brings to the body?

The purpose of considering such questions is not, however, simply to chart people's different social and cultural responses to the ultimate inevitability of physical decline, whether chronic or acute. Nor is it purely an acknowledgement that, across different cultures, the life course as lived may be very different from a western life course, given, for example, the high rates of child mortality in less developed economies, their populations' shorter average life expectancy and the impact of disease and natural disasters such as famine on people's lives (Phillips and Verhasselt 1994; Scheper-Hughes 1992). All these are of course critical to acknowledge. However, this chapter also sets out to develop this book's ongoing arguments about the contribution of structure and agency perspectives to medical sociology and anthropology and the ways in which each of these might be drawn on to explore the relationship between health and identity at the site of the body. In so doing, it returns us to the question of medical power and the social knowledges it produces for our embodiment (B.S. Turner 1987:3–4). Importantly, it also permits exploration of the issue of how, as embodied beings, we discursively construct the body's health across the life course. In this chapter our focus will be primarily on the early and the later periods of the life course – childhood and old age – since it is at these times that the body's instability, and therefore its negotiation, can become particularly pressing.

What is the Life Course?

The concept of the life course, as used by social scientists, draws attention to the ways in which the lifelong process of ageing is both understood and experienced. As we have discussed in detail elsewhere, both cross-cultural and historical perspectives highlight the mutable nature of the social categories through which the life course is constructed and, therefore, through which we come to know that we are ageing (Hockey and James 1993; 2003). For example, as we noted, key transitional moments between different stages within the life course will occur at different chronological ages, depending upon the individual's historical and cultural location:

> There is a social dimension to human life which cannot be reduced to a set of bodily imperatives. Thus .... 'ageing' is not simply a matter of organic matura-tion and decay, for the way in which these processes are understood and their import for societies' members differ cross-culturally (Hockey and James 2003:23).

For example, taking an historical perspective on the changed dimensions of the life course in the UK, those who were born at the end of the nineteenth century will recall not only starting paid employment in their early teens but also its symbolic status as a transition to adulthood: 'we were men then' (Hockey n.d.). By contrast, Brannen and Nilsen (2002) also note that in the early twenty-first century, western adulthood has become increasingly deferred as young people continue to live at home with parents into their 20s, returning there after higher education or between jobs and relationships. In addition, age of first marriage has varied across quite brief historical periods. Early marriage was the norm in the 1950s and 1960s, but was occurring later, and often after cohabitation, by the 1970s and 1980s (Elliott 1991). In addition, as Featherstone and Hepworth (1991) argue, a period called 'mid-life' has now emerged, extending from the early 30s right through until the individual displays unambiguous physical or psychological indicators of being 'elderly', perhaps only after they have passed the age of 70.

Thus, not only are life course transitions such as the entry to adulthood or 'old age' subject to cross-cultural and historical variation, but the very categories through which age-based identities are assumed or attributed, are themselves mutable across time. And in this respect, as we shall explore through this chapter, how medical specialisms of different kinds, together with changing social policies and laws, help structure the passage of the life course. They also, therefore, shape what we think of as the building blocks of our social identities – childhood, adulthood and old age.

However, as soon as we begin to examine this temporal profile more closely, in social, medical and legal terms, it becomes apparent that even the boundaries to the life course, and the stages within it, are neither fixed nor self-evident. Instead they emerge as the outcome of a range of different negotiations with and about the body. Lock (2002), for example, compares Western and Japanese conceptions of the point of 'death'. She shows that contemporary western medicine strives to define a *moment* after which death can be said to have occurred in order to legitimate the harvesting of organs from the 'dead' for transplantation to the bodies of the living. Such a perspective, as Smith points out, has led some individuals to feel 'increasingly troubled by the present attitude of the medical profession: "You're dead when your doctor says you are"' (cited in Lock 2002:78). Japanese 'death', by contrast, is a family-defined *process*, rather than a particular point in time. This, Lock argues, accounts for Japan's comparatively low rate of transplant surgery. As she notes, in Japan '[e]fforts to assign death scientifically to a specific moment are frequently rejected outright by both medical and lay people' (2002:8). Thus, as we acknowledge throughout this book, although western medicine is increasingly influential throughout the world, its whole-scale adoption is far from universal. Other models of health, illness and, indeed, dying remain in place. In Japan, Lock reports, '[a]s of the end of 2000, organs for transplant had been procured from only 9 brain-dead donors' (2002:3).

Even within the West, however, there are ambiguities surrounding what De Vries (1981) refers to as the twin gate-posts of 'birth' and 'death'. A position that assumes that '[a]t birth a previously non-existent individual appears, at death an existing individual passes into non-existence' is at odds, for example, with the potential *social* presence of unborn children and dead family members whose life-to-be or life-that-was can be a prominent dimension of everyday experience among the living (1981:1075). Morgan describes how in western societies unborn children have long been regarded as, in some senses, already in the world through the commonly held idea that prenatal influences can result in 'birth defects such as cleft palate and club foot, behavioral idiosyncrasies, food likes and dislikes, personality characteristics, and so on' (2003:272). And indeed, pregnant women increasingly constitute a large section of the newly worried well (see Chapter 4). Held morally responsible for the health of their as yet unborn child, it is a responsibility that, in effect, endows the foetus with the social status of family member who needs to be cared for. As Layne describes with reference to women in America:

> Women may now actively construct the personhood of their wished-for child from the moment they do a home pregnancy test. Each cup of coffee or glass of wine abstained from, and each person informed of the impending birth adds to the 'realness' of the baby they are growing within (2000:322).

Constructing the Object Body across the Life Course

The examples above suggest therefore that 'life', which is often viewed in contra-distinction to 'death', is indeterminate, rather than clear-cut. They show that what might, at first glance, appear to be 'self-evident', naturalised identity characteristics and boundaries are subject to interpretation and do in fact shift across historical and cross-cultural time and space. In line with our arguments about the embodied nature of human life (see Chapter 3) models of the 'life course' have, therefore, also to be seen as the outcome of perceptual and inter-pretative processes. These *terminate* in the production of a range of 'object', aged bodies – young, middle aged and elderly. That is to say, these different types of bodies are not simply descriptions of a pre-existing, pre-defined set of changing bodies; instead, they arise and become construed as 'objects', in and through social practices of different kinds. In addition, they are models of bodily change that represent particular, often politicised, positions that mobilise specific moral, legal, emotional and biological evidence in laying rhetorical claims about the status of that body as 'real'. This is not, of course, to deny the material effects upon the body that the ageing process has. Instead, it underscores the point that how that process is understood and taken note of is subject to variation. We are therefore concerned to understand, once again, both the first person perspective of the ageing body-as-experiencer *and*, as Leder describes, 'the body as it regis-ters in public experience' and to account for the relationship between these perspectives (1990:5).

That said, even the *material* bodily indicators that 'life' has started, or stopped, turn out to be highly contingent, depending upon political position or historical location. For example, within the understanding provided by western medicine, over time 'life' has begun at conception or at the quicken-ing, a mutability of life's start point that is evidenced in the increasingly early age of foetal viability (see Human Fertilisation and Embryology Act 1990). Similarly, the point of death has been variously identified, as the cessation of breathing, or of heartbeat, or of brainstem function (Arnold *et al* 1997). And we find only a thin line sometimes being drawn between a late period and an early miscarriage (Johnson and Puddifoot 1998).

Such discursive 'readings' of the body are, however, not without their material outcomes as the debates about abortion and pro-life campaigns in western societies make abundantly clear. But they also reveal, precisely, the ambiguous, indeterminate nature of the perceptual processes that terminate in the object body. So although medical interventions into bodily processes may testify to professionals' capacity to save life, in so doing they can also reveal the very uncertainty of that relationship between 'life' and 'death'. Thus in Harvey's (1996, 1997) ethnographies of two Intensive Care Units and a Maternity Hospital labour ward, both medical science and medical technology are used by physicians first in the proactive technical management of birth. This is justified by the range of clinical uncertainties of childbirth that have become subsumed within the concept of 'risk'. Similarly, when faced with the unpredictable outcome of critical illness in ICU, the busy use of technology by medical professionals again shores up a spurious appearance of their control over the potential premature ending of the life course. This is described by Grieg from the perspective of a patient who recalls being 'in shadowlands, in a blue room where spectral figures hurried with an urgency I could not feel' (2004:11).

The above examples have shown, then, that medical ownership of unstable bodily processes has to be actively secured through the use of medical science and medical technology (see also Chapter 8) and, as such, this illustrates the immense challenge to medical science posed by the indeterminacy of the body as it changes over time. Indeed, as Armstrong (1981) shows, and as we discuss in detail below, the historical development of the medical specialisms of paediatrics and geriatrics within western medicine can be seen as the outcome of medicine's attempts to engage with the very instability of human embodiment during the twentieth century. Given the mutability of the body over the life course, the question for medical science became one of 'objectifying' it, of rendering it more stable, and of making its processes of change more statistically predictable.

As we have argued elsewhere (Hockey and James 1993; 2003), however, across the life course, the body as object is achieved through the intertwining of social, economic and *medical* framings. Together, these render the body's chronological age a central feature of social identity, a process of identification that, in turn, has implications for the (sexual and emotional) life of the object body. Thus, for example, when a woman bereaved of her male partner, asked the 'Private Lives' page of the *Guardian* (29th July 2005) whether she should fulfil her desire for 'physical affection' by introducing a sexual dimension into her five year friendship with a widowed man, the selection of readers' replies were far from encouraging. They included warning statements such as: 'be careful!'; 'conserve what you now enjoy?'; 'by turning your relationship into a physical one, you are setting in transit feelings which may be difficult to control once they are unleashed'. Had she been 30 or 40 years old, these replies would have resonated oddly among readers since they would have been more likely to pathologise her hesitancy – as a failure to let go of the dead, or as a sexual inhibition. However, the woman begins her letter 'I am a widow, aged 60', and the accompanying illustration depicts a portly woman with plump, solidly planted legs. Her chronological age thus begets a social identity that excludes the sexual mores of younger adults, rendering them dangerous and inappropriate. Only one reader advocates 'taking the risk'.

This example underscores the social construction of the body in relation to life course categories that confer age-related identities and, as such, reveals how the changing materiality of the body is not only differentially framed, but also differently experienced, over the course of a life, a point which we return to explore in detail later in this chapter. However, this example also provides evidence of the indeterminacy of the ageing body, an indeterminacy that illness can then exacerbate as both lay people and professionals struggle to interpret the body via, for example, statistical predictions of a 'normal' trajectory of change over time. Such objectifications of the body are, then, critical to the identification of the body as well or ill at different points in the life course. To illustrate this process, we now examine three cross-cultural examples of the different ways in which children's health and well-being is negotiated and rendered meaningful.

Determining the Health of 'the Child' through the Body

Einarsdottir notes that 'research demonstrates that responses to dysfunctional bodies or minds may range from extermination to the attribution of positive qualities' (2005:31). This observation, in itself, underscores the indeterminacy of the body and in her work among the Papel of Guinea-Bissau in West Africa she shows, for example, how the birth of 'anomalous' children are dealt with. Whether they have motor problems, blindness, epilepsy, ambiguous genitalia, or facial deformities, the key to these newborn children's treatment is to be found in processes that allow differentiation to be made between 'human' and 'non-human' children. Those who fall into the latter category are known as *iran* children. This refers to a body possessed by a spirit and therefore lacking a human soul. Such children are killed and buried without any of the funerary ritual that confers or sustains human identity and what Einarsdottir (2005) explores are the difficulties generated precisely through the ambiguities – or indeterminacy – of *iran* children's bodies. In that they fail to conform to accepted models of the child and its body, they cannot easily be identified as human. In this sense, the mere fact of their birth does not guarantee these children a place in human society. As Einarsdottir's (2005) data document, this process has, instead, to be established *after* birth and she shows how different members of Papel society, particularly the child's mother, seek to establish that child's identity – and therefore its fate, through, for example, refusing to stop breastfeeding the child and maintaining their hopes for a cure.

This example can be compared with Talle's (1995) account of the birth of children with disabilities among the Maasai of Kenya. Though regarded as a misfortune, and explained variously as an act of God (*Enkai*) – as caused by an inherited sin, sorcery or the misbehaviour of the child's mother during pregnancy – for the Maasai

> to give birth to a disabled child is not culturally defined as a crisis, requiring specific actions and precautions. It is part of life's experience … and thus, while marking the difference, they normalise it (Talle 1995:71).

In this case, then, the failure of the child's body to conform makes little difference. As the child matures, the fact that he or she 'is impaired in one way or another is just an aspect of his or her person and does not make any differences in social and cultural terms' (Talle 1995:71).

Fadiman's (1997) account of Lia, an Hmong child born in California, reveals a rather different story of the negotiations that take place in and around the child's body in relation to health and identity. From the perspective of western medicine, which was the framework within which Lia is born and receives healthcare and social welfare, she is seen as having serious congenital health problems. The doctors do not expect her to live. Her 'problems' include quadriplegia, spasticity and incontinence and together constitute the diagnosis that Lia is in a 'persistent vegetative state' (Fadiman 1997:210). From her family's point of view, however, the condition she is born with, and which translates as epilepsy, is 'an illness of some distinction', as Fadiman (1997:21) describes it. Among the Hmong, epilepsy can be an indicator of an individual's fitness for divine office and, traditionally, those who suffer from it often become shamans. Fadiman's account documents the treatment Lia receives at the hands of both her parents and her western doctors. While her parents are concerned about her fits and the possibility that she may die, they are more suspicious of the many western treatments that she is offered, treatments that, from a western perspective, aim to stabilise her body in different ways. For Lia's parents, however, such treatments pose a risk for the child's eternal soul and they actively resist them: 'they see a definite possibility of eternal damnation for their child if she dies from the surgery ... next to that, death might not seem so important' (Fadiman 1997:277).

Thus in Einarsdottir (2005), Talle (1995) and Fadiman's (1997) work, a child is perceived as *different* from others of the same age-based category and so provokes an account. It is an account that, in terms of the particular embodied location of the child and its parents, produces a particular kind of body out of an unstable materiality. Then, as an *iran*, a child with a disability, or an epileptic child, children take up positions within the life course with varying consequent embodied experiences.

Old Bodies, Young Bodies

As illustrated above, ambiguities associated with the body's mutability are differently negotiated in different cultural contexts through particular kinds of social interactions – and in relation to varying beliefs about the causes of illness and their treatment (see Chapter 4). We turn now, therefore, to explore in more detail the contrasting hegemonic role that western medical science has played in helping to objectify and produce a concept of *stable* and universalising trajectories of change. Once again our focus will be on the bodies of children and old people.

As Armstrong (1981; 1983) details, in western societies, paediatrics developed in the early twentieth century, after an almost complete absence of medical or social policy interest in infant health until the late nineteenth century. After the Second World War, a similar specialism – geriatrics – grew up around later life, and as Armstrong (1981) argues, each one, in their own way, produced particular conceptualisations, or objectifications, of the young and old body as it either grew up or grew old. However, both disciplines can also be seen as forms of medical pathologisation in that both childhood and later life came to be regarded as periods of the life course when people are especially vulnerable to disease and death. If medical science produces the concept of the 'healthy' body via objectifications which privilege its stability, so providing a set of criteria from which 'sick' bodies can be demonstrated to deviate (see Chapters 1 and 2), then the relatively rapid processes of change that occur in young and old bodies, in particular, make these bodies potentially difficult to categorise as either 'healthy', 'normal' or 'natural'.

Thus, for example, with respect to later life, Armstrong notes how the instabilities of an ageing body came to be seen as a kind of illness. He describes their medical construction as follows:

> Age made multiple pathology the rule rather than the exception and age altered the resistance of the old to disease processes. Management, too, had to be different as defects accumulated with age (Armstrong 1981:253).

As he goes on to suggest,' in geriatric patients the ageing process constituted a vital dimension of the medical problem' and later life in its entirety came to be viewed as the sufficient grounds for pathologies waiting to happen (1981:253).

What becomes problematic for geriatricians, however, are the social implications of this medicalised perspective of old age in everyday life. As Harari notes, for any medical practitioner the transition from teaching to consultation and treatment can be experienced as 'a descent from an ordered world of precision and rationality into a maelstrom of uncertainty and ambiguity' (2001:724). This he attributes to a 'widespread misunderstanding of the nature of science and its methods' that are experienced by the doctor as 'a struggle with ambiguous observations and competing, equally plausible interpretations of phenomena, arrived at by different methodologies' (2002:724–5). And in the case of geriatric medicine this uncertainty is amplified by a medicalised framing of the life course that pathologises 'old age', a perspective which stands in marked contrast to a more contemporary discursive construction of the old body found in the related discipline of social gerontology. Here the imperative is to represent the bodily changes which occur during later life as *natural*, to promote the possibility of a 'positive', active social life, despite chronological age (see Featherstone and Hepworth 1995).

Thus, as Coupland and Coupland show, in the medical encounters between elderly people and geriatricians that take place in the consulting room,' identity negotiation .... [is] ... a real-time and multi-party process' (1994:101). Using data collected in a geriatric outpatient clinic in Wales, they reveal that many elderly patients have multiple symptoms that are not amenable to cure, but simply have to be managed. Thus what takes place between doctor and patient is the active and ongoing social construction of health or illness – or indeed something in-between – in relation to a conversation that, in essence, is about old age and its place within the life course. This leads some elderly people to take comfort in a diagnosis that confirms the 'natural' frailty of old age, since this protects against the possibility of their being diagnosed with a 'more rapidly or unaccountably decremental and ultimately more fear-ridden or debilitating disease' (1994:122). Given the continuing criticism of the role that geriatric medicine plays in pathologising the end of the life course, however, as Coupland and Coupland show,' in their ideologically purest moments, doctors ... will go so far as to explicitly deny their patients' complaints are in any sense age-salient' (1994:120). As a result, other elderly people find that the doctor aggressively counters their claim that 'old age' and 'ill-health' are a natural consequence of the ageing process. Thus, although Leder argues for the body's capacity to *recede* from direct experience as the source, rather than the focus, of the perceptual process, he also acknowledges that, when its functioning is disrupted in some way, the body, or a part of it, 'speaks up' (1990:71). For those who are experiencing diminishing physiological capacities in old age, medicalised models of a stable, object body are, however, less likely to be persuasive – and geriatric medicine's acknowledgement of decline, whilst problematically pathologising, is thus potentially in harmony with the bodily processes which older adults are already learning to accommodate.

In the case of paediatrics, too, conceptions of age-related health play an important part in the ways in which the child's body is produced as an object within the medical encounter. As Bluebond-Langner's classic account of dying children in the US in the 1970s reveals, the onset of leukemia disrupts ideas about normal childhood because the children 'will not "become", they have no future' (1978:213; see also Jenks 1996). Thus, at a time when death from childhood leukemia was far greater than it now is, what took place in hospital encounters between children and those adults who cared for them was a game of mutual pretense that denied that death was imminent:

> Leukemics are an affront to the doctors' sense of mastery, to their training, their professions, and their self-concept …. They can neither cure these children nor, as the disease progresses, insure their comfort …. Mutual pretense allows physicians to salvage some of what is expected of them (1978:219).

Mutual pretense allowed the change to children's bodies wrought by leukemia to be, momentarily, avoided and ignored by children, parents and doctors; the unstable, dying body was rendered conceptually stable through a mutual, yet implicit and unacknowledged, process of bodily negotiation.

Yet, in western societies, medicine's core business is the prevention, diagnosis and treatment of pathological bodily changes. Thus, De Swaan (1990) traces a continuum of unstable bodies. This encompasses heart patients and 'psychotics in crisis', out-patients with a health problem who 'live according to the doctor's precepts and regulate their existence and their expectations of the future accordingly' and 'the rest of the population (which) is not so much healthy as not-yet-sick and live under a light medical regime' (1990:57). However, into this range De Swaan inserts *another* category: those for whom 'there may not even be a danger signal, but … their youth or advanced age is in itself a reason for increased watchfulness in medical matters' (1990:57). What De Swaan's analysis draws attention to, therefore, is that the body's ageing process, whether in childhood or later life, has become, in itself, problematic during the course of the twentieth century in western societies. The instability of the ageing body, coupled with a decline in childhood mortality and increasing life expectancy, has worked to blur bio-medicine's normal division between natural and pathological bodily changes. And, in so doing, it has produced a range of new uncertainties about the life course as lived.

A good illustration of this is the ways in which the menopause is contemporarily understood. As a bodily change which is intrinsic to the ageing female body, it has, nonetheless, become increasingly medicalised, and problematised within western medical science, its 'cure' being identified as the use of HRT (Greer 1999). What was once a normal aspect of female embodiment, known simply as 'the change', has now become recast as medical problem that needs to be dealt with. Similarly, within contemporary western societies, declining infant mortality has led to the expectation that all children will survive, that bodily changes will only be those associated with normal development and that professional attention will be on hand for any child who appears to deviate from the standard pattern. Ironically, however, the more surveillance that has taken place to guard against the occurrence of potential (pathological) change in children's bodies, the more new illnesses, such as Attention Deficit Disorder (ADD), have been discovered. Explaining how and why such reconstructions of health take place in relation to changes in the body across the life course is the task of the next section, a case study which demonstrates the production of the western child's body through the process of medicalisation.

The Medicalisation of the Child's Body

Wright's (1987) account of the social construction of babyhood in the UK asks how infant care came to be defined as a problem, and how the everyday lives, the feeding and behaviours of babies, came to be construed as subjects of medical enquiry and activity. Like Armstrong (1983), Wright (1987) posits the early twentieth century as the period in which the specialism of paediatrics is rooted. From the 1890s onwards, it was doctors and no longer mothers, or grandmothers, who were seen to possess authentic expertise in caring for babies. Even though the primary carer has extensive exposure to the baby's patterns of behaviour, the doctor, whose knowledge was inaccessible to a lay public, became seen as the person who 'knows best'.

If the medicalisation of babyhood occurred between 1890 and 1915, it was, however, not only changes in medical science which contributed to the emergence of this specialism. These new healthcare practices were part of broader ideological and cultural shifts that were occurring, particularly in relation to political definitions of the working class. As Wright documents, for the first time, the deaths of infants became seen as a problem needing to be addressed and dealt with, rather than simply a sad fact of life. During the 1850s and 1860s, for example, 40% of infants under the age of five died, yet at that time social responses to their deaths were non-medical. Instead, working class mothers were morally exhorted to do better, by the clergy or middle-class lady philanthropists. By 1915, however, infant death was seen as a medical problem.

In making sense of this shift Wright takes account of a range of factors such as the introduction of the registration of deaths in 1877, a move which, for the first time, exposed infant mortality statistically and so revealed geographical and social variation in the death rate. This underscored the links between child death and specific social conditions. However, in Wright's (1987) view, the resulting changes in social policy and practice stemmed from their core *medical* framework. The new germ pathogen theory redefined child death as an avoidable outcome of poor hygiene. This helped make doctors, rather than any other professional group, the experts in this domain of the life course.

What Wright's account reveals, therefore, is the way in which medical science expanded its remit. Infant mortality became constituted as a 'problem' which a newly professionalised group were then able to 'solve'. Despite the effects of public health improvements, which may in themselves have lessened infant mortality, childrearing was newly medicalised. Technical skill took hold, and existing practices of domestic culture were warned against: kissing, demand feeding, dummies, masturbation, babies' sleeping positions.

As Armstrong (1983) notes, by the 1940s, the child-health surveys and clinics that followed on from this medicalising of childcare were beginning to yield medical evidence that could be used to generate the profile of the 'normal' child. This provided a universalising yardstick against which all children could be measured and, as such, also led to the many ways in which some children might be identified as *different* (James 2004). Thus, increasingly, through the expansion of what Armstrong (1995) terms surveillance medicine, the risks to child health intensified and led to the creation of a statistically derived objectification: the stable child's body. Thus he argues:

> the techniques of Surveillance Medicine – screening, surveys, and public health campaigns – would all address this problem in terms of searching for temporal regularities, offering anticipatory care, and attempting to transform the future by changing the health and health behaviours of the present (1995:402).

For contemporary children, however, the body of this standardised child can become a tyrannical model *of* and *for* their own bodies, one which evokes the risk that such differences will become regarded as deviant (James 2004).

It might, therefore, be that the periods during which the body is at its most changeable and unstable, youth and old age, are the most challenging for medical science. However, what we argue on the basis of the evidence presented here is that, on the contrary, such instabilities in fact provide grist to the medical scientific mill. They have helped shore up the elite professional status of medicine because, as we have seen, if children's bodies are in a process of constant but not necessarily even growth, their conformity to a fixed albeit unfolding schema of 'child development' provides scope for medical surveillance and intervention.

Health and Ageing across the Life Course?

The case study of the development of baby-care has provided us with a route into exploring the structural processes through which health and identity are brought into a relationship across the life course – and how these age-based social identities then structure the life course into identifiable stages. The question of life course transitions between 'stages' raises the related issue of how *continuities* across the life course have been identified. We now turn, therefore, to examine this process in more detail, beginning with Wadsworth's (1991) longitudinal study of five and half thousand children born in the UK in 1946. This work helps explain the enduring correlation, noted since at least the 1840s, that exists between health and social class, whereby the poorest health is experienced by working class people (Blane *et al* 1998). Wadsworth is able to show that social and material advantage has a clear cumulative effect on health which becomes more marked after middle-age. This health gradient is evident across the whole population and demonstrates the effects of maternal health, particularly diet, on birth weight and on the subsequent lifetime's health of the child. So, for example, tests of cognitive ability among Wadsworth's (1991) sample showed differences at the ages of 8, 11, 15 and 26 which mapped on to birthweight differences. This is not, of course, to assume any simple causal connection, since account also needs to be taken of independent variables such as poverty and material deprivation which would result in both a lower birthweight *and* poorer educational achievement.

Situated in historical and social time, variations of this kind are, however, intrinsic to the nature of the ageing body and mind. Longitudinal studies, such as Wadsworth's, which compare age cohorts, underscore therefore the locatedness of human embodiment, rather than any easy universality. So, for example, cohorts born in 1958 were taller than those born in 1946, their children in turn being taller than their parents (Kuh and Wadsworth and Kuh *et al*, cited in Davey 2001:281).

But as well as the economic or material aspects of everyday life, we need to take account of how particular ways of (health-related) thinking may also have given progressive shape to the identity of the ageing individual. Comparisons can be made, for example, between those Westerners who grew up 70 years ago during the Depression; who aged during the world war which followed it and lived within a close-knit industrial community; or who experienced forced migration, and today's young adults, growing up in relative affluence and in communities that are scattered. Each will have experienced different expectations of everyday embodied life and different ways of making sense of the causes and the cures of illness.

Returning to Wadsworth's study, different trends in infant health illustrate this well. He points out such that while 20 children per 1,000 had tonsillectomies in 1946, that number had dropped to seven per 1,000 in 1958 (cited in Davey 2001:280). However, although an historical, particularly longitudinal, perspective can highlight the apparent contingency of such medical interventions, it cannot necessarily identify the underlying *reasons* for such changes. Was this change in tonsillectomy rate simply a reflection of changes in medical fashion? Or did it, instead, reflect the effects of the 1956 Clean Air Act which restricted the use of coal domestically and industrially, coupled with the post-war decline in cigarette smoking (Davey 2001:280)? With the rate of lower respiratory tract infection falling from 250 per 1,000 in 1946 to 130 per 1,000 for those children's children, were tonsillectomies simply no longer called for?

Alongside the detail of particular approaches to the management of child health and illness and the broader political and economic context of growing up and growing older, must therefore be set the changing demographic profile within which the individual is ageing. Thus, for example, even the *size* of age cohorts varies with historical peaks and troughs in the birth rate and this may, in itself, be important for an individual's health across the life course.

Gray (2001), for example, has suggested that being born when the birthrate is high can put pressure on resources such as welfare provision and access to employment. Thus, in western societies, individuals who are currently approaching later life – the post World War Two 'baby boomers' – face membership of a large cohort of potentially dependent people. In the UK in 1901 there were less than two million people alive over the age of 65; by 1991 there were nine million. And while the demographic profile may shift across time, the socioeconomic differences within this fluctuation that might impact differentially on health, also need to be taken into account.

For example, in 1921 60% of men aged 65 and over were still working, compared with 1990 when this proportion had fallen to 8%. So within the smaller 1921 cohort of older adults, more were in paid work. The same picture is true of women, despite the marriage bar which drove many women out of paid work. Thus, while 11% of women of 65 and over were employed in 1911, this proportion had fallen to 3% in 1990 (Gray 2001).

Looking at the global context, a comparable contemporary example might be the AIDS crisis in Africa. We can suppose, for example, that children born in the early part of the twenty-first century, and whose parents died of AIDS, may expect their economic and social conditions to become increasingly impoverished, with consequent knock-on effects for their health status as they mature into adulthood (UNICEF 2002).

A focus on the structural factors that can impact upon the relationship between health and identity across the life course therefore provides a valuable corrective to notions of health identity across the life course as voluntaristic. Instead, it calls attention to the importance of materialities such as wealth, poverty, the environments of paid employment and domestic life. It also gives some insights into the ways in which passage through particular historical eras produce particular kinds of health experiences in relation to the ageing body for the embodied individual. As Phillips and Verhasselt note, in respect of the developing world, 'a complex interrelationship exists between health and development; it is certainly not a one way relationship and there are surely reciprocal and synergistic elements to it.' (1994:4). If the health status of the population of a country is poor, individuals are unable to contribute fully to the country's economic development, a situation which in turn exacerbates poor health care provision for individuals. Conversely, where economic development takes place it 'has almost invariably been associated with improved health status via improved nutrition, hygiene and reproductive health' (1994:5).

Health Experiences across the Life Course

Although recognition of the range of structural issues that shape the ways in which the health of the body changes across the life course is clearly important, this does not explain how that life course is embodied and experienced through a series of age-related identities. As we saw in Chapter 4, although the body may be experienced as ever changing, in ways which evoke the spectres of either illness or unwanted ageing, the body also endures, carrying forward the accumulation of the changes that it has undergone. Indeed, as Hallam *et al* point out with respect to the dead body, if its 'life' ends suddenly and it becomes subject to an investigation by a coroner, then 'the body itself provides the material evidence of the life that was lived' (1999:88). It is the starting point for the construction of 'retrospective biographies' (Hallam *et al* 1999:89). Not only the bodily and emotional events immediately surrounding the death, but also 'the presence of old scars or wounds, or the marks left by medical interventions such as surgery' can, for example, all figure within the pathologist's report (Halllam *et al* 1999:99), contributing to the processes of 'identification' with which the coroner's court engages.

This suggests, therefore, that as the life course progresses so this kind of biographical information accumulates upon the body, a suggestion confirmed in a study of later life in residential care (Hockey 1990). Here interview data was supplemented with material sources of biographical information, some of them bodily:

In addition to scrapbooks, still noticeable consequences of industrial injuries to Albert's eyes and feet provided prompts for the re-telling of dramatic incidents from his working life (Hockey 1990:134).

In another case, it was his service in war time, over 60 years previously, which contributed to an elderly man's experience of embodied life in a residential home in the 1980s:

> ... it's very noticeable now, that the three of us in here that were in the First World War – there's George, big Jimmy and meself – all our legs, they're going. Sometimes we can't walk. They're afflicted in the same way ... nobody would believe it, nobody would believe it. We're suffering for it now, but there we are. It comes back now and again. I don't wake up screaming or anything like that, you know, but it doesn't affect me in that way at all. But I know when the malaria comes back and I know when the gas comes back. Feel rotten. Just have to square up to it, that's all. Frostbite. All for sixpence a day (Hockey 1990: 130–1).

These examples therefore highlight that bodily ageing across the life course, while apparently following a 'natural' path, is highly contingent, the body itself being formed precisely through its participation in the social and economic activities of everyday life. Thus, as noted in Chapter 3, the body that we *have* and *are* is not just, or only, the outcome of a biologically driven process of maturation and decline.

Such a perspective on the ageing body is, however, not only of interest for social scientists. It is also of concern for medical science itself, in revealing those factors which impact cumulatively on health and illness. Such data are, however, relatively scarce since longitudinal research requires an enormous commitment of resources. Wadsworth's (1991) study, cited above, is therefore an important example of work of this kind and illustrates the richness of the data which it can yield. In his view:

> Just as a core sample of glacial ice or pond mud can show layers of matter deposited at earlier times, when climate and foliage were not as they are today, so an age slice through the population reveals the different impacts of influences from earlier times, in the same way that layers of earlier influences accumulate and interact in the individual (Wadsworth, cited in Davey 2001:278).

In this layering up of 'influences from earlier times' we find, as in the ethnographic examples above, powerful illustration of how health and illness experiences can become core features of embodied identity. At the same time, we can also see how the changing political, social and economic environment of particular life courses acts directly upon, with and through the body itself to result in persons with different cultural and class-based social identities. This provides further evidence that, as already noted, identification is always *becoming* and is 'never a final or settled matter' (Jenkins 2004:5) for, when we examine health and illness from a life course perspective, its processual, unfinished nature becomes sovereign. Thus, while postmodernists argue that we can reinvent ourselves, discarding old identities and animating new ones, a focus on the body reminds us of its capacity to resist such processes, and the limitations of any would-be pick-and-mix life course (Hockey and James 2003).

This returns us once more, therefore, to consider the links between identity and the negotiated body by exploring the ways in which embodied individuals experience health and illness during the life course. We turn first to consider how 'old age' and illness are negotiated and embodied, mindful that, as noted above, ageing itself can take on the status of an illness as an outcome of what Armstrong (1981) refers to as the 'geriatric gaze'.

Feeling and Being Old

Conway and Hockey's (1998) study among older people living in the community in East Yorkshire shows, for example, that if people did not actually feel ill, they found it hard to identify themselves as 'elderly'. One man said that he had only started feeling his age when he had a heart attack: 'I felt too young before ... I am 71 ... how are you expected to feel when you are 71?' Here it is the concurrence of the man's chronological age and his embodied experience of a medical condition, which together create his sense of self-identity. Thus, although heart attacks are by no means restricted to older adults, as Siddell (1995) argues, in such an example old age is constructed as both the *cause* of illness *and* the time of the life when illness is expected to occur.

Medical knowledge and medical practitioners may thus constitute key reference points in older westerners' perceptions of their bodies. This provides a stark contrast with experiences of ageing in other societies where the physical signs of ageing are evaluated within cultural, rather than medicalised, frameworks and are taken to be important indicators of the elderly person approaching the 'real' world of the ancestors (Sankar 1984). Yet, in western societies, the implications of illness for age-based identity, may also be managed socially through the institutionalisation of chronological age (see Hockey and James 2003). So, as Conway and Hockey go on to show (1998), older adults might rationalise being ill as inevitable, given their chronological age; however, they would also proclaim their age with pride, in order to demonstrate that they were fitter and healthier than their peers. For example, they would assert that they were 'as well as I can be … I'll tell you first I'm going on 90' or, conversely, 'not on top of the world, but … when you come to 83 years of age you can't expect to be a spring chicken can you?' In addition, although the illness/ageing elision led some older people to assert their well-being as a way of resisting a stigmatised social identity, it also allowed them to sidestep recent health promotion's moral requirement that the individual should take responsibility for their own health (see Chapters 4 and 5). At their age, they implied, illness was not something for which they could be blamed.

Such ambivalence towards a medical pathologisation of later life is evident in many sources of data. Pound *et al*'s (1998) study of stroke among elderly Eastenders, for example, showed that it was perceived as a 'normal crisis' in people over 70. Indeed life skills built up over time enabled them to cope with it. For them, stroke posed no threat to biographical continuity, their life course narratives constituting a kind of 'social clock' used to guide expectations of such events. Indeed, paradoxically therefore, *improved* health in later life can provide a source of biographical disruption (Hockey n.d.). When interviewed, 81-year-old Louisa first described finding that her everyday activities were taking her longer:

> I don't know where that time's gone now, but I suppose I am four years older, I'm 81 … sounds silly to say I found a difference in my health, I am that much older and I know it, I'm puffing, puffing, walking down hill never mind going uphill.

However, she had recently been widowed after a long period of caring for her husband who suffered from dementia. It was this, which she drew on, when seeking to explain what was otherwise a biographically disruptive upturn in her health status:

> I feel so much better, because I was up at night for the last two years … his mind had gone … I felt so tired, so ill … and look at me now, I'm going out, and you know it's so different now … I've got a second wind you know …

Such data give insights, therefore, into the ways in which, in western societies, medicine informs older adults' perceptions of their bodies and evidences the pre-abstract, though not pre-social, starting point for seeking to make sense of changes occurring within their bodies. While the externalities of the wrinkled skin and grey hair of the object body might result in someone being ascribed the identity of 'old', data such as these suggest that an individual's encounters with health and illness may be a crucial element of the subjective *experience* of being old. For example, Ros, a 69-year-old woman interviewed in Conway's East Yorkshire study (Conway and Hockey 1998), said

> as you get older, your body gets older, and you look older. But, if you had no mirrors and no clocks you would never know that you are getting older, because the inside of your brain is still exactly the same (1998:480).

Her point was born out by another interviewee, 78-year-old Hettie, who said

> The thing is that bits of your body wear out, but inside, the essential me is still the same. The physical me is the envelope in which the letter is, and the envelope gets worn out (Conway and Hockey 1998:481).

The embodied engagement of older adults with medical knowledge and medical practice has, however, to be understood within the context where, as noted earlier, western medicine has *divided* normality from pathology by collapsing later life into illness. Thus, within the conditions of modernism it becomes apparent how both the chronologisation of the life course and the hegemony of medical knowledge together help shore up distinctive age-based identities for older people in western societies. A parallel process can be noted at the other end of the life course and it is children's embodied experiences of illness that we now go on to explore.

Being Sick as a Child

As implied above, not only are life course transitions such as the entry into adulthood or 'old age' subject to historical variation, but also the very categories through which age-based identities are assumed or attributed, are themselves mutable across time (Hockey and James 2003). Rather than emerging spontaneously or 'naturally', they are instead the outcome of extended social processes which, latterly, have made the body, as an object, increasingly central to age-based identities. Hendrick (1990), for example, has traced an entire history of western childhood which includes incommensurate notions such as the seventeenth century sinful, almost animal-like child who was in need of taming; and the nineteenth century Romantic child who personified purity and innocence. With these changing conceptions came the gradual social differentiation of children from adults. And as we have seen, the medical specialism of paediatrics, through its surveillance of the child population, gradually refined definitions of what a normal, healthy childhood should be like.

In the context of contemporary western societies to be sick as a child has therefore to be set against a view that constructs childhood as a period of dependency, marked by a joyful innocence, in which children will develop, physically and mentally, into healthy, well-rounded adults (James and Prout 1990; Jenks 1996). Unlike the case of old age, where illness confirms the aged identity of old, a sharp division is made between the well and sick child, with the latter arousing great concern. To be sick as a child, in western society, is in some senses therefore to transgress the identity of 'child'.

Thus, as Bluebond-Langner (1996) shows in her study of the impact that cystic fibrosis has on family life:

> whenever possible parents call attention to how much the child is like other children. They continue to point out the child's interest and involvement in numerous extracurricular activities, often alluding to how much more active they are then their healthy siblings (1996:174).

This is one of the many strategies that parents use to redefine what is 'normal' and, as the illness progresses, so the body has to be negotiated anew (see also Vosey 1975; Burton 1975). For example, Bluebond-Langner suggests that the child's first hospitalisation is a major change that undermines parents' identification of their child as normal and engenders a process of reidentification that intensifies as the disease takes hold. In the case of the UK baby who was 'declared blind, deaf, severely disabled and with only a 5% chance of surviving the winter' when she was born in 2003, her parents have similarly highlighted her 'normal' social behaviour in their appeals against the ruling that she should not be ventilated if her condition deteriorates. 'Charlotte can see and hear and show enjoyment when she is bathed or tickled', they point out, noting that what the hospital trust's lawyer describes as a 'perilously sick child' can sit in a chair, be taken outside the hospital building and potentially be taken home (*The Guardian*, 26th August 2005).

Elsewhere, however, ill-health and sickness during childhood is, if not expected, certainly more commonplace as evidenced by high child mortality figures. Scheper-Hughes (1992) argues that among the poorest people in Brazil who live in the shantytown of Alto do Cruzeiro, childhood is regarded as a time when children die, rather than a time for growth and development, as in the more affluent parts of the country. Thus, for example, she describes the answer given by Nailza de Arruda, a Brazilian woman of mixed Indian and white ancestry, to her question 'Why do the church bells ring so often?': 'It's nothing … just another little angel gone to heaven' said Nailza (1992:268). The woman herself had had many children who had died, few surviving for more than a month. This 'indifference' was absent only in the case of a child called Joana, who, Scheper-Hughes says, 'Nailza had dangerously allowed herself to love' (1992:268). She had lived for a year and at baptism had been optimistically placed under the protection of Joan of Arc whose care was expected to ensure her survival. Unlike her other dead children, Joana occupied Nailza's thoughts and inspired emotional outpourings.

In trying to make sense of the 'indifference' to child deaths which she observes everywhere among the poor women of Brazil, Scheper-Hughes notes that the medicalised concept of 'child mortality' tends to emerge only in specific conditions. Referring to 'the mundaneness and ubiquitousness of child death – a fairly permanent feature of the history of childhood until quite recently' – she points out that it was, in part, the inclusion of women into the western medical profession which led to the 'discovery of child mortality' (1992:273). Malnutrition and diarrhea are the two conditions which contribute most to infant death – and in the first case, Scheper-Hughes (1992) argues, its *social* nature, as an aspect of poverty went unrecognised, frailty being seen as intrinsic to certain children. In the second case, of diarrhea, its pervasiveness and popularly perceived 'triviality', led doctors to obscure its potency as a killer, for fear that their failure to treat it effectively would make them seem incompetent. Thus, while 'child mortality' may have emerged as a cause for concern during the twentieth century, its presence among some populations was more at issue than among others. Scheper-Hughes cites Foucault's statement about the rural and urban poor: 'It was of little importance whether *these* people lived or died, since their reproduction was [thought of] as something that took care of itself in any case' (1992:275). She goes on to discuss the many Third World countries where:

> The naturalness of infant and child mortality has yet to be questioned, and parents may understand a baby's life as a provisional and undependable thing – a candle whose flame is likely to flicker and go out as to burn brightly and continuously. There, child death may be viewed less as a tragedy than as a predictable and relatively minor misfortune, one to be accepted with equanimity and resignation as an unalterable fact of human existence (1992:275).

In radical contrast to such a view, contemporary western conceptions of childhood are predominantly bound to notions of health, an inverted mirror-image of the way in which ideas of old age blur with those of illness. Given this emphasis, it is therefore important to consider how children themselves experience sickness and ill-health in western societies.

Alderson's (1993) work on children's consent to surgery in England provides some initial insights. In her study of children undergoing orthopaedic surgery for leg-lengthening she shows how adult conceptions of children's dependency and incompetence, combined with a desire to protect them, can limit the amount of information children are given about their medical condition and subsequent operations. This leaves children feeling not only confused and frightened, but also angry when they are not consulted about their wishes and feelings in respect of the surgical procedures they will have to undergo.

The majority of children, however, will not experience lengthy and painful surgery; nor will they have to come to terms with serious illness. It is important, therefore, to consider children's experiences of more common complaints in order to understand how it is that they come to know that they are ill and what that bodily experience of illness means to them. As we explored in Chapter 6 it is through their everyday interactions with adults that children come to recognise what the signs of illness are (Prout and Christensen 1996). However, importantly, as Christensen (1993) showed in her earlier study of children's playground accidents, once we pay attention to children's embodied experience of illness we gain insight into the ways in which they participate in the negotiations that take place around the instability of the body during illness. She suggests, for example, that when children ask adults to look at cuts and bruises they are simply asking that – that adults should look, and note, the changes their body has undergone. Children are not necessarily seeking help or interventions. However, adults' greater experience in dealing with the body's instability and propensity for change – and their lack of 'child-like' curiosity – explains why adults often dismiss children's claims for attention. Adults only regard bodily symptoms that endure as warranting attention as 'illness'; unlike children, they are not interested in the minor cuts and bruises that simply reveal the indeterminacy of the body.

As in the case of older adults, children's embodied experiences of illness therefore have to be contextualised by both the expectations of their categorical position in the life course and their everyday engagement with medicine and medical professionals as well as with authoritative others, such as parents or teachers, for it is through these social relationships that the body's identity – as well or ill – is produced.

Conclusion

This chapter has sought to explain the ways in which the body is negotiated across the life course as individuals come to know whether they are well or ill. As we saw, while the diagnosis of illness acts to confirm the social identity of 'elderly', it renders the sick child transgressive. However, the chapter has also explored the ways in which knowledge of age-specific well-being is produced and reproduced, through the hegemonic power of medicine in providing particular medicalised framings of illness and, indeed, of the life course itself. While structural inequalities and cultural differences contribute to the different life courses that individuals take, it is also clear that these have to be situated in historical time. Thus, through the course of a life, an individual may not only experience illness in different ways, given the different meanings attached to age and the range of different resources that individuals may have to draw on, but may also have to negotiate the materiality of the body itself which, unstable and ever changing, resists attempts to fix and tame it.

8

Negotiating the Body's Limits

Writing about the role of genetics in the context of race and identity in contemporary Brazil, Santos (2004) shows that a survey carried out on the DNA of Brazilians, designed to reveal their genetic history, had unforeseen consequences in that it provoked an intense public debate in 2000. The 'Molecular Portrait of Brazil', as the study was called, sought to identify how much Amerindian, European and African elements were present in contemporary Brazilians. The geneticists argued that since their results proved the prevalence of miscegenation in Brazil, this had contributed significantly to Brazilian identity and their research should therefore be used to support resistance to racism in Brazilian society. It was an argument, however, that was 'far from being perceived as the only (or preferred) path to be followed' and, indeed, 'in the opinion of certain social segments it [was] actually seen as potentially oppressive' (2004:351). Santos therefore demonstrates that an advance in medical science, such as genetics, potentially 'not only reshapes the biological, cultural and social loci in the immediate surroundings of individuals, but also reconfigures wide-ranging, macro-social, historical and political relations' (2004:347–8).

While this seems a very large claim to make about the reach of a microcosmic body 'part', what it alerts us to are the ways in which technology is reconfiguring the materiality of the body, as well as our ideas about its capacities and potential. In addition, Santos' statement draws attention to the fact that the body's health or illness is, in a very real sense, no longer confined within and by the individual body. In the context of the global, technological changes that have and will continue to make a difference to experiences of health and illness, the concept of the negotiated body, that we have been exploring through this volume, therefore takes on a new significance for our identities as embodied individuals.

A focus on medical technology therefore allows us to consider what happens when the materiality of the body is changed as a result of technolo-

156

gical interventions of different kinds. However, whilst we have opened our discussion by referring to the new genetics and its implications, we need to bear in mind that medical technology has a history. It comprises far more than simply the latest high tech developments that, seemingly, give scientists deeper and deeper access into the body's interior. Though recent examples of how medical science can monitor and intervene in our bodily lives do offer more condensed and powerful examples of what technology might do to and with the body, at present their availability is limited outside western societies. Alongside them, therefore, we need to consider the role of more mundane and commonplace technologies – the blood test, the x-ray, the ultrasound, the stethoscope, the inhaler – and how these also might shape our health and identities. Although now very much taken for granted and unremarkable, such devices are also the outcome of technical knowledge. They too reflect the application of science in finding solutions to the health-related problems of the body that all people experience at some time in their lives:

> Medicine forms an archaeology of layer upon layer of technologies from the most mundane band-aids and pencils to sophisticated machines such as MRIs and artificial hearts, from virtually neutral infusion pumps to highly symbolic procedures such as the drug Viagra or genetic tests (Timmermans and Berg 2003:98–9)

However, although this chapter's discussion acknowledges the broad sweep of available technologies, we do not consider the full range. Rather, what we wish to highlight is the role of medical technologies within the dynamic negotiation of the body, embodiment and social identity. And in so doing, we show how medical technology can bring the body's materiality into question by offering scope for the creation of new kinds of bodies and therefore new forms of embodiment. Here, therefore, we not only insist that the body's indeterminate materiality must reside at the core of any sociological attempt to explain how we come to know that we are ill – but we are also exploring bio-medicine's potential for radically *transforming* that materiality. Thus, in the course of this chapter we will be examining the implications of medical technology for embodied life and how these are perceived by different individuals and interest groups.

Technology in Practice

We begin with Timmermans and Berg's (2003) account of three positions which social scientists have adopted *vis-à-vis* technology's relationship with medicine. The first they term, technological determinism, a critical approach in which technology is understood to enhance medical control and provide an additional tool in the armoury of the weapons that sustain the hegemony of western medical science. A second approach identified by Timmermans and Berg is social essentialism. Here, in direct contrast to technological determinism, 'medical technologies are viewed as blank slates to be interpreted and rendered meaningful by culture' (2003:101). However, the third perspective – the one we adopt here – is concerned with exploring technology *in practice*, a view which argues that 'technology might *do* things ... but what it does and how it accomplishes something remains an open empirical question' (Timmermans and Berg 2003).

Combining a technology-in-practice approach with the insights of cultural phenomenology, this chapter therefore considers agency and experience as valuable points from which to understand the way that technology shapes social identity. In this sense, as in previous chapters, rather than seeking to write the body *into* existing sociological understandings of structure and agency, and examine their relationship or inter-meshing, we view 'the body' as the *product* of embodied engagement with the span of health technologies. As already argued in Chapter 3, embodied experience in different cultural and social contexts is likely to produce a diversity of understandings of the body. Thus, for example, what many westerners understand by 'the body' is something which emerges out of their experience of embodiment within the technologised environment of contemporary western society and which constitutes what Shildrick calls 'the sovereign self, and ... the bounded body' (2002:5).

As we shall show, this is because technology works powerfully to obscure individuals' awareness that 'corporeality is a dynamic process', something that is hidden by 'the static universalisation of the body image' (Shildrick 2002:4). We are asking, therefore, how technology operates to produce 'the body' as a stable entity and how the social positioning of bodies is a negotiated, and indeed sometimes highly contested, process. What we reveal here, then, is the scope of medical technology to occupy a mediating role within the process of social identification, and the implications that this has for our embodiment.

In the previous chapter, for example, we saw how age-based social identities, and their associated life course categories, were in part the outcome of nineteenth and twentieth century medicalising processes that began to incorporate aspects of human life previously seen as being beyond the limits of curative medicine – childhood and later life. In this chapter we retain this concern with the life course, but place it within the context of other aspects of embodied identity, to explore how medical technologies have, in practice, the potential to transform not only our categories of 'health' and 'illness' but also a whole range of associated social identities, at both the local and a more global level. In this respect, therefore, medical technologies have the capacity to mediate and diversify identities across the life course – creating life, sustaining a youthful appearance, enabling mobility and independence, prolonging life, and averting death.

The Medical Encounter Resituated

We begin by exploring the links between 'medicine' and 'technology' and how they might be situated within the relationship that exists between the doctor and the patient, discussed in earlier chapters (see Chapters 2 and 4). Is there a discrepancy, for example, between the intersubjective quality of the consultation process, which relies on conversational exchanges that are, potentially, open to a variety of interpretations (see Chapters 1 and 7), and the high tech interventions of scanners and surgery that appear to offer greater precision and certainty, leaving little scope for interpretation? If so, does technology therefore work to reframe the medical encounter and the production of medical knowledge by augmenting the doctor's power? And what outcomes might that have for the doctor and for the patient?

In addressing these questions, we draw on Foucault's (1973) conception of the medical gaze (see Chapter 2). This suggests that, as the doctor examines the patient in particular ways and diagnoses their disease, so the patient's body and their management of it are constructed accordingly (see also Good 1994). This raises the question of what difference the results of scans and blood tests, for example, might make to that encounter. While, it is clear that scientific knowledge is core to the doctor's training and is echoed in technologies whose design and use are based on the principles of scientific rationality, we can still ask what outcomes technologies have for medical *practice*? For Willis (1994) the answer is clear. While in other occupations technology typically puts jobs at risk by replacing the worker themself, in medicine, technology *augments* the power of the 'worker'. It extends the scope of the medical gaze and of its role in constructing the patient's body.

It comes as no surprise, therefore, that even within forms of alternative or complementary medicine, practitioners can find themselves in thrall to technology, despite its oppositional stance to bio-medicine. Thus, as McClean shows in his ethnographic study of the work of crystal healers at a healing centre in the north-east of England, the practitioners reveal 'a degree of engagement with the language and science of biomedicine' (2003:487). For example, when beginning work on a patient, healers purify or cleanse their instruments – the crystals – in a small hand basin, one of a range of ritual actions that mimic the practices of bio-medical practitioners. Healers also use, what they call 'laser crystals' or 'laser wands' as part of their practice. The points of these long thin crystals are said to emit healing energy that can both open up and close the spiritual body which is suffering from sickness. As McClean argues:

> The image of crystal healing energy pouring into the spiritual body makes it seem more akin to the penetrative act of certain biomedical instruments – for example, the surgeon's scalpel (2003:489).

In another example, McClean describes the 'injection' given to Teresa, a client, by Charlie, a crystal healer:

> Then he appeared to grasp what seemed like an imaginary hypodermic needle, and started to enact the filling of it and the subsequent injection of the imaginary substance into the lump. This was performed in an exaggerated manner and was repeated three times. Each time he pulled the needle away he seemed to empty it onto the floor, before refilling and pressing it back into the lump (2003:492).

For McClean, such practices can be seen to parody bio-medicine through a kind of metaphorisation, so demonstrating its continued hegemony even within the context of complementary or alternative medical regimes.

Indeed, it is a hegemony that is increasingly sustained by the use of technologies of all kinds. As Willis (1994) argues, technology is now a fundamental part of patients' expectations of professionals' expert resources. Thus, although many medical tasks involve the kind of technology which can be delegated to lower status nursing staff – applying dressings, dispensing drugs, giving injections, taking specimens – Willis suggests there is a division between these *mechanical* technical tasks and those technologies whose uses are much more indeterminate. These are said to involve interpersonal skills, clinical judgements, and 'flair' or 'knack'. It is these latter technologies that sustain the power of the doctor in particular.

In the case of surgery, for example, there is a high ratio of indeterminate to technical or mechanical elements. These include technologies such as the stethoscope, the ophthalmoscope and x-rays. All of these technological resources allow the inside of the patient's body to be scrutinised, monitored and subsequently interpreted – with skill – by the doctor. Thus, rather than the patient being the source of knowledge through narrating their illness to the doctor, it is their body – in the form of an object – which is, quite literally, 'looked into'. Through the power of *looking*, rather than hearing, scientific evidence of the patient's condition is achieved by the use of these technologies. This constitutes a powerful enhancement, therefore, of the 'medical gaze' since it is the doctor who assesses and interprets the evidence that the technologies produce.

Coming into clinical use in 1896, x-rays, for example, allowed doctors, for the first time, to diagnose in the absence of the patient. Their body, or a part of it, became objectified in the x-ray image which could then travel around the hospital for scrutiny elsewhere. This technology paved the way for later ultrasound scanning, particularly of the foetus, CT scanning and then nuclear magnetic resonance imaging (NMR) of potential tumours. Thus, in hospital medicine, where the bedside and the ceremonial ward round have been, and indeed remain, the fixed sites at which doctor and patient encounter one another, and where medical knowledge of the body is created, Willis (1994) reminds us that the patient's body is now nonetheless technologically dispersed around the hospital. Images and samples of body parts and other organic material are sent to different specialist departments. In this sense, therefore, it would seem that the patient's own embodied experience becomes less significant, the greater the number of technologies that are employed to comprehend it.

For example, as Atkinson's (1995) work on haematology laboratories demonstrates, the samples of blood and bone marrow that are taken from a patient's body act as texts that have to be interpreted by haematologists. Though apparently taking place according to scientific principles of rationality and objectivity, reading the material through the microscope is revealed as an indeterminate process. As Atkinson shows, *negotiations* take place among haematologists seeking a consensus, the vocabulary, skill and the reputation of these high status individuals uncannily resembling that of wine buffs:

> the haematologist needs to be able to describe blood, its constituents and traces. These registers of practical recognition are learned and reinforced through the shared talk of instruction and rounds. They are organized socially through the vocabularies and imagery that are shared among physicians and scientists (1995:73).

This sharing of knowledge and experience, which helps medical professionals to determine the body and its ills, is facilitated, of course, by a shared training and Good (1994) shows how medical students' learning about the body is augmented by their experiences in the anatomy laboratory (see Chapter 3). Here students learn to read the body differently; it is a different world where a 'phenomenological reconstruction of the body' takes place (see also Chapter 3). As Good suggests, what is going on in the anatomy laboratory, through the use of a range of technologies such as the scalpel and the microscope, is the 'reconstruction of the person appropriate to the medical gaze, identified as a body, a case, a patient or a cadaver ... [which] ... is essential to a student becoming a competent physician' (1994:73).

Such examples might, therefore, suggest that the dispersal and fragmenta-tion of the sick body – whether through its distillation into smaller and smaller units of observation and analysis, or through its distribution in and across dif-ferent departments of a hospital – simply enhances the power of the medical profession, at the expense of the embodied experiences of individuals. However, the research presented below reveals that this is too simplistic an account.

Indeterminacy and Interpretation

Although Draper's (2002a; 2002b) work on ultrasound imaging shows how medical technologies can enhance the doctor's professional status and exper-tise, ultrasound imaging of the foetus also opens up interpretive opportunities for parents-to-be and their families by allowing their familial identities to shift and develop. Ultrasound is not, therefore, simply a diagnostic tool that helps doctors to increase their monopoly over the body. What Draper's work details are the ways in which this technology enables child and parental identities to materialise *prior* to birth, simultaneously calling into question how the life course is experienced and understood (see Chapter 7). Ultrasound screening is therefore an important resource in transforming the meaning of the birth of 'the body'. No longer does this signal the birth of the child's *social* identity, since, thanks to the scanned image, it already has one. Through interviews with men during and after their female partners' pregnancies, it became apparent that men saw ultrasound as a window into the pregnant body. Steve, a man about to become a father for the first time, said:

> Afterwards I was sort of, a couple of days, completely dazed because that was the first time that it (fatherhood) really crystallised into anything. Up until then it was just a sort of vague blobby thing that was going to happen seven months away. It was going to happen at the end of the summer. And since then it has felt real, it has felt as though there's a human being (2002b:780).

This example underscores our argument that the categories of health and illness have a wider social resonance, one which extends beyond simply iden-tifying the patient's *medical* condition or status. Many of the men whom Draper interviewed had placed the ultrasound scan in the new family album, a practice fostered by hospitals as they hand out a copy in a gift card frame. That the image has a primarily *diagnostic* purpose, however, is something which can escape fathers, as the man below indicates:

> And it was only while I was there that I realised that it was to check the well-being of the baby. Has it got all its limbs and is it the right shape and eyes and

everything else. So it suddenly became a bit scary. Erm, because you start thinking 'shit' you know, this could be a problem (2002b:787).

In addition to enabling or enhancing identification as a 'parent', the ultrasound image also abstracts the baby from the mother, giving it an independent identity as 'fetal patient', with a status and rights that can conflict very directly with those of the mother (see Chapter 7).

Yet, as Hockey and Draper (2005) argue, while the ultrasound image, like the x-ray, has the status of the real, as Sawday (1995) points out, the ultrasound 'baby' is simply a technologically generated representation which has to be read and interpreted by technicians, in a similar fashion to the blood samples around which haematologists cluster (Atkinson 1995). In this sense, therefore, 'power' might be said to remain with the medical profession since it is they who are skilled in making such readings. However, precisely because ultrasound technology makes it possible for the child to be *seen*, it secures for the foetus an embodied social identity which is shared by fathers and other family members who lack the mother's sensory experiences of the child's *in utero* activities. The materiality of the ultrasound image thus resources the imaginative processes through which partners, other family members and healthcare professionals transcend the boundaries of the mother's 'container' body to access embodied knowledge of the child-to-be.

What this example therefore reveals is that the indeterminacy of the body plays a key part in the network of power that medical technology sustains and enhances. Just as the body is an entity in continual flux (see Chapters 1 and 3), one which medical science then seeks to know and stabilise via a technologically based, universalising and normalising canon of knowledge, so the *products* and *applications* of medical technology are also powerful extensions of a kind of medical mystique into the social realm of everyday life. As noted in the previous chapter, for example, intensive care units and maternity wards are sites where the indeterminacy of the bodily processes of birth and death are managed via technological imperatives (Harvey 1996, 1997). But when that management fails, the body's indeterminacy is suddenly exposed in ways that put the individual's embodied identity at risk. Thus, for example, premature babies and older adults who are kept alive through technological means can become the problematic and protracted focus of legal disputes. Their embodiment depends not just on being and having a body (see Chapter 3), but on the technological extensions to the body that enable, and indeed, permit the materiality of their body to be sustained. In such cases, though the boundaries and the limits of the body are extended, they remain ill-defined. Embodiment and social identity become, themselves, matters for negotiation.

Place (2000:172), for example, describes the ways in which, within the paediatric intensive care unit, the embodiment of very sick children becomes radically transformed. Through a form of rite of passage (see Chapter 6) which involves attaching the child to a whole variety of machines and monitors, children 'lie enigmatically between being alive and being dead, and between being social and non-social entities' (2000:174). Motionless on the bed, the corporeal body of the sick child becomes, he suggests, 'technomorphic', its boundaries:

> delineated by the mathematical rationality of the PICU. Cardiac monitors display heart *rates*, urinary catheter bags collect *amounts* of urine, mechanical ventilators deliver breaths of particular *sizes*, intravenous drips infuse various *volumes* of fluid, electronic pumps deliver specific *quantities* of drugs, temperature probes indicate varying *degrees* of heat, blood pressure transducers display varying *numbers* etc (2000:177).

Attending to the sick child, the nurses read these signs and numbers, Place (2000) argues, translating and inscribing them onto the large paper observation chart, while also observing the child. This means that although this chart then has a direct relationship to the corporeal child, it has been constructed by the nurses. In this sense, the chart comes to 'represent' or constitute the child. As a result, experienced nurses have to work hard to maintain the *human* elements of this network of relationships since it now contains a new and ambiguous kind of body.

That advances in medical technology open up the possibility of new forms of embodiment is also shown by Lock (2003). She suggests that what has been produced by medical technology is a new kind of hybrid body/corpse, one that is 'as-good-as-dead'. As she notes, within western medical science brain death has, over the last 30 years, come to be regarded as the end of life. However, this clinical concept can, in practice, be difficult to establish as an embodied, rather than a technically ascribed identity. Thus, Lock argues, for many physicians and others caring for those who are living in a permanent vegetative state, 'it is difficult to ignore the signs of life that constantly bombard the senses', such as the warmth of the skin and lengthening hair and nails (2003:172). When such patients are declared dead and professionals working in ICUs have 'to participate in transforming patients into organ donors', the indeterminacy of the body then brings on radical doubt. Lock says:

> One physician with more than fifteen years experience said that he sometimes lies in bed at night after sending a brain-dead body for organ procurement and asks himself, 'Was that patient *really* dead? It is irreversible – I know that, and the clinical tests are infallible. My rational mind is sure, but some nagging, irrational doubt seeps in' (2003:173).

It is to unpacking such difficulties that we now turn, through an exploration of some of the more recent developments in medical technology – and the debates which they stimulate about the body and its health and identity.

Bodies and Technology as Embodied Practice

Just as this book draws extensively on social scientists' critiques of a biologically determined view of health, so we view the actions and technologies of medical science as not simply instrumental. Instead, we see them occupying a place within complex social networks (Latour 1993) that contain both animate and inanimate elements, and consider the extent to which medical technologies themselves have a capacity for agency in relation to the body. Having therefore examined the place of technologies within more or less professionalised hierarchies, we now move on to focus more specifically on their *effects*, following the example of Prout's (1996) analysis of the metred dose inhaler used by asthma sufferers.

What Prout's (1996) work shows is that changes in the inhaler's design come about as result of ongoing relationships between doctors, patients and the technology itself. In other words, medical technologies of this kind have an agency of *effect*, if not intention and, according to Latour, *all* the elements of such a network have effects, by virtue of their position of relatedness to one another. For our purposes, this means that not only doctors, but also medical technologies and the human body itself, have their own effects – or agency – and therefore the view of the body as a stable or predictable object *itself* has effects.

Shildrick, for example, demonstrates an elision between the western container body and 'the normalcy and closure of the centred self' (2002:3). The *effect* of this objectification of the body, in her view, therefore, is not simply to create difference between what she terms 'monstrous' bodies, such as conjoined twins and others whose bodies more closely adhere to the ideal of morphological containment. Rather, she argues, those bodies categorised as 'monstrous' destabilise individuals' embodied perceptions of their own autonomous corporeality, by reflecting back to them 'the leaks and flows, the vulnerabilities' of their own embodied being (2002:4). Hence the fascination and fear inspired by the 'deviant' body, its stigmatisation and indeed the conceptual and social distances which this introduces between people.

In discussing the effects of advances in medical science and technology, then, we need to take account of the agency of different objectifications of the body and as a result, the different social and moral values that are attached to them. Importantly, then, these views of the body need to be recognised as both integral to the development of medical technologies *and* an outcome of their design and implementation. Indeed, as we shall go on to detail, recent advances in medical technology have raised questions about the body's limits, both in terms of the fleshy boundaries that are usually conceptualised as the limits of the self, and also about the body's scope for modification, cloning and transplantation.

This therefore problematises the social scientific notion that the western container body is a particular form of embodiment that is different from others. Thus, although comparisons are commonly made within anthropology between the western container body and a more traditional, usually non-western form of interdependent embodiment (Becker 1995; Lakoff and Johnson 1980) (see Chapter 3), this comparison may no longer be useful.

For example, describing the relation of the self to the body in Fiji Becker says: 'in the context of an intensified degree of embeddedness in social relations (and perhaps less in one's body), cultivation of the body is not legitimated as an exclusively personal enterprise' (1995:37; see also Chapter 3). In the west, however, as she describes, the notion is that the self has jurisdiction over the body. Citing Giddens, she argues that the (western) body is reflexively appropriated as part of the 'project of the self' and in this sense is a fundamental part of the individuals that we think ourselves to be. However, as this chapter goes on to explore, this western commitment to achieving autonomous corporeality (Shildrick 2002) may no longer be achievable in the context of global medical science and technology.

To begin to make sense of what this might mean for our experiences of embodiment, Fernandez's account of rhetorical metaphoric strategies that 'make manageable objects of the self or of others and facilitate performance' proves useful (1972:42). For Fernandez, these strategies reside in the figures of speech or metaphors that we use in everyday life to explain or comprehend phenomena. Such devices provide 'a way of avoiding building up precise intellectual structures' (1972:42). They therefore introduce a degree of flexibility into the kinds of concepts and ideas that we use to understand the world.

Thus, for example, as we shall see in this chapter, medical technology is able to reposition the body in the social space of the life course: it breathes new life into a body that was almost dead. This means the body can no longer be made to take up a fixed position by medical science, in the way it once was. What the potentialities of new forms of medical technology open up, therefore, are contexts which demand that new metaphors or models of the body are brought into play, as a kind of rhetorical metaphoric strategy, at different points in the life course. In this sense, negotiations about the body may be intensifying. In the network that combines, at a very minimum, patients, bodies, doctors and technologies the body is opened up for contestation, rather than simply being directed towards stability as it once was. The result is, as Fernandez argues, that we metaphorically change the 'ballgame' as the perspectives through which the body is seen and understood begin to shift (1972:45).

We see this exemplified in the high profile debates that surround the use of advanced technologies that radically transform the body. For example, the once stable gendered body becomes destabilised by transsexuals seeking surgical gender reassignment in order to have a different kind of life course. Similarly post-menopausal women are now able to conceive a child and become a parent in later life through new reproductive technologies (see *The Times* 9th March 2004). Other body-focused innovations, made available via medical technology, centre around commodified body parts and the organic material that passes between individuals – organ transplantation; donor insemination; surrogate pregnancy; gene therapy; and designer babies with organs destined for a sick sibling. In almost all cases, these developments have attracted intense and polarised arguments.

In an extended example, explored below, we show that these debates hinge on the rhetorical use of the following models or metaphors of the body: the *individualised* body; the *commodified* body; and the *relational* body. The intervention of medical technology therefore stimulates conceptual and rhetorical shifts and slippages, between sets of cultural and moral values associated with these different kinds of bodies.

However, in claiming this relationship between medical technology and the body we are not embracing a purely discursive account. Rather, our intention is to look more closely into the production of the body via engagement-within-the-world. And in this case, it is a world where medical technologies can shape human reproduction and survival in previously unimaginable ways. What we explore here, therefore, is the play of contestation or conflict within the processes of perception and objectification that arise out of the existential condition of embodiment.

Individual Bodies, Commodified Bodies and Relational Bodies

We focus first on the commodified body that has been made visible through techniques of organ transplantation. This body now occupies an important place within the arena of global capitalism, its value constituted by 'the incredible expansion of possibilities through recent advances in biomedicine, transplant surgery, experimental genetic medicine, biotechnology and the science of genomics' (Scheper-Hughes 2002:3). As Scheper-Hughes argues, commodified bodies are '*both* objects and semi-magical and symbolic representations' and, like commodities everywhere, she says, they are 'heavy with social meanings and significations' (2002:2). And yet, as she also notes, neo-classical economists and certain bioethicists see no discontinuities between the market in bodies and their parts and the exchange of any other kinds of goods and services. Autonomous control over one's own body, the freedom to buy and to sell parts thereof, would seem therefore to be a liberating aspect of the contemporary global free market. Indeed, as Scheper-Hughes describes, people wishing to sell their kidneys and brokers seeking kidneys to buy, are all now part of a well-established 'black market in organ and tissue sales' such that the kidney has now become 'an *organ of opportunity* for the buyer and an *organ of last resort* for the seller' (2002:51). And, as Scheper-Hughes observes, 'commercialized transplant medicine has allowed global society to be divided into two decidedly unequal populations – organ givers and organ receivers' which mostly, though not exclusively, mirrors the usual economic division between the rich North and poor South (2002:4).

However, at the same time, what this new spirit of liberation with regard to the body has also effected is the paradoxical dissolution of the boundaries *between* bodies. Thus, while the integrity of the individual body remains highly valued – and indeed, as we have seen in previous chapters, may be increasing in its value in western consumer societies (Featherstone and Hepworth 1991) – its achievement may only be possible, for some individuals, through technologies which have simultaneously exploited the commodified bodies of others. And, thus, in this way, the individual body inevitably becomes a relational one. So, while for some, surgery replaces the failed features of the individual body, for others, whose organs are their only capital, surgery commoditises the body.

But this is not the only effect that the technology of transplantation can have. When organs are transplanted from the bodies of relatives – and indeed we now have the possibility of creating foetuses through artificial insemination which carry the organic material necessary to save or enhance a sibling's life – the boundaries between the individual body and the embodied bodies of others become particularly confused. More profound questions about social identity and the individual body are therefore raised. In the process of transplantation, *each* body becomes relational through the exchange of tissues, one to another.

Lock (2002), in her work on organ transplantation from the dead to the living, describes this kind of relatedness existing between donor and recipient. Data from a 37-year-old man who had been given a liver transplant reveals this. He says: 'I'd really like to know more about the donor. I dream about it … I feel an emotion for him that I can't even describe, and I don't think I want to lose that, ever' (2002:30). Yet this form of relatedness somehow disturbs broader cultural conceptions of autonomous corporeality. As the interviewee goes on to say: 'the donor family sometimes wants to build up a lasting relationship with the recipient, and the authorities don't want that' (2002:30).

The implications that this kind of technological application can have for social identity – the question as to where one body/person starts and another ends – becomes particularly poignant in cases of so-called designer babies. In 2003, for example, an embryologist applied to the human fertilisation and embryology authority (HFEA) on behalf of the Hashimi family whose four-year-old son suffers an ultimately terminal inherited blood disorder (Dyer 2003). The embryologist wanted permission to perform the pre-implantation genetic diagnosis (PGD) necessary to choose the embryo of a child without this disorder so that blood from their umbilical cord could be used to cure the sick child. After initial, unprecedented agreement, the HFEA was then taken to court by Core (Comment on Reproductive Ethics) on the grounds that only treatment designed to 'assist women to carry children' is sanctioned, not procedures which might help a sick child. In play here are the individualised and relational bodies of a four-year-old boy and his parents as the child faces 'a miserable quality of life with an unknown demise at any stage' (Dyer 2003:17). In addition, the generation of embryos in order to assist with medical treatment – as well as the discarding of these embryos if the match is incorrect – problematically also transforms the embryo into a commodified body.

What the above examples draw to our attention, therefore, are the ways in which, as decisions about the use of technology are being made, the competing agendas of different interest groups are articulated through different metaphors of the body. Each metaphor has a different kind of moral entailment in relation to identity, personhood and the embodied self.

Health, Identity and New Reproductive Technologies

While the status of the embryo is a familiar focus for contestation (see Chapter 7), new reproductive technologies have added extra layers to these debates. However, the seriousness with which the choice to abort a foetus is treated – by both its potential parents and by the legal and medical profession – reveals the conceptual, rather than technological, difficulties of abstracting this small collection of cells from the *individual* embodied personhoods of both its parents and its *individual* future embodied self. But once there exists scope for arresting the development of the embryo, whilst maintaining its viability through freezing, new and more pressing problems arise. Its potential life can only be realised through its *commodification* in different ways.

First, stem cells taken from the embryos under 14-days-old and generated via in vitro fertilisation (IVF) can be used to repair damaged organs or bodily systems in other people. Their pluripotency enables them to transform themselves into specialised cells in any part of the body. This strategy has been condemned as the *commodification* of human life by the Vatican and by anti-abortion groups. One campaigner described this practice as nothing more than expediency 'simply because we have the most permissive environment in the world for this kind of research' (*Independent* 29th April 2003). Such a view sees human life as embodied within these cells and that to employ them in medicine in this way is to misuse them, to treat them simply as if they were a commodity. Comparably, as Lock says of the transplantation of organs from the dead to the living: 'Only when corpses could be conceptualised as neutral biological objects, as part of nature and therefore autonomous and without cultural baggage, was it possible (for medical men, at least) to divest them of social, moral, and religious worth' (2002:39).

However, in a newspaper article (*Independent* 29th April 2003) which cautiously reported on the development of stem cell research, the commodification of this embryonic cellular material was downplayed. Instead, it became imbued with positive and moral worth through the use of particular images – of children or famous people, tragically disabled by illnesses that such new technologies might relieve. Examples here included Christopher Reeves, accidentally paralysed, and Iris Murdoch, mentally incapacitated through Alzheimers. Both these people might have benefited from such technological developments. Arguably, therefore, these highly personalised images were being used to frame one of the most exciting areas of medical research (*Independent* 29th April 2003), in order to obviate concern or moral outrage that what this practice rests upon, in fact, is the medical profession's capacity to mobilise commodified bodies.

But what exactly is taking place here and how and why might the personification of this technology by famous people seem to take the sting out of the commodified tail? The answer would seem to lie in the ways in which social identification takes place within the life course, in and round the different valuations of the different kinds of bodies. When the developing bodies of children, or the 'superman' body of Christopher Reeves, become the site of incurable damage, we find the moral worth attached to the *relational* body being mobilised. That is to say, identification with the plight of children or Christopher Reeves is achieved by emphasising that part of another individual with which we identify or invest ourselves. We put ourselves, metaphorically, into their shoes, into their position within the life course. By doing this, the associated *commodification* of other unknown bodies and their cellular material is thereby strategically downplayed.

Thus, when the newspaper also cautiously reports the use of stem cells from the patient's *own* healthy organs, all objections disappear. Now, the possibility of using cells from the patient's *own* body, becomes newsworthy in a different way, since through this internal cellular transfer no material need leave the bounded, enselved body of the western individual. Here, then, investment in cure is not only personalised but also managed within the framework of more traditional conceptualisations of medical interventions and of western notions of the individual body. Social identity remains intact and moreover can be made to endure across the life course – the mediation of identity here being between a 'sick' and a 'well' self, rather than between one person and another.

The new reproductive technologies described here also enable the birth of children who began life as 'spare' embryos (*Independent* 29th April 2003), 'left over from IVF treatment' (*Guardian* 12th June 2003). Out of *commodified* cellular material, therefore, identity or personhood becomes possible through the development of another *individualised* body. This move from commodity to person might, at first, seem unproblematic for, in comparison with the use of stem cells, discussed above, a reverse process is in operation. Here, however, we become aware of the values attached to the body and just how 'heavy with social meanings and signification' (Scheper-Hughes 2002:2), the *commodified* body can become. When it comes to 'spare' IVF embryos, described as the 'left-over specks of life' (Weale 2003), these by-products of assisted conception are seen as posing a threat. Rather than being encompassed within the boundary of the mother's individual body, these frozen embryos have the potential in the course of time – in their own life course, as it were – to themselves have an effect as *commodified* bodies, by putting in motion a set of uneasy relationships between the egg donor, their family and the embryo recipient.

Thus, for example, Sarah Parks who had five embryos left in store after she finished her IVF cycle said 'It was a very strange feeling, to think we could donate an embryo and our children could have a brother or sister somewhere in the world' (Weale 2003). Using a bodily metaphor to connote relational embodiment, she went on to say, 'I had not realised how it would tug at my heart strings'. Another woman, Michele Hodgkiss, who had also donated embryos, discovered precise information from her consultant's casual remarks at a garden party about who they had been implanted in, the sex of the child and when she was born. Michele said, 'I started to have these horrible dreams that I was actually having this baby, and I could feel the baby moving in me' (Weale 2003). Though the girl is now nine years old, Michele went on to say, 'After all this time I still think about her. Not a week goes by. I worry about her. I know she is out there'.

Comparable 'effects' are noted by Lock (2002) in her discussions of transplant surgery, where she describes the 'animation' of commodified body parts. Hearts and kidneys are accepted by donors, not simply as life-saving commodities, but also as objects which stand in a metonymic relationship with the individual or enslaved body from which they have been removed. Something of the individual donor remains, embodied within the organ. Lock (2002:72) reports, for example, the difficulties involved in operationalising a plan to transplant the hearts of men put to death for murder in the US. Something of their malevolence would be felt by those who receive them, it is believed. The commodified body part therefore poses the threat of producing an undesirable relational body, once it is meshed with the new recipient's individual body. Similarly, as noted in the example of conjoined twins, what disturbs us most about this kind of 'monstrosity' is the undermining of autonomous corporeality as the relational and the individual body are made one (Shildrick 2002).

What we have described therefore are the outcomes of a network which encompasses both a western commitment to autonomous corporeality and a proliferation of medical technologies which can powerfully amend previous shapings of the life course, setting in motion a whole series of negotiations and moral concerns. While the reproduction of the life course inevitably involves not only the processes of individual bodily growth, maturation and decline, but also the embodied relational processes of conception, birth and child rearing, the desire for autonomous corporeality persists, very often in tension with processes of technological change across time. What we have shown, therefore, is that given the availability of medical technologies this can involve the problematic transfer of commodified organic matter between bodies in order that one individual body may survive or reproduce itself; and conversely that, as the time of the life course unfolds on both an individual and a generational basis, relational bodies can impose themselves and have an effect, intervening in the abstraction of bodily matter from the enselved corporeality of individuals. What we have here, therefore, is an example of fluid discursive practices within which both metaphoric strategies *and* the fleshy stuff of the body can be made to combine and recombine.

The Global Politics of Technology

The network of relations within which different kinds of bodies and medical technology are embroiled are not, however, solely limited to mere local effects. Indeed, as noted above in the case of kidney transplants, there is a global trade in these body parts. This provides evidence of a network of interdependent relationships that in some senses reflects the broader global environment within which the body's limits are everywhere continually negotiated within the networks which encompass the medical technologies that are now available.

Thus, for example, as Strathern (2001) has shown, what, in 1997, became known as the 'Hagahai blood saga' reveals the international dimension of such negotiations. The Hagahai, a tribal community living in Papua New Guinea, were discovered to have a virus which, in other people, leads to severe leukaemia, and yet they appeared not to develop this disease.

Antibodies were separated from the blood and 'a cell line was cultured in an American laboratory' (2001:150). Following this 'invention' a patent application was made and was signed by the anthropologist who made the discovery on behalf of the Hagahai people. The interest that these events generated within the media not only raised issues about the commodification of the body but also about its ownership. Strathern cites an emotive description of this dispute that was broadcast on an American news network: 'He's out there somewhere in the wild gorges of the Yuat River, hunting pig, harvesting yam, a young tribesman whose heart belongs to the jungle – but whose blood belongs to the US government' (2001:153–4). As Strathern observes, the Hagahai became a 'global icon of people's everywhere exploited by the new technologies' (2001:158).

This example shows not only the global relationships that medical technology can embrace but also, as Strathern is keen to explore, how such relationships may be experienced, translated and understood, more locally. This exploration is also part of Hogle's (1996) concern in her discussion of the use of body parts in the context of medical practice in Germany. As she argues, any understanding of the practice and effects of medical science have always to be socially and culturally situated because 'transformations of the body are made at the level of everyday activities *in interaction* with particular social, economic and historical contexts' (1996:676). In the context of the US, and much of Europe, she argues that

> the high cultural value placed on technological progress and commoditization is relatively unproblematic, as evidenced by the number of explicit market mechanisms currently proposed for the exchange of bodily tissues (1996:676).

However, given the specific historical, social and political contexts of Nazism in Germany, when experiments were carried out on living humans and their body parts were used for a variety of different purposes, these practices are contemporarily seen as much more problematic. Organ donation rates are therefore far lower than other European countries and skin and bone donations are rare. As Hogle notes:

> physicians rarely request these tissues from families as they feel that such requests are too 'disturbing' and will negatively affect the acquisition of organs as well. As a result, almost all skin is acquired from foreign banks (1996:677).

In addition, however, Hogle argues that different cultural ideas about the body's inviolability also shapes the way such technological work is carried out by German surgeons. Within the US, body parts are transformed into standard 'tools' and technological products that can be used for a variety of individuals. Their preoccupation is with the kind of 'donor' that can produce a 'quality' body part. In Germany, by contrast, body parts remain viewed as essentially natural products, with surgeons seeing the 'quality' of the organ as dependent upon the team who removed it and its regenerative capacity within the recipient's body.

In this example, therefore, what we see are two rather different views of embodiment that reflect particular local contexts, illustrating the role that medical technology plays in relation to the body and identity. This under-scores the argument that medical technology cannot be comprehended simply as an outcome of medical science because its effects depend upon the net-works within which it – and the body – are located. Thus even in the mundane example of the use of condoms for the prevention of spread of AIDS and HIV infection in Mozambique we find, within the same population, different kinds of effects in terms of particular embodied identities. As Pfeifer (2004) shows, the health education campaign promoting the use of Jeito condoms succeeded in alienating, rather than enrolling large sections of the population because it failed to recognise the ways in which condom use was interpreted within the framework of the Pentecostal church. For churchgoers, the use of condoms is discouraged since condoms are 'identified as sinful primarily because it is thought that if one is faithful, there is no need for condoms' (Pfeifer 2004:91). Given this context, as Pfeifer notes, rumours abounded about the agency of the Jeito condom itself in the spread, rather than prevention, of HIV infection:

> Informants had heard it said that if one hangs a Jeito condom up to dry in the sunlight for a day, one can eventually see the HIV virus squirming inside, and for this reason these condoms should be avoided (2004:94).

Conclusion

This chapter has illustrated the subtleties that have to be embraced in explor-ing the ways in which medical technologies of different kinds participate in the network of social, cultural, economic and political relationships through which the body's health identity is negotiated. What it demonstrates is both the hegemony of the western container body, a model of the body that is becoming increasingly globalised, and its implications for identification. It has also shown the emergence of new thinking about the body, as one outcome of the development and use of medical technologies. Thus the visions of commodified and relational bodies throw up new moral and ethical debates that raise questions about the relationship between health and identity. But, like the idea of the individualised body, these too must be recognised as objectifications of the otherwise indeterminate materiality of the body which provides the grounds of human being.

9

Conclusion

This volume has drawn together the range of approaches through which both anthropologists and sociologists have sought to understand health and illness. As Chapter 2 noted, this task was originally one of uncovering and highlighting the social dimensions of what were seen, unquestioningly, as medical matters – for example, the mortality and morbidity rates in the UK; the efficacy of traditional societies' indigenous systems of healing and their relationship with western medicine; the compliance of patients with a medical regime; the changing nature of UK healthcare provision; epidemics and the role of immunisation; the problem of communicating medical diagnoses to patients. In areas such as these, medical anthropologists and sociologists sought to support the growth of medical science by expanding practitioners' understanding of the challenges with which they were faced. If medicine approached illness as some kind of malfunctioning that was located in the body or the brain, then social scientists could enhance its effectiveness by drawing attention to social divisions such as class, gender and ethnicity, the ways in which these are manifested in inequalities in housing, income, education and lifestyle, for example, and the threats such inequalities pose to the nation's health.

From the 1970s onwards, however, alongside an ongoing concern with health inequalities, we have seen the growth of a more critical position which has led medical sociology and anthropology to draw more heavily on social constructionist frameworks. These have allowed the very categories of health, illness and the body to be problematised, so generating a position from which to critique some of the assumptions of medical science.

We would locate this volume within this more recent approach and, to this end, we selected as its primary focus 'the body' as understood within a medicalised western culture, using historically and cross-culturally located examples to demonstrate how this kind of body can become the end point of

individuals' embodied perceptual processes. Having acquired a global hegemony, this is the body that many of us may come to think and feel ourselves
to *be* and to *have*. It is this body, we suggest, that informs not only a wide
range of western ideas and practices associated with health and illness but can
also be discovered to compete with, if not displace, indigenous healthcare
systems throughout the world.

The approach which this volume has developed in seeking to understand
the implications of the 'body' which so influences experiences of health and
illness throughout the world derives from cultural phenomenology and its
emphasis on the embodied nature of human life. Thus, rather than simply
uncovering evermore examples of historical and cross-cultural variability in
the ways in which health and illness and the body have been and are conceived of and treated, our aim has been to revisit many of the familiar territo-
ries of medical sociology and anthropology, but to do so from the perspective
of the embodied social life which constitutes the experience of individuals,
families, communities, organisations and indeed nations that we all, in fact,
recognise. Thus we have revisited familiar questions as to how illness comes
into being, suggesting that changes in the body and its cognitive, perceptual
and motor facilities are insufficient as an account of illness.

What we have explored, instead, are the ways in which illness becomes
manifest, whether through the interpretive processes of individuals, the interactions between children and parents, women and men, families and friendship groups, lay people and healthcare practitioners, or through the social and
technical processes of screening, divination and exorcism. What we have suggested is that issues of identity not only inform these embodied, interactive
social processes, as they unfold in ways which are particular to our age,
gender, class and ethnicity, but that the ever incomplete process of identification involves the negotiation of *changes* in our health status and therefore
our identity. As the examples showed, illness can curtail a professional career,
radically change a personal relationship and undermine an individual's participation in neighbourhood or community affairs. Alongside such changes,
however, it can also provide the basis for new social affiliations as, for
example, fundraiser, environmental activist or simply friend and chauffeur to
individuals who share one's condition. Moreover, the implications of illness
for identity can be contingent. Rather than becoming an inevitable 'master
status', even stigmatising illnesses can be managed in ways which, for
example, allow the individual to 'pass' as healthy, to foreground other aspects
of their life, or indeed to challenge prevailing assumptions about stigma.

Alison Lapper, for example, an artist who was born without arms and with
only stunted legs, chose to model naked for a statue when eight months pregnant. In 2005 the 12 foot high work was erected in London's Trafalgar Square
to mixed responses. Winston Churchill, the UK war-time prime minister who

suffered from depression, was the subject of another statue. This was unveiled in 2006 by the charity Rethink and showed the former leader with his arms trapped across his chest in a straitjacket, so demonstrating that mental illness does not preclude participation in public life. In both these cases a stigmatising disability or illness is made highly visible, yet within a complex piece of art which aligns that condition with other aspects of the individual's identity in order to disrupt conceptions such as 'disabled', 'prime minister', 'mother', and 'mental illness'. In both cases it is the body which arrests the attention by encompassing powerfully dissonant sets of meanings.

Representations such as these are located within a social environment where images and texts of all kinds work to position the embodied individual in relation to prevailing conceptions and experiences of healthcare provision, to the practices which constitute their individual 'lifestyle', from diet and exercise through to sexual practices and working hours, and to the health status of other people, whether family members of the casualties of war and famine in other parts of the world. What we have explored, however, are the ways in which the embodied consumer of such representations actually engages with their potential meaning and how this may be subverted, accommodated – or indeed provide the stimulus for alternative health or illness narratives. While the experience of health and illness is both embodied and interactive, we argue that it is only via representation – and the particular metaphors which inform and underpin that representation – that the essentially inchoate, private nature of that experience can be made knowable, both to the individual themself, to their family and friends, and to their healthcare provider. This focus on representation inevitably highlights, therefore, the impossibility of 'neutrality' or objectivity in the ways in which both health and illness are represented. As such, it forms part of contemporary social scientists' more critical engagement with such issues. However, as noted above, the social 'factors' which engaged an earlier cohort of sociologists and anthropologists nonetheless remain an important aspect of this more critical position.

What we have also chosen to foreground in this book are the implications of *age*, highlighting not only the age-based social divisions which can act to dispossess both children and older adults of their capacity to exercise choice in relation to their bodies, but also the ways in which medicalised conceptions of the chronologised life course manifest themselves in age-specific assumptions about the distribution of health and illness across the population. For those who are young and those who are elderly, a chronology which meshes with medicalised assumptions about the ageing body carries powerful implications for identity. Thus while children are seen to be vulnerable to illness and injury, a conception which informs health, social, educational and legal policy-making, older adults have become defined through an elision of 'old age' and 'illness' which can result in the restriction of employment opportunities, poorer healthcare and limited access to costly surgical techniques, low self-esteem, and the largely unchallenged depredations of ageism. As the examples presented demonstrate, however, both children and older adults, as embodied social beings, engage with such representations of themselves and their bodies in a whole variety of ways, not only challenging their salience but also, at times, deploying them as a resource.

In making embodiment our starting point, then, we not only overcome the mind-body distinction that undermines attempts to provide theoretically adequate accounts of health and illness, but we also find a surer route towards understanding the complexities and ambiguities of experiences of health and illness within the context of particular medical regimes. As Chapter 8 argued, medical technology may have implications for the very nature of the human body, its scope and its limitations, yet as embodied beings, we as the consumers of such technology are faced with the ethical and therefore *social* implications of what can be done to and with that body. In the case of the egg, sperm and embryo, for example, whilst seen as the very essence of human embodied life, these have become susceptible to technological interventions which have disrupted many of the values and beliefs which are core to particular kinship systems. Whilst the fertilisation of the egg through sexual intercourse is seen as a normally consensual practice which unproblematically confers the identities of 'mother' and 'father' upon the woman and man involved once a child is born, the clinical possibility of *freezing* the egg, sperm and embryo raise legal, moral and ethical issues of the kind which took Diane Blood to the Court of Appeal in order that she and her (dead) husband might conceive a child in 1998; and in 2006 left Natallie Evans, infertile after cancer treatment, without the independent right to bring to full term the embryos which she and her previous partner had allowed to be conceived in a Petri dish.

Embodiment, as shown in the examples presented throughout this book, has therefore to be understood as part of the ongoing negotiations that take place both within the body and in social interaction, between conceptions of health and illness and body-based experience. Given this evidence, we argue that the body is not simply the passive site where 'illness' and 'health' are located. Instead, as each chapter shows, we propose a notion of the body's materiality as in constant flux, one that changes imperceptibly during the process of ageing, or more rapidly when illness or injury intervene. Providing critical reflection on many of the areas which both medical anthropology and medical sociology have been exploring from the middle of the twentieth century onwards, then, this book has placed the body – in whatever shape, state or form – at the centre of its enquiry. In asking, for example, about the implications of illness for the functioning of society; the varying nature of illness categories cross-culturally and historically; and the issue of power as manifested within the doctor-patient encounter we have continually returned to the body.

However, as argued, the remit of the book has been broader than this; we have also asked more focused questions about the part played by the body in the ways in which health, illness and *identity* relate to one another and have explored how illness might impact upon our existing social identities – or, more specifically, upon the unfolding process of identification. And, in parallel, we have sought to explore how our identities as gendered, aged individuals, occupying particular class positions, shape not only our health and illness statuses, but also the ways in which we understand and respond to the mental and physical conditions and bodily changes which ground those statuses.

In addressing such questions – and particularly in light of the bodily location of that which we understand as health and as illness – we have drawn on the insights of cultural phenomenology. However, as we have argued, this is not simply a matter of including the patient's experience and conceptions of illness – an approach therefore restricted to the analysis of micro-level actions and interactions. On the contrary cultural phenomenology can provide a way of examining culture and history far more broadly (Csordas 2002:87). It is fitting, therefore, that we have drawn this book to its close with a chapter that explored the intra-cultural exchange of bodies and body parts that medical technology now facilitates and that asks questions about the effects that such new bodies might have upon the world.

But, more than this, as have argued strongly throughout this volume, any understanding of both bodily and mental health and illness has to be grounded in the irreducible fact of human embodiment. Though much of the theoretical and substantive material we have drawn upon reflects a social constructionist perspective, this is not to deny the material reality which is the body. Rather, following Csordas (2002), what we have proposed is that the body, in illness and in health, be recognised as the *endpoint* of embodied perceptual processes, as the outcome of unfolding processes of negotiation. That these, in turn, stem from and feed back into the sometimes competing perceptions of different embodied individuals in 'an indefinite series of perspectival views, none of which exhausts the given objects' (Csordas 2002:86) simply makes this kind of approach the more significant for, core to this entire enterprise, is the notion that the indeterminacy of human life stems from its grounding in lived, embodied experience – rather than the free-floating constructions of discourse theory. 'The body', whether defined in terms of traditional or lay health beliefs, medical science, or the exigencies of manual labour or military service, has therefore to be treated as the objective outcome of perceptual processes which are rooted in the indeterminacy of human embodiment.

10

Bibliography

Ablon, J. (1986) 'Reactions of Samoan burn patients and their families to severe burns'. In C. Currer and M. Stacey (eds) *Concepts of Health, Illness and Disease*. Leamington Spa: Berg.

Alderson, P. (1993) *Children's Consent to Surgery*. Buckingham: Open University Press.

Archer, L. and Francis, B. (2006) 'Challenging classes? Exploring the role of social class within the identities and achievements of British Chinese pupils', *Sociology*, 40(1):29–51.

Armstrong, D. (1980) *An Outline of Sociology as Applied to Medicine*. Bristol: John Wright.

Armstrong, D. (1981) 'Pathological life and death: medical spatialisation and geriatrics', *Social Science and Medicine*, 15(A):253–7.

Armstrong, D. (1983) *Political Anatomy of the Body: medical knowledge in Britain in the twentieth century*. Cambridge: Cambridge University Press.

Armstrong, D. (1987) 'Bodies of knowledge: Foucault and the problem of human anatomy'. In G. Scambler (ed.) *Sociological Theory and Medical Sociology*. London: Tavistock.

Armstrong, D. (1995) 'The rise of surveillance medicine', *Sociology of Health and Illness*, 17(3):393–404.

Arnold, K., Hurwitz, B., McKee, F. and Richardson, R. (1997) *Doctor Death: Medicine at the End of Life*. London: The Wellcome Trust.

Atkinson, P. (1995) *Medical Talk and Medical work: the liturgy of the clinic*. London: Sage.

Bauby, J. (1998) *The Diving Bell and the Butterfly*. London: Fourth Estate.

Beattie, J. (1960) *Bunyoro. An African Kingdom*. New York: Holt, Rinehart and Winston.

Beck, U. (1992) *Risk Society: towards a new modernity*. London: Sage.

Becker, A. (1995) *Body Self and Society: the view from Fiji*. Philadelphia: University of Pennsylvania Press.

Becker, A.E. (1994) 'Nurturing and negligence: working on others' bodies in Fiji'. In T. Csordas (ed.) *Embodiment and Experience: the existential ground of culture and self*. Cambridge: Cambridge University Press.

Bellerby, P. (1993) 'The world of illness of the closed head injured'. In A. Radley (ed.) *Worlds of Illness*. London: Routledge.

Bendelow, G.A. (1996) 'A "failure" of modern medicine? Lay perspectives on a pain relief clinic'. In S.J. Williams and M. Calnan (eds) *Modern Medicine: lay perspectives and experiences*. London: UCL Press.

Benton, T. (1991) 'Biology and Social Science: Why the return of the repressed should be given a (cautious) welcome', *Sociology*, 25(1):1–31.

Blane, D., Bartley, M. and Davey Smith, G. (1998) 'Making sense of socio-economic health inequalities'. In D. Field and S. Taylor (eds) *Sociological Perspectives on Health, Illness and Health Care*. Oxford: Blackwell.

Blaxter, M. and Patterson, E. (1982) *Mothers and Daughters: A Three-Generational Study of Health Attitudes and Behaviour*. London: Heinemann.

Bluebond-Langner, M. (1978) *The Private Worlds of Dying Children*. Princeton: Princeton University Press.

Bluebond-Langner, M. (1996) *In the Shadow of Illness: parents and siblings of the chronically ill child*. Princeton: Princeton University Press.

Bode, M. (2002) 'Indian indigenous pharmaceuticals: tradition, modernity and nature'. In W. Ernst (ed.) *Plural Medicine: Orthodox and heteredox medicine in western and colonial countries during the 19th and 20th Centuries*. London: Routledge.

Bourdieu, P. (1977) *Outline of a Theory of Practice*. Cambridge: Cambridge University Press.

Bourdieu, P. (1984) *Distinction. A Social Critique of the Judgement of Taste*. London: Routledge and Kegan Paul.

Brannen, J. and Nilsen, B. (2002) 'Young People's Time Perspectives: From Youth to Adulthood', *Sociology*, 36(3):513–37.

Brown, G.W. and Harris, T.O. (1989) *Life Events and Illness*. London: Unwin and Allen.

Brooks, D.H.M. (1990) 'The route to home ventilation: a patient's perspective', *Care of the Critically Ill*, 6(3):96–7.

Buckingham, D. (2000) *After the Death of Childhood*. Cambridge: Polity Press.

Bunton, R., Nettleton, S. and Burrows, R. (1995) 'Consumption and health in the "epidemiological" clinic of late modern medicine'. In R. Bunton, S. Nettleton and R. Burrows (eds) *The Sociology of Health Promotion*. London: Routledge.

Burton, L. (1975) *The Family Life of Sick Children*. London: Routledge and Kegan Paul.

Bury, M.R. (1982) 'Chronic illness as biological disruption', *Sociology of Health and Illness*, 4(2):167–82.

Bury, M.R. (1986) 'Social constructionism and the development of medical sociology', *Sociology of Health and Illness*, 8:137–69.

Bury, M.R. (1991) 'The sociology of chronic illness: a review of research and prospects', *Sociology of Health and Illness*, 13(4):451–68.

Bury, M.R. (2001) 'Illness narratives: fact or fiction', *Sociology of Health and Illness*, 23(3):263–85.

Busfield, J. (1996) *Men, Women and Madness. Understanding gender and mental disorder*. Basingstoke: Macmillan.

Cassell, E. (1976) *The Healer's Art: A new approach to the Doctor-Patient Relationship*. New York: Lippincott.

Chapman, R.R. (2003) 'Endangering safe motherhood in Mozambique: prenatal care as pregnancy risk', *Social Science and Medicine*, 57:355–74.

Chesler, P. (1972) *Women and Madness*. New York: Doubleday.

Christensen, C. (1993) 'The social construction of help among Danish children', *Sociology of Health and Illness*, 15:488–502.

Christensen, P., Hockey, J. and James, A. (1999) '"That's farming, Rosie …": Power and Familial Relations in an Agricultural Community'. In J. Seymour and P. Bagguley (eds) *Relating Intimacies. Power and Resistance*. Basingstoke: Macmillan Press Ltd.

Christensen, P. (1997) 'Difference and similarity: how children are constituted in illness and its treatment'. In I. Hutchby and J. Moran-Ellis (eds) *Children and Social Competence: arenas of action*. London: Falmer.

Clifford, J. and Marcus, G. (1986) *Writing Culture. The Poetics and Politics of Ethnography.* Berkeley: University of California Press.

Conway, S. and Hockey, J. (1998) 'Resisting the "mask" of old age?: the social meaning of lay health beliefs in later life', *Ageing and Society*, 18:469–94.

Cooley, C.H. ([1902] 1964) *Human Nature and the Social Order*. New York: Scribner's.

Copson, R.W. (2005) *Aids in Africa*, CRS Issue Brief for Congress (www.fas.org/sgp/crs/roro/IBI0050.pdf – 20th October 2005).

Corker, M. and French, S. (eds) (1999) *Disability Discourse*. Buckingham: Open University Press.

Coupland, N. and Coupland, J. (1994) 'Age-identity and health identity in geriatric medical discourse'. In S. Lauritzen and L. Sachs (eds) *Health Care Encounters: interdisciplinary perspectives*. Stockholm: Multicultural Centre, Botkyrka.

Craib, I. (1998) *Experiencing Identity*. London: Sage.

Craig, D. (2000) 'Practical logics: the shapes and lessons of popular medical knowledge and practice – examples from Vietnam and Indigenous Australia', *Social Science and Medicine*, 51:703–11.

Csordas, T. (1994) 'Introduction: the body as representation and being-in-the-world'. In T. Csordas (ed.) *Embodiment and Experience*. Cambridge: Cambridge University Press.

Csordas, T. (2002) *Body/Meaning/Healing*. Basingstoke: Palgrave Macmillan.

Damasio, A.R. (1994) *Descartes' Error. Emotion, Reason and the Human Brain*. London: Papermac.

Davey, B. (2001) 'Health in Transition'. In B. Davey (ed.) *Birth to Old Age: Health in Transition*. Buckingham: Open University Press.

Davies, C. (1995) *Gender and the Professional Predicament in Nursing*. Buckingham: Open University Press.

Davin, S. (2005) 'Public medicine: the reception of a medical drama'. In M. King and K. Watson (eds) *Representing Health: Discourses of Health and Illness in the Media*. London: Palgrave.

Davin, S. (2003) 'Healthy viewing: the reception of medical narratives', *Sociology of Health and Illness*, 25(6):662–79.

Davis, K. (1991) 'Critical sociology and gender relations'. In K. Davis and M. Leijenaar (eds) *The Gender of Power*. London: Sage.

Davis, K. (1995) *Reshaping the Female Body. The dilemma of cosmetic surgery*. New York: Routledge.

Davison, C., Smith, G.D. and Frankel, S. (1991) 'Lay epidemiology and the prevention paradox: the implications of coronary candidacy for health education', *Social Health and Illness*, 13:1–19.

Davison, C., Frankel, S. and Smith, G.D. (1992) 'The limits of life-style: reassessing "fatalism" in the popular culture of illness prevention', *Social Science and Medicine*, 34:675–85.

Daykin, N. and Naidoo, J. (1995) 'Feminist critiques of health promotion'. In R. Bunton, S. Nettleton and R. Burrows (eds) *The Sociology of Health Promotion.S* London: Routledge.

De Swaan, A. (1990) *The Management of Normality*. London: Routledge.

De Vries, R. (1981) 'Birth and Death: Social Construction at the Poles of Existence', *Social Forces*, 59(4):1074–93.

Denny, E. (1996) 'New Reproductive Technologies: the views of women undergoing treatment'. In S. Williams and M. Calnan (eds) *Modern Medicine. Lay perspectives and experiences*. London: UCL Press.

Diamond, J. (1998) *C: Because cowards get cancer too....* London: Vermilion.

Doi, Y. (2005) 'Health promotion campaigns for ethnic minority groups: the case of the radio campaign for Asian populations in the UK'. In M. King and K. Watson (eds) *Representing Health*. London: Palgrave.

Douglas, M. (1966) *Purity and Danger*. London: Routledge and Kegan Paul.

Doyal, L. (1979) *The Political Economy of Health*. London: Archway.

Doyal, L. (2002) 'Gender equity in health debates and dilemmas'. In G. Bendelow, M. Carpenter, C. Vautier and S. Williams (eds) *Gender Health and Healing*: London: Routledge.

Draper, J. (2002a) '"It's the First Scientific Evidence": Men's Experiences of Pregnancy Confirmation – Some Findings from a Longitudinal Ethnographic Study of Transition to Fatherhood', *Journal of Advanced Nursing*, 39(6):563–70.

Draper, J. (2002b) '"It was a Real Good Show": The Ultrasound Scan, Fathers and the Power of Visual Knowledge', *Sociology of Health and Illness*, 24(6):771–95.

Draper, J. (2003) 'Men's Passage to Fatherhood: An Analysis of the Contemporary Relevance of Transition Theory', *Nursing Enquiry*, 10(1):66–78.

Dyer, C. (2003) 'All we wanted was to save our son', *The Guardian*, 14th January 2003.

Einarsdottir, J. (2005) 'Restoration of social order through the extinction of non-human children'. In R. Jenkins, H. Jessen and V. Steffen (eds) *Managing Uncertainty. Ethnographic Studies of Illness, Risk and the Struggle for Control*. Copenhagen: Museum Tusculanum Press, University of Copenhagen.

Elliott, B.J. (1991) 'Demographic trends in domestic life, 1945–87'. In D. Clark (ed.) *Marriage, Domestic Life and Social Change*. London: Routledge.

Evans, M. and Lee, E. (2002) *Real Bodies*. Basingstoke: Palgrave.

Evans-Pritchard, E. (1937) *Witchcraft, Oracles and Magic among the Azande*. Oxford: Oxford University Press.

Fadiman, A. (1997) *The Spirit Catches You and You Fall Down: A Hmong child, her American doctors, and the collision of two cultures*. New York: The Noonday Press.

Featherstone, M. (1991) 'The body in consumer culture'. In M. Featherstone, M. Hepworth and B.S. Turner (eds) *The Body. Social Process and Cultural Theory*. London: Sage.

Featherstone, M. and Hepworth, M. (1991) 'The mask of ageing and the postmodern lifecourse'. In M. Featherstone, M. Hepworth and B.S. Turner (eds) *The Body, Social Process and Cultural Theory*. London: Sage.

Featherstone, M. and Hepworth, M. (1995) 'Images of positive aging: a case study of *Retirement Choice* magazine'. In M. Featherstone and A. Wernick (eds) *Images of Aging: Cultural Representations of Later Life*. London: Routledge.

Fernandez, J.W. (1972) 'Persuasions and Performances: Of the Beast in Every Body … and the Metaphors of Everyman', *Daedalus*, 101(1), Winter, pp. 39–60.

Fitzpatrick, M. (2001) *The Tyranny of Health*. London: Routledge.

Foucault, M. (1972) *The Archaeology of Knowledge*. London: Tavistock.

Foucault, M. (1973) *The Birth of the Clinic: an archaeology of medical perception*. London: Tavistock.

Foucault, M. (1979) *Discipline and Punish*. Harmondsworth: Penguin.

Fox, N. (1993) *Postmodernism, Sociology and Health*. Buckingham: Open University Press.

Frank, A.W. (1995) *The Wounded Storyteller*. Chicago: University of Chicago Press.

Frankenberg, R. (1980) 'Medical anthropology and development: a theoretical perspective', *Social Science and Medicine*, 14b:197–207.

Frankenberg, R. (1992) '"Your time or mine": temporal contradictions of biomedical practice'. In R. Frankenberg (ed.) *Time, Health and Medicine*. London: Sage.

Freund, P. and McGuire, M. (1991) *Health, Illness and the Social Body*. Englewood Cliffs, NJ: Prentice-Hall, Inc.

Friedson, E. (1970) *Profession of Medicine: A study of the sociology of applied knowledge*. New York: Dodd, Mead and Co.

Froggatt, K. (1997) 'Rites of passage and the hospice culture', *Mortality*, 2(2):123–6.

Gabe, J. (ed.) (1995) *Medicine, health and risk*. Oxford: Blackwell.

Gabe, J. and Bury, M. (1996) 'Risking tranquillizer use: cultural and lay dimensions'. In S.J. Williams and M. Calnan (eds) *Modern Medicine: lay perspectives and experiences*. London: UCL Press.

Geertz, C. (1966) 'Religion as a cultural system'. In M. Banton (ed.) *Anthropological Approaches to the Study of Religion*. London: Tavistock Publications.

Gerhardt, S. (2004) *Why Love Matters. How affection shapes a baby's brain*. London: Routledge.

Giddens, A. (1979) *Central Problems in Social Theory: Action, structure and contradiction in social analysis*. London: Macmillan.

Giddens, A. (1991) *Modernity and Self Identity*. Cambridge: Polity.

Gillet, J. (2003) 'Media activism and Internet use by people with HIV/AIDS', *Sociology of Health and Illness*, 25(6):608–24.

Glaser, B. and Strauss, A. (1968) *Time for Dying*. Chicago: Aldine.

Goffman, E. (1968) *Stigma, Notes on the Management of a Spoiled Identity*. London: Penguin.

Goffman, E. (1969) *The Presentation of Self in Everyday Life*. London: Allen Lane.

Good, B. (1994) *Medicine, Rationality and Experience*. Cambridge: Cambridge University Press.

Goudsmit, E.M. (1994) 'All in her mind! Stereotypic views and the psychologisation of women's illness'. In S. Wilkinson and C. Kitzinger (eds) *Women and Health. Feminist perspectives*. London: Taylor and Francis.

Graham, H. (1987) 'Women's Smoking and Family Health', *Social Science and Medicine*, 25(1):47–56.

Gray, A. (2001) 'The changing fortunes of the life course'. In B. Davey (ed.) *Birth to Old Age: Health in Transition*. Buckingham: Open University Press.

Greer, G. (1999) *The Whole Woman*. London: Doubleday.

Grieg, A. (2004) *In Another Light*. London: Phoenix.

Grue, L. and Laerum, K.T. (2002) 'Doing motherhood: some experiences of mothers with physical disabilities', *Disability and Society*, 17(6):671–83.

Grundfest Schoepf, B. (1998) 'Inscribing the body politic: women and AIDS in Africa'. In M. Lock and P. Kauffert (eds) *Pragmatic Women and Body Politics*. Cambridge: Cambridge University Press.

Hacking, I. (1999) *The Social Construction of what?* Cambridge, MA: Harvard University Press.

Hall, S. (1996) 'Introduction: who needs identity?' In S. Hall and P. du Gay (eds) *Questions of Cultural Identity*. London: Sage.

Hallam, E., Hockey, J. and Howarth, G. (1999) *Beyond the Body. Death and Social Identity*. London: Routledge.

Harari, E. (2001) 'Whose evidence? Lessons from the philosophy of science and the epistemology of medicine', *Australian and New Zealand Journal of Psychiatry*, 35:724–30.

Hardey, M. (2005) 'Writing digital selves: Narratives of health and illness on the Internet', In M. King and K. Watson (eds) *Representing Health*. London: Palgrave.

Harvey, J. (1996) 'Achieving the Indeterminate: Accomplishing Degrees of Certainty in Life and Death Situation', *Sociological Review*, 44:78–98.

Harvey, J. (1997) 'The Technological Regulation of Death: With Reference to the Technological Regulation of Birth', *Sociology*, 31(4):719–35.

Helander, B. (1995) 'Disability as incurable illness: health, process and personhood in Southern Somalia'. In S. Reynolds Whyte and B. Ingstad (eds) *Disability and Culture*. Berkeley: University of California Press.

Helman, C. ([1978] 1986) 'Feed a cold, starve a fever: Folk models of infection in an English surburban community and their relation to medical treatment'. In C. Currer and M. Stacey (eds) *Concepts of Health, Illness and Disease: a comparative perspective*. Oxford: Berg.

Helman, C. (1984) *Culture, Health and Illness*. Bristol: Wright.

Helman, C. (1990) *Culture, Health and Illness* 2nd edn. Oxford: Butterworth-Heinemann Ltd.

Hendrick, H. (1990) 'Constructions and reconstructions of British childhood: an interpretative survey, 1800 to the present'. In A. James and A. Prout (eds) *Constructing and Reconstructing Childhood*. Lewes: Falmer Press.

Henwood, F. Wyatt, S., Hart, A. and Smith, J. (2003) '"Ignorance is bliss sometimes": constraints on the emergence of the "informed patient" in the changing landscapes of health information', *Sociology of Health and Illness*, 25(6):589–607.

Hepworth, M. (2000) *Stories of Ageing*. Buckingham: Open University Press.

Herzlich, C. (1973) *Health and Illness: A social psychological approach*. London: Academic Press.

Higgs, P. and Scambler, G. (1998) 'Explaining health inequalities: how useful are concepts of social class?' In G. Scambler and P. Higgs (eds) *Modernity, Medicine and Health: Medical Sociology towards 2000*. London: Routledge.

Hockey, J. (1990) *Experiences of Death. An anthropological account*. Edinburgh: Edinburgh University Press.

Hockey, J. (2002) 'The importance of being intuitive: Arnold Van Gennep's Rites of Passage' (Classics Revisited), *Mortality*, 7(2):210–17.

Hockey, J. and Draper, J. (2005) 'Beyond the Womb and the Tomb: Identity, (Dis)embodiment and the Life Course', *Body and Society*, 11(2):41–58.

Hockey, J. and James, A. (1993) *Growing Up and Growing Old*. London: Sage.

Hockey, J. and James, A. (2003) *Social identities Across the Life Course*. London: Palgrave.

Hockey, J., Penhale, B. and Sibley, D. (2001) 'Landscapes of loss: spaces of memory, times of bereavement', *Ageing and Society*, 21:739–57.

Hogle, L.F. (1996) 'Transforming "body parts" into therapeutic tools: a report from Germany', *Medical Anthropology Quarterly* 10(4):675–82.

Illich, I. (1976) *Limits to Medicine*. London: Marion Boyars.

Jackson, J. (1994) 'Chronic pain and the tension between the body as subject and object'. In T. Csordas (ed.) *Embodiment and Experience: the existential ground of culture and self*. Cambridge: Cambridge University Press.

James, A. (1993) *Childhood Identities: self and social relationships in the experience of the child*. Edinburgh: Edinburgh University Press.

James, A. (2004) 'The Standardized Child: Issues of Openness, Objectivity and Agency in promoting child health', *Anthropological Journal of European Cultures*, 13:93–111.

James, A. and Prout, A. (eds) (1990) *Constructing and Reconstructing Childhood*. Lewes: Falmer Press.

Janes, C.R. and Chuluundori, O. (2004) 'Free markets and dead mothers: the social ecology of maternal mortality', *Medical Anthropology Quarterly*, 18(2):230–58.

Jenkins, R. (1996) *Social Identity*. London: Routledge.

Jenkins, R. (2002) *Foundations of Sociology*. Basingstoke: Palgrave Macmillan.

Jenkins, R. (2004) *Social Identity: second edition*. London: Routledge.

Jenks, C. (1996) *Childhood*. London: Routledge.

Johnson, M. and Puddifoot, J. (1998) 'Miscarriage: Is Vividness of Visual Imagery a Factor in the Grief Reaction of a Partner?', *British Journal of Health Psychology*, 3:137–46.

Jerome, J.K. ([1889] 2004) *Three Men in a Boat*. London: Penguin.

Karasek, R.A. and Theorell, T. (1990) *Healthy Work*. New York: Basic Books.

Karpf, A. (1988) *Doctoring the Media*. London: Routledge.

Keane, A. (1997) 'The palatability of healthy eating advice'. In P. Caplan (ed.) *Food, Health and Identity*. London: Routledge.

Kelleher, D. (1994) 'Self-help groups and medicine'. In J. Gabe, D. Kelleher and G. Williams (eds) *Challenging Medicine*. London: Routledge.

King, M. and Watson, K. (eds) (2005) *Representing Health: Discourses of Health and Illness in the Media*. London: Palgrave.

Kingsolver, B. (1998) *The Poisonwood Bible*. London: Faber and Faber.

Kleinman, A. (1978) 'Concepts and a model for the comparison of medical systems as cultural systems', *Social Science Medicine B*, 12:85–93.

Kleinman, A. (1980) *Patients and Healers in the Context of Culture*. California: University of California Press.

Kleinman, A. (1988) *The Illness Narratives: Suffering, Healing and the Humans Condition*. New York: Basic Books.

Knowles, C. (2000) *Bedlam on the Streets*. London: Routledge.

Laing, R.D. and Esterson, A. (1973) *Sanity and Madness in the Family* 2nd edn. Harmondsworth: Penguin.

Lakoff, G. and Johnson, M. (1980) *Metaphors We Live By*. Chicago: University of Chicago Press.

Lambert, H. (1998) 'Methods and meanings in anthropological, epidemiological and clinical encounters: the case of sexually transmitted disease and human immunodeficiency virus control and prevention in India', *Tropical Medicine and International Health*, 3(12):1002–10.

Lane, K. (1995) 'The medical model of the body as a site of risk: a case study of childbirth'. In J. Gabe (ed.) *Medicine, Health and Risk*. Oxford: Blackwell Publishers.

Lane, S. (1997) 'Television mini-dramas: social marketing and evaluation Egypt', *Medical Anthropology Quarterly*, NS 11 (2), Knowledge and Practice in International Health, 164–82.

Lane, J. (2001) *A Social History of Medicine: health, healing and disease in England, 1750–1950*. London: Routledge.

Latour, B. (1993) *We Have Never Been Modern*. New York: Harvester Wheatsheaf.

Latour, B. (2004) 'How to talk about the body? The normative dimension of Science', *Body and Society*, 10(2–3):205–29.

Lawrence, C. (1994) *Medicine in the Making of Modern Britain 1700–1920*. London: Routledge.

Layne, L. (2000) 'He Was a Real Baby with Baby Things', *Journal of Material Culture*, 5(3):321–45.

Leder, D. (1990) *The Absent Body*. Chicago and London: University of Chicago Press.

Leve, A. (2005) 'One Google search and I was a goner', *The Guardian*, 26th July.

Lock, M. (2002) *Twice Dead. Organ Transplants and the Reinvention of Death*. Berkeley: University of California Press.

Lock, M. (2003) 'On making up the good-as-dead in a utilitarian world'. In S. Franklin and M. Lock (eds) *Remaking Life and Death*. Oxford: James Curry.

Lonsdale, S. (1990) *Women and Disability. The experience of physical disability among women*. Basingstoke: Macmillan.

Lupton, D. (1994) *Medicine as Culture*. London: Sage.

Lupton, D. (2004) *Medicine as Culture* 2nd edn. London: Sage.

Lyon, M.L. and Barbalet, J.M. (1994) 'Society's body: emotion and the "somatization" of social theory'. In T. Csordas (ed.) *Embodiment and Experience: the existential ground of culture and self*. Cambridge: Cambridge University Press.

Macure, J. (1994) 'Cold turkey for television's mythic medics', *The Observer*, 17th April.

Marmot, M. (2001) 'A social view of health and disease'. In T. Heller, R. Muston, M. Siddell and C. Lloyd (eds) *Working for Health*. London: Sage.

Martin, E. (1987) *The Woman in the Body*. Milton Keynes: Open University Press.

Mauss, M. ([1934] 1973) 'Techniques of the Body', *Economy and Society*, 2:70–88.

McCartney, M. (2005) 'Take with a pinch of sodium chloride', *The Guardian*, 18th August.

Mayall, B. (2002) *Towards a Sociology of Childhood*. Buckingham: Open University Press.

McClean, S. (2003) 'Doctoring the spirit: exploring the use and meaning of mimicry and parody at a healing centre in the North of England', *Health: An Interdisciplinary Journal for the Social Study of Health, Illness and Medicine*, 7(4):483–500.

McGowen, R. (1994) 'Power and humanity, or Foucault among the historians'. In C. Jones and R. Porter (eds) *Reassessing Foucault: power, medicine and the body*. London: Routledge.

Mead, G.H. (1934) *Mind, Self and Society: from the standpoint of a social behaviourist*. Chicago: Chicago University Press.

Meador, C.K. (1995) 'The last well person'. In B. Davey, A. Gray and C. Seale (eds) *Health and Disease. A Reader*. Buckingham: Open University Press.

Merleau-Ponty, M. (1962) *The Phenomenology of Perception*. London: Routledge and Kegan Paul.

Merleau-Ponty, M. (1974) *Phenomenology, Language and Society*. London: Heinemann.

Mogensen, H.O. (2005) 'Medicalized experience and the active use of biomedicine'. In V. Steffen, R. Jenkins and H. Jessen (eds) *Managing Uncertainty: ethnographic studies of illness, risk and the struggle for control*. Copenhagen: Museum Tuscalnum Press.

Morgan, D. (2002) 'The Body in Pain'. In M. Evans and E. Lee (eds) *Real Bodies*. London: Palgrave.

Morris, J. (1991) *Pride against Prejudice. Transforming Attitudes to Disability*. London: The Women's Press.

Mulkay, M. (1993) 'Social death in Britain'. In D. Clark (ed.) *The Sociology of Death*. Oxford: Blackwell Publishers.

Murphy, R. (1995) 'Encounters: the body silent in America'. In B. Ingstad and S. Reynolds Whyte (eds) *Disability and Culture*. Berkeley: University of California Press.

Navarro, V. (1976) *Medicine under Capitalism*. London: Croom Helm.

Nettleton, S. (1995) *The Sociology of Health and Illness*. Cambridge: Polity Press.

Nettleton, S. and Bunton, R. (1995) 'Sociological critiques of health promotion'. In R. Bunton, S. Nettleton and R. Burrows (eds) *The Sociology of Health Promotion*. London: Routledge.

Nettleton, S. and Watson, J. (eds) (1998) *The Body in Everyday Life*. London: Routledge.

Newton, E. (1984) 'This bed my centre'. In N. Black, D. Boswell, A. Gray, S. Murphy and J. Popay (eds) *Health and Disease*. Milton Keynes: Open University Press.

Nicholaisen, I. (1995) 'Persons and nonpersons. Disability and personhood among the Punah Bah of Central Borneo'. In S. Reynolds Whyte and B. Ingstad (eds) *Disability and Culture*. Berkeley: University of California Press.

Nicholson, M. and McLaughlin, C. (1987) 'Social constructionism and medical sociology', *Sociology of Health and Illness*, 9(2):107–26.

Oakley, A. (1995) 'Doctor knows best'. In B. Davey, A. Gray and C. Seale (eds) *Health and Disease. A Reader*. Buckingham: Open University Press.

Oliver, M. (1990) *The Politics of Disablement*. London: Macmillan.

Oliver, M. (1996) *Understanding Disability*. London: Macmillan.

Parish, R. (1995) 'Health promotion: rhetoric and reality'. In R. Bunton, S. Nettleton and R. Burrows (eds) *The Sociology of Health Promotion*. London: Routledge.

Parsons, T. (1951) *The Social System*. Glencoe: Free Press.

Pfeifer, J. (2004) 'Condom social marketing, Pentacostalism, and structural adjustment in Mozambique: a clash of AIDS prevention messages', *Medical Anthropology Quarterly*, 18(1):77–103.

Phillips, D.R. and Verhasselt, Y. (eds) (1994) *Health and Development*. London: Routledge.

Place, B. (2000) 'Constructing the bodies of ill children in the intensive care unit'. In A. Prout (ed.) *The Body, Childhood and Society*. London: Macmillan.

Porter, R. (2002) *Blood and Guts: a short history of medicine*. London: Allen Lane.

Pound, P., Gompertz, P. and Ebrahim, S. (1998) 'Illness in the context of older age: the case of stroke', *Sociology of Health and Illness*, 20(4):489–506.

Price, P. (1994) 'Maternal and child health care strategies'. In D.R. Phillips and Y. Verhasselt (eds) *Health and Development*. London: Routledge.

Prior, L. (1989) *The Social Organisation of Death: Medical Discourses and Social Practices in Belfast*. London: Macmillan.

Prout, A. (1996) 'Actor-network theory, technology and medical sociology: an illustrative analysis of the metred dose inhaler', *Sociology of Health and Illness*, 18(2):198–219.

Prout, A. and Christensen, P. (1996) 'Hierarchies, boundaries and symbols: medicine use and the cultural performance of childhood sickness'. In P. Bush et al (eds) *Children, Medicine and Culture*. Birmingham: Haworth.

Pryce, A. (2005) 'Planting landmines in their sex lives: Governmentality, iconography of sexual disease and the duties of the STD clinic'. In M. King and K. Watson (eds) *Representing Health: Discourses of Health and Illness in the Media*. London: Palgrave.

Radley, A. (1994) *Making Sense of Illness. The Social Psychology of Health and Disease*. London: Sage.

Radley, A. (1996) 'The critical moment: time, information and medical expertise in the experience of patients receiving coronary bypass surgery'. In S.J. Williams and M. Calnan (eds) *Modern Medicine: Lay perspectives and experiences*. London: UCL Press.

Reynolds Whyte, S. (2005) 'Uncertain undertakings: practicing health care in the subjunctive'. In V. Steffen, R. Jenkins and H. Jessen (eds) *Managing Uncertainty: ethnographic studies of illness, risk and the struggle for control*. Copenhagen: Museum Tuscalnum Press.

Richards, A. (1956) *Chisungu: A Girls' Initiation Ceremony among the Bemba of Northern Rhodesia*. London: Faber.

Robinson, V., Hockey, J. and Meah, A. (2004) '"What I Used to Do ... On My Mother's Settee": spatial and emotional aspects of heterosexuality in England', *Gender, Place and Culture*, 11(3):417–35.

Rogers, A. and Pilgrim, D. (1995) 'The risk of resistance: perspectives on the mass childhood immunization programme'. In J. Gabe (ed.) *Medicine, Health and Risk*. Oxford: Blackwell Publishers.

Sankar, A. (1984) '"It's just old age": Old age as a diagnosis in American and Chinese medicine'. In D.I. Kertzer and J. Keith (eds) *Age and Anthropological Theory*. Ithaca, NY: Cornell University Press.

Santos, R.V. (2004) 'Race, genomics, identities and politics in contemporary Brazil', *Critique of Anthropology*, 24(4):347–78.

Sawday, J. (1995) *The Body Emblazoned: Dissection and the Human Body in Renaissance Culture*. London: Routledge.

Scambler, G. (1989) *Epilepsy*. London: Routledge.

Scarry, E. (1985) *The Body in Pain*. Oxford: Oxford University Press.

Scheper-Hughes, N. (1992) *Death Without Weeping*. Berkley: University of California Press.

Scheper-Hughes, N. (2002) 'Commodity festishism in organs trafficking'. In N. Scheper-Hughes and L. Wacquant (eds) *Commodifying Bodies*. London: Sage.

Seale, C. (2003) 'Health and Media: an overview', *Sociology of Health and Illness*, 25(6):513–31.

Seale, C. (2005) 'New directions for critical internet health studies: representing cancer experience on the web', *Sociology of Health and Illness*, 27(4):515–40.

Seale, C., Pattison, S. and Davey, B. (eds) (2001) *Medical Knowledge: Doubt and Uncertainty*. Buckingham: Open University Press.

Segar, J. (1997) 'Hard lives and evil winds: illness aeitology and the search for healing amongst Ciskeian villagers', *Social Science and Medicine*, 44(10):1585–600.

Seremetakis, C.N. (1991) *The Last Word. Women, death and divination in Inner Mani*. Chicago: University of Chicago Press.

Shakespeare, T. (1997) 'Cultural representations of disabled people: dustbins of disavowal'. In L. Barton and M. Oliver (eds) *Disability Studies: past, present and future*. Leeds: Disability Press.

Shakespeare, T. (1999) 'Arts and Lies? Representations of disability on film'. In M. Corker and S. French (eds) *Disability Discourse*. Buckingham: Open University Press.

Sharma, U. (1994) *Complementary Medicine Today*. London: Tavistock.

Sharma, U. (1996) 'Using complementary therapies: a challenge to orthodox medicine?'. In S.J. Williams and M. Calnan (eds) *Modern Medicine. Lay perspectives and experiences*. London: UCL Press Ltd.

Shildrick, M. (1997) *Leaky Bodies and Boundaries. Feminism, Postmodernism and (bio)ethics*. London: Routledge.

Shildrick, M. (2002) *Embodying the Monster. Encounters with the vulnerable self*. London: Sage.

Shilling, C. (1993) *The Body and Social Theory*. London: Sage.

Shilling, C. (2005) *The Body in Culture, Technology and Society*. London: Sage.

Showalter, E. (1987) *The Female Malady*. London: Virago.

Siddell, M. (1995) *Health in Old Age*. Buckingham: Open University Press.

Simpson, J. (1998) *Touching the Void*. London: Vintage.

Sinclair, S. (1997) *Making Doctors. An institutional apprenticeship*. Oxford: Berg.

Small, N. (1998) 'Death of the authors', *Mortality*, 3(3):215–28.

Sontag, S. (1988) *Aids and its Metaphors*. London: Penguin.

Sontag, S. (1978) *Illness as Metaphor*. Harmondsworth: Penguin.

Stewart, S. (1999) 'From the museum of touch'. In M. Kwint, C. Breward and J. Aynsley (eds) *Material Memories. Design and evocation*. Oxford: Berg.

Strathern, M. (2001) 'Global and local contexts'. In L. Kalinoe and J. Leach (eds) *Rationales of Ownership*. New Delhi: UBS Publishers Distributors Ltd.

Strong, P. (1994) 'Two types of ceremonial order'. In S. Lauritzen and L. Sachs (eds) *Health Care Encounters and Culture*. Botyrka, Sweden: Multicultural Centre.

Svendsen, M.N. (2005) 'Pursuing knowledge about agenetic risk of cancer'. In V. Steffen, R. Jenkins and H. Jessen (eds) *Managing Uncertainty: ethnographic studies of illness, risk and the struggle for control*. Copenhagen: Museum Tusculanum Press.

Synnnott, A. (1993) *The Body Social: Symbolism, Self and Society*. London: Routledge.

Talle, A. (1995) 'A child is a child: disability and equality among the Kenya Maasai'. In B. Ingstaad and S. Reynolds Whyte (eds) *Disability and Culture*. Berkeley: University of California Press.

Thomas, C. (2002) 'The "disabled" body'. In M. Evans and E. Lee (eds) *Real Bodies*. London: Palgrave.

Thomas-Maclean, R. (2004) 'Understanding breast cancer stories via Frank's narrative types', *Social Science and Medicine*, 58:1647–57.

Timmermans, S. and Berg, M. (2003) 'The practice of medical technology', *Sociology of Health and Illness*, 25:97–114.

Townsend, P. and Davidson, N. (1982) *Inequalities in Health: the Black Report*. Harmondsworth: Penguin.

Townsend, P., Phillimore, P. and Beattie, A. (1988) *Health and Deprivation: Inequality and the North*. London: Routledge.

Trostle, J.A. and Summerfield, J. (1996) 'Medical Anthropology and Epidemiology', *Annual Review of Anthropology*, 25:253–74.

Turner, B.S. (1987) *Medical Power and Social Knowledge*. London: Sage.

Turner, B.S. (1992) *Regulating Bodies: Essays in medical sociology*. London: Routledge.

Turner, V.W. (1969) *The Ritual Process*. Chicago: Aldine.

Turner, V.W. (1974) *Dramas, Fields and Metaphors*. Ithaca: Cornell University Press.

UNICEF (2002) *Orphans and Other Children Affected by AIDS*. New York: UNICEF.

Urla, J. and Terry, J. (1995) 'Introduction: Mapping embodied deviance'. In J. Terry and J. Urla (eds) *Deviant Bodies*. Bloomington: Indiana University Press.

Usher, J. (1991) *Women's Madness: misogyny or mental illness*. London: Harvester Wheatsheaf.

Van Gennep, A. ([1909] 1960) *The Rites of Passage*. Chicago: Chicago University Press.

Vosey, M. (1975) *A Constant Burden: the reconstitution of family life*. London: Routledge and Kegan Paul.

Wadsworth, M. (1991) *The Imprint of Time: Childhood, History and Adult Life*. Oxford: Clarendon Press.

Waitzkin, H. (1989) 'A critical theory of medical discourse: ideology, social control and the processing of social context in medical encounters', *Journal of Health and Social Behaviour*, 30(2): 220–39.

Waitzkin, H. (1991) *The Politics of Medical Encounters: how patients and doctors deal with social problems*. New York: Yale University Press.

Waitzkin, H. (2000) *The Second Sickness: contradictions of capitalist health care*. Oxford: Rowman and Littlefield.

Watson, J. (2000) *Male Bodies: Health, culture and identity*. Buckingham: Open University Press.

Watt, B. (1996) *Patient. The true story of a rare illness*. London: Penguin.

Weale, S. (2003) 'What happens to all those frozen embryos?', *The Guardian*, G2, 10–11.

Wenzel Geissler, P. (1998) '"Worms are our life", part II: Luo children's thoughts about worms and illness', *Anthropology and Medicine*, 5(2):133–44.

White, S. (2005) 'Uncertain undertakings: practicing health care in the Subjunctive mood'. In V. Steffen, R. Jenkins and H. Jessen (eds) *Managing Uncertainty: ethnographic studies of illness, risk and the struggle for control*. Copenhagen: Museum Tusculanum Press.

Whyte, S., van der Geest, J. and Hardon, A. (2002) *Social Lives of Medicine*. Cambridge: Cambridge University Press.

Wilde, A. (2005) 'Performing disability: Impairment, disability and soap opera viewing'. In M. King and K. Watson (eds) *Representing Health: Discourses of Health and Illness in the Media*. London: Palgrave.

Wilkinson, S.R. (1988) *The Child's World of Illness*. Cambridge: Cambridge University Press.

Williams, G.H. (1984) 'The genesis of chronic illness: narrative reconstruction', *Sociology of Health and Illness*, 6(2):175–200.

Williams, S. (2003) *Medicine and the Body*. London: Sage.

Williams, S.J. and Bendelow, G. (1998) *The Lived Body*. London: Routledge.

Willis, E. (1994) *Illness and Social Relations*. St Leonards NSW: Allen and Unwin.

Wright, P. (1987) 'The social construction of babyhood: the definition of infant care as a medical problem'. In A. Bryman, B. Bytheway, P. Allatt and T. Keil (eds) *Rethinking the Life Cycle*. Basingstoke: Macmillan.

Young, A. (1976) 'Some implications of medical beliefs and practices for social anthropology', *American Anthropologist*, 78:5–23.

Young, A. (1982) 'The anthropologies of illness and sickness', *Annual Review of Anthropology*, 11:257–85.

Zola, I.K. (1973) 'Pathways to the doctor – from person to patient', *Social Science and Medicine*, 7:677–89.

Index